# THE VIRGIN OF ALDERMANBURY

*Books by Mrs Robert Henrey*

THE LITTLE MADELEINE (*her girlhood*)

AN EXILE IN SOHO (*her adolescence*)

MADELEINE GROWN UP (*her love story and marriage*)

A FARM IN NORMANDY (*the birth of her child*)

MATILDA AND THE CHICKENS (*a winter on her farm*)

LONDON (*with water colours by Phyllis Ginger*)

THE JOURNEY TO VIENNA (*the making of a film*)

PALOMA (*the story of a friend*)

MADELEINE'S JOURNAL (*London during Coronation year*)

A MONTH IN PARIS (*she revisits the city of her birth*)

MILOU'S DAUGHTER (*a winter in the Midi*)

BLOOMSBURY FAIR (*three London families*)

THIS FEMININE WORLD (*Paris dressmakers*)

A DAUGHTER FOR A FORTNIGHT

THE VIRGIN OF ALDERMANBURY (*rebirth of the City of London*)

In America *A Farm in Normandy* is published under the title *Madeleine Young Wife*

*St Mary the Virgin, Aldermanbury*

# THE VIRGIN OF ALDERMANBURY

*Rebirth of the City of London*

by

MRS ROBERT HENREY

*Water-colour and drawings by*

PHYLLIS GINGER

LONDON: J. M. DENT & SONS LTD

Made in Great Britain
at the
Aldine Press · Letchworth · Herts
for
J. M. DENT & SONS LTD
Aldine House · Bedford Street · London
First published 1958

For

Edmund de Rothschild

# I

WHAT A fine sight the bracken makes this spring in the countrified regions beyond London's Guildhall!

From the bastion of the Roman Wall at Cripplegate, for instance, to Moorgate, are patches of bracken as tough stalked and as delicately leafed as you will find in Richmond Park. Quiet lanes lead to patches of wild flowers and undergrowth not seen in these parts since the days of Henry VIII.

Take a deep breath, for ragwort scents the air, and from walled and suspended gardens come breezes laden with the perfume of white and mauve lilac in full bloom. There are also tender lilies of the valley. If the gardens of Semiramis were really one of the seven wonders of the ancient world, here before us is one of the wonders of the modern world. But bear this in mind. Just as Babylon, its gardens, and its fabulous queen are now mere legends, so this countrified scene, within the precincts of the Roman Wall, and just beyond it toward Barbican, is transient. In a few moments a new picture will arise before us. Gone will be the delights of wild flowers, peaceful gardens, and Roman remains.

I am sad to think that these young trees of sixteen years' growth, sturdy willows, London plane-trees, and trees of heaven, will not be allowed to thrive, to invite rooks to nest in their branches, or to give shade to the traveller. They have so bravely got over their formative years. The rest would be so easy. They would grow into giants. Already under spreading boughs dandelion clocks, swaying gently in hot sunshine, are as willing to tell the hour when blown upon as any of the rusty timepieces which cling to the battered towers and spires of wrecked City churches.

There was one part of the City more effectively given back to pre-medievalism than any other. Most of this was razed to the ground by the great incendiary raids of the nights of 29th December 1940 and 10th May 1941, and then lying fallow became a habitat, as the botanists would say, for Oxford ragwort, rosebay, Canadian fleabane, and 'pussy' willows. Archaeologists found remains of Roman occupation, temples and statues, coins, and hitherto hidden sections of the Roman Wall. Ornithologists noted strange birds like the black redstart, a robin-like bird with a red tail, which nests on high ledges and feeds on just those insects which reappeared with this sudden vegetation. Poets who liked the macabre could philosophize amongst the churned-up graveyards of historic City churches or wander around in search of Milton's skull. Others with more present-day interests went 'borrowing' seventeenth-century gravestones to decorate their rockeries.

The area of which I speak runs from the bastion of the Roman Wall at Cripplegate (with the church of St Giles hard against it) along the Roman Wall to Moorgate at the north, and from St Paul's Churchyard along Cannon Street to Bow Lane at the south. The map shows it as an untidy rectangle rather wider at the top than at the bottom, about a quarter of a mile at its widest and a third of a mile in depth.

A love for what is lonely and strange—for what is on the point of dissolving into something else—made me adopt this area for a few months as my own. I lived in it three-dimensionally—in the past, in the present, and in the future. In no other environment had these three periods of time ever been so inextricably mixed together.

Now I hesitated about the most suitable day on which to begin this account. Somehow my starting point chose itself—Easter morning 1957. On this day, although I had set out intending to go elsewhere, I found myself walking beside the Roman Wall at Cripplegate.

After looking in at the Jesuit church at Farm Street, which was filled to overflowing on this Easter morning, I had felt a sudden desire to attend morning service at St-Botolph-without-Aldersgate, where my father-in-law had been curate at the end of the last century. I could not bring myself to see anything reprehensible in the way that I had come to terms with the two faiths in which I had been alternately brought up. Though born a Catholic I had as a child received great sympathy and kindness from the Protestant pastor of our parish. My father-in-law was a parson in the English tradition and he passed on to me some of his own affection for St Botolph and the atmosphere of the City streets through which as a young man he had so often walked both by day when they are crowded and by night when one meets only the policeman on his beat and the lamp-lighter riding his bicycle. I liked the photograph he so often showed me of himself, slim, moustached, and wearing a surplice, preaching from the pulpit of St Botolph, and I imagined that the church on this Easter morning would be full of lilac and white tulips to enhance the particular beauty of its communion table above which hangs the strangely luminous picture of Christ's agony in the Garden. It is painted on glass by James Pierson. I had since my marriage, however, lost the resentment that as a very young woman I had unjustly felt against the older faith, and I am not sure that what drew me especially to the City was not the eternal juxtaposition one discovered at every step of the two beliefs which, however bitter were their struggles for power, have yet over the centuries combined to make the greatness of England.

St Botolph was almost entirely remodelled in 1754. There had been a previous church dating from Edward III, and little of the fourteenth-century building, which escaped the Great Fire of 1666, remains.

Then too it is inextricably connected with Aldersgate, one of the seven famous gates of the Roman Wall, and like the church of St Giles, Cripplegate, it stood just outside the City enclosure, though in both cases the remains of the Roman Wall are to be found in their churchyards.

Some say that Aldersgate was named after Aldrich, the Saxon, who built it; others, says Stow, attribute the name to the alder-trees which grew round it. It had an arch in the centre with rooms above it. During Queen Elizabeth I's reign John Day lived here. It was he who printed the folio Bible dedicated to the Queen's brother and predecessor, Edward VI. Through this gate rode James I when he first entered London to take possession of the crown.

Shortly after this, on 9th December 1608, John Milton was born over a shop bearing the sign of the Spread Eagle in Bread Street, Cheapside. His family came from Oxfordshire and his father was the first of the Miltons to conform to the new faith, which disgraced him in the eyes of his own father. He was a man of probity and had already made a plentiful fortune as a scrivener, the seventeenth-century equivalent of a solicitor. The young Milton was to grow up with a great love for books and later admitted that from the age of twelve he read so much that he 'scarce ever went to bed before midnight.' Though he spent seven years at Cambridge, taking his M.A. degree in 1632, he could not make up his mind on a profession, and at the age of twenty-four returned to his father's house bringing nothing with him but his education and a silent purpose.

His father, who was now living in retirement at Horton in Buckinghamshire, in a house surrounded by thickets and woods, never tried to influence his son in the choice of a vocation but allowed him quietly to enjoy unbroken leisure, solitude, and that tranquillity of mind which Pliny thought indispensable to poetic meditation. In due course he gave his son £350 to enable him to travel in Italy for a year. Before leaving he was advised by Sir Henry Wotton, the ageing provost of Eton, on how to deport himself as a Protestant in a country so Catholic. As yet he was far from intolerant. He points out that it was not his policy to introduce the topic of religion in such surroundings, but that if interrogated respecting the faith, then, 'whatsoever I should suffer, to dissemble nothing.'

He was back in England in 1639, and though he decided not to go on living at Horton but to take lodgings in the house of a tailor in St Bride's Churchyard, his father continued to give him ample funds. There were no public libraries in London at that time and he had to provide his own store of books, which must have taken up an increasing amount of space. Soon the lodging at St Bride's was too small for the poet, who removed to a house of his own—'a pretty, garden-house in Aldersgate.'

The gate was no longer the same through which James I had passed on his arrival from Scotland. One William Parker, a merchant tailor, had left a legacy of more than £1,000 for a new one to be built, the Saxon gate being dilapidated and dangerous. The new gate had two square towers of four storeys on either side with portals for foot-passengers and a main archway in the centre. The whole was decorated with sculpture designed to flatter King James. A plaque against the façade of Alder House to-day commemorates the site of this gate.

In Milton's time there lay nearly a third of a mile of fine buildings on either side of the street in the direction of Islington. Milton resided in what was known as the second precinct of St Botolph's parish. Taking a walk along Aldersgate Street toward the country, he would pass the town houses of the Earls of Thanet and Kingston, also the Bell Inn and one or two other inns, and quite soon he would be in open fields. Milton's two nephews, sons of his sister Anne, came to his quiet and pleasant house to be tutored by their uncle. Many of the notes he made at this time are now preserved at Cambridge.

Early in the summer of 1643, when he was thirty-five, he set off on a short visit to friends in Oxfordshire. Squire Powell and his wife, Ann Moulton, had a large family and a fine house near the pretty church and vicarage of Forest Hill. There was a hall, a great parlour, a little parlour, a matted chamber, a chamber over the hall, a chamber over the little parlour, two little chambers over the kitchen, and one over the pantry, a study or boys' den, Mrs Powell's own room and her closet, a room next to this, a room over the wash-house, and Mr Powell's study. Added to these were the kitchen quarters, with a pastry, pantry, bakehouse, brewhouse, dairy, cellar, stilling-house, cheese-press house, and wool-house. There were also stables, yards, barns, and gardens, two coaches, one wain, and four carts. Unfortunately the Civil War was on and since the previous November Oxford had become the king's headquarters. He held his court in Christ Church, and the city was full of his wildly enthusiastic followers. Communication between London and Oxford was not easy. Passes were required and the journey was not without risk.

The Powells were Royalists both by choice and necessity. The family had been friendly with the Miltons for many years, and though Mr Powell had an income of some £300 a year, which would be the equivalent of some £4,000 a year to-day, he had on several occasions borrowed money from the scrivener and his son.

Milton in going to visit his friends was travelling into the heart of the Royalist camp, and it may seem strange that he, one of the most marked of extreme Parliamentarians out of Parliament, should be doing so. Was there any connection between this journey and a debt of £500 which Squire Powell had owed him for sixteen years? If so, Milton appears quickly to have dismissed the matter from his mind. The Powells had, amongst other children, a seventeen-year-old daughter Mary. Brought up in such rural surroundings she must have been shy at first with Milton, but their walks in the woods and fields and along lanes filled with the song of the nightingale during this post-Whitsun holiday soon had their effect. Milton returned to Aldersgate from his post-Whitsun holiday with a seventeen-year-old bride and accompanied by 'some of her nearest relations,' who filled his pretty garden-house with laughter and feasting.

As soon as Mary's relations returned to Forest Hill she was unhappy. Brought up where there had been a great deal of company, merriment, and dancing, and the gay atmosphere of a Royalist country house, she found life austere and lonely with a Puritan husband. After only a month in London she decided to return to Mama, though on the understanding that she would be back at Michaelmas. When the appointed time came, however, a messenger whom Milton had dispatched to bring her home from the Powells was dismissed perfunctorily.

Two years passed and things were going badly for the Royalists. Oxford was invested, Forest Hill occupied, and the Powells were alarmed about the future. They began to think that Milton's political views made him of value as a son-in-law! Friends of both families were anxious to effect a reconciliation. Milton was in the habit of dropping in almost daily on a kinsman of his, Mr Blackborough, who had a house in St Martin's-le-Grand, not a hundred yards from Aldersgate. Mary was brought to London, and one day in July or August 1645 when Milton called there he was surprised to see his young wife suddenly enter the room, throw herself on her knees, and ask his forgiveness. He is said later to have remembered this scene when he wrote in *Paradise Lost* (x. 943–4):

> Now at his feet submissive in distress
> Creature so fair his reconcilement seeking.

He quickly forgave his young wife. During her absence his father, who no longer had a place in the country, had come to live with his son in Aldersgate Street. The Civil War was making things miserable for everybody. On the surrender of Oxford the following June (1646), and the sequestration of Forest Hill, Squire Powell, utterly broken down with the accumulation of his misfortunes, also arrived with his family to seek refuge with his daughter and son-in-law. He refused to be comforted or persuaded that things could improve. Mrs Powell found comfort in the news that her daughter was about to have her first baby. She did not have long to wait. On 29th July Mary Milton gave birth to a daughter, Anne.

Old Mr Powell and old Mr Milton were a good deal together, and at length, when Mr Powell was dying, Mr Milton, good scrivener that he was, helped him to frame his will. Two months later Milton's own father died, and was buried on 15th March 1647, in the chancel of nearby St Giles's Church, Cripplegate.

The new regime was in need of a man who could translate foreign dispatches and carry out propaganda work. Pamphlets written in Latin reached the widest public because Latin was an international tongue. Milton had proved himself to be a good party man and in 1649 he accepted the post of Latin secretary at a salary of £288 a year.

For some time his eyes had been giving him trouble. Within a year of becoming a government servant he lost the sight of his left eye and his doctor warned him that if he went on using the remaining eye for bookwork he would lose that too. 'The choice lay before me,' he wrote in the *Second Defence*,

> between dereliction of a supreme duty and loss of eyesight; in such a case I could not listen to the physician, not if Æsculapius himself had spoken from his sanctuary; I could not but obey that inward monitor, I know not what, that spake to me from heaven. I considered with myself that many had purchased less good with worse ill, as they who give their lives to reap only glory. . . .

By 1652 the worst had happened. At the age of forty-three he was in total darkness, and hardly had this happened than his young wife, who was only twenty-six, died in childbirth. Thus he was robbed not only of his sight but also of the tenderness of a woman's hand. He found himself with three little girls, one in the cradle, the other two already facing little feminine problems with which he was neither willing nor able to sympathize. He was persuaded to marry Katherine Woodcock, whose goodness he has immortalized in a sonnet, but after only fifteen months she died, and he was once more left alone with nobody to console him in moments of loneliness.

Great indeed must have been his despair. The Commonwealth was over and there were exulting prophecies in the newspapers that Milton would soon be seen going to Tyburn in a cart. He would have to seek refuge with friends as the Powells had done when they had been robbed of their lovely home and chased out of Oxfordshire. Milton, who in Latin pamphlets had so vilified Charles I, now waited in the utter darkness about him to learn his fate. During three months and three weeks he was hidden by a friend in Bartholomew Close, during which time his nights must on occasion have been disturbed by imaginings of the hangman's rope. Had he not been the first to justify the regicide and the institution of the republic? Milton may even for a while have known the inside of a prison. Several copies of the books justifying the murder of the late king were solemnly burned at the Session House in the Old Bailey by the hand of the common hangman. When finally by some miracle he was allowed to rent a house of his own and feel free once more, he learned that many of his close friends were prisoners for life, others were objects of suspicion, while a few had signified abject submission to the Restoration.

In 1663 he married a third time. His new wife, Elizabeth Minshull, made him comfortable and cooked his meals. He hired servants to read aloud to him in Hebrew, Greek, Latin, and English. They did it badly and were so incapable of writing Latin that when he dictated to them in that tongue he had to spell the words out letter by letter.

As he had always regarded women with biblical disdain he had not allowed his daughters to go to school or learn languages. Now he would have liked them to read aloud to him and he tried to train them to do so in five or six languages of which they understood not a word. One is not surprised to learn of their revolt.

The Great Plague struck London early in 1665 and spread

alarmingly through the months of sea-fighting with the Dutch. By August the red-spot pestilence had claimed over 20,000 victims, the number of houses shut up was past counting, corpses were being carried along the streets, and Pepys was exclaiming: 'Lord! how sad a sight it is to see the streets empty of people, and very few upon the Change.'

For Milton, though blind and now engrossed in the great poem which was to make him famous throughout the ages, the Fire was an actual and tremendous experience. 'For three days or so,' writes David Masson in his magnificient biography,

Milton and his household were among the huddled myriads on the edge of that roaring, crackling, conflagration, which was reducing two-thirds of the entire City to ashes, drawing down the vast bulk of St Paul's and a hundred other towers and steeples from their familiar solidity on the old sky-line, hurling burning timbers and scorching smoke whichever way the wind blew, turning the sun overhead by day into a blood-coloured ball, and lighting up the sky at night over four counties with a lurid glare like that from a thousand furnaces. Helpless on the edge of this horror and commotion, only the sounds of which could come into his own sensation, while the sights had to be reported to him, the blind man sat for three days and three nights. Not till the third or fourth day could it be known where, in any direction, the conflagration would stop, or whether it would ever stop. Then it was known that the area of the fire included the 436 square acres from the Tower to Temple Bar, and from the river to Aldersgate, Cripplegate, and Moorgate, and that what remained of London was but the irregular fringe of built ground round this desolated space. . . . It had spared the Aldersgate Street suburb, including Aldersgate Street itself, where he had lived from 1640 to 1645, the Barbican, where he had lived from 1645 to 1647, and Jewin Street, where he had lived more recently. It had spared, and only just spared, the church of St Giles, Cripplegate, immediately outside the walls, the church which had been Milton's parish church in his Barbican days, again his parish church when he was in Jewin Street, and which was his parish church still. . . . Among the ruins, in the very centre of the map of the fire, there lay, as Milton knew, whatever remained distinguishable or indistinguishable of what had formerly been his native

Bread Street, with the rest of the neighbourhood of old Cheapside. His house in Bread Street, the Spread Eagle of his birth and boyhood, 'which was all the real estate he had then left,' as Wood expressly tells us, was of course totally gone.

*Paradise Lost* was probably finished by Milton at the height of the Great Plague. Permission to print it, held up during the Great Fire, was granted early in 1667. It was a bad time for the book trade. Milton signed up with Samuel Simmons, printer and publisher, next door to the Golden Lion in Aldersgate Street, and this agreement may be seen in the British Museum.

Milton died late at night on 8th November 1674, 'with so little pain that the time of his expiring was not perceived by those in the room.' He was buried in his own parish church of St Giles, Cripplegate, beside his father. The funeral was on Thursday, 12th November. 'All his learned and great friends in London, not without a concourse of the vulgar,' says Toland, 'accompanied his body to the church of St Giles, near Cripplegate, where he was buried in the chancel.'

The City on this fine Easter morning of 1957 was glaringly hot and to all appearances deserted. Traffic was almost non-existent, only a few buses emerged from the direction of Cheapside into Newgate Street where I stood. No bells within hearing pealed out the wondrous message. The air was oppressive and joyless.

From here was a view—which surely would soon disappear—of St Paul's, whose golden cross and mighty dome stood out against the sky-line beyond low brick-hedged fields of chickweed and coltsfoot which had once been Paternoster Row. The premises of thirty publishers and over four million books were destroyed here during the great fire raid of 29th December 1940, thus repeating on a larger scale what happened in Milton's time when, according to Pepys, books to the value of £150,000 were burned in and around St Paul's and 'all the great booksellers almost undone.'

Nearer to Newgate Street and facing the bus stop,

caravans were exposed for sale on a piece of waste ground. They would sleep undisturbed this Easter. There was nobody to sell them or to buy them.

King Edward Street leads to the gardens of St Botolph. One passes the burned-out shell of Christ Church, which Wren had built on the site of the fourteenth-century Greyfriars. There was not even grass in the charred interior. Unsightly wreckage with the mould and rubbish of seventeen years' neglect could be seen through cracks in the boards. A hundred yards farther along is that part of the General Post Office which is kept open to the public day and night, and even on Sundays and holidays; it is a beautiful example of the more ornate decorative architecture popular during the reign of Edward VII. On the other side of the road are the gardens of St Botolph, through which one can walk to reach the entrance to the church in Aldersgate Street.

These gardens, skirted here and there by fragments of the Roman Wall as it ran from Aldersgate to Newgate, are composed not only of the original burial ground of St Botolph but of those also of Christ Church and of St Leonard's Foster to which was added a piece of land purchased by public subscription in 1880. Because of their proximity to the earlier General Post Office, which still exists and comprises the entire block between St Martin's-le-Grand and King Edward Street, they were nicknamed *The Postman's Park*.

Here under the shade of beautiful old trees my father-in-law made a great stir in the nineties by inaugurating open-air services. He and his vicar, the impressive white-bearded Rev. S. Flood-Jones, chaplain to Queen Victoria and one of the last Anglican divines to favour the skull-cap, took turns to preach to immense congregations from a pulpit outside their church as was the custom in certain towns and villages in Elizabethan days.

I remembered this garden from a previous visit of which I once wrote:

There is an oasis, a lovely garden with fig-trees whose milky juice, touched by the sun, fills the air with the perfume of the countryside. Several postmen are sitting round the sun-dial, smoking their pipes and blinking at the lilac and the blue irises. My goodness! How the birds in London can chirrup and sing! How sweet it is to hear the sound of water falling from a fountain into the dark waters of a pond skirted by long grass and bulrushes.

There is an arbour with tablets commemorating brave, every-day deeds done sixty and seventy years ago. I am intrigued and look up and down the wall on which they are displayed.

Walter Peart, the driver, and Harry Dean, the fireman, of the Windsor express 'whilst being scalded and burnt, sacrificed their lives in saving the train.' This deed, recorded in curious English, took place on a summer's day in 1898. Samuel Rabbeth of the Royal Free Hospital tried to save a child suffering from diphtheria at the cost of his own life in 1884, while two years later a little boy of twelve supported his drowning playfellow and sank with him clasped in his arms. Alfred Smith, a police constable, was killed in an air-raid while saving the lives of women and girls—in June 1917! These tablets were to do with a memorial to G. F. Watts, the painter, but the money ran out and no more brave deeds were recorded. The black-trunked tree full of sprouting leaves is a black poplar. In the pond there lives a 4½-lb. carp that a retired police inspector gave to Charles Bennett, the gardener. There are also some goldfish.

The garden, I thought, must be looking at its loveliest this Easter, but the bells are silent and I shall miss the beginning of the service.

A warm wind blew softly through the leaves of the fig-tree, but the iron gates of the garden were closed. Puzzled, I turned into Little Britain which, skirting the garden and the north wall of the church, leads into Aldersgate Street, but here another surprise awaited me. The church door was securely locked and no sign of any life within answered my knocking. Was it possible that this famous City church, miraculously saved during the Great Fire of 1940 as its predecessor had been during the Great Fire of 1666, was closed on Easter morning, *the* morning in the whole year when music should be bursting out in strains of joy?

'Welcome, happy morning!' age to age shall say.

Had the good citizens of Aldersgate no more gratitude than this, and was it nothing to them that whereas their church was unscathed and a lovely place in which to worship, the church of St Giles, Cripplegate, to the east and Christ Church to the west, as well as so many other City churches, were in ruins? In vain had the miracle happened. This jewel of a church had been saved from the flames. And what did the parishioners do with it? They bolted the doors on Easter morning.

Still in my ears was the music of rejoicing at the Jesuit church in Farm Street, the packed congregation, the rich vestments, the magnificence of the flowers. I fell to dreaming of the bitter fights between Catholics and Protestants which had taken place on the very ground on which I stood. Those antagonists of the papists, those men like Milton's father who had turned with such fanaticism from the old faith to the new—could they have guessed how little their descendants would profit by their change of heart?

Having read on the notice-board outside the church that on every Tuesday from 12.30 to 1.30 there was a lunch-time talk with prayers I decided to return at that time and on that day, and for the moment, as the sun was still shining, to continue my walk in the direction of the wild countrified area about Cripplegate and London Wall.

The Roman Wall, passing north-east from Aldersgate, has left traces in Falcon Street, and one merely needs to take this turning to come into full view of what is perhaps the most romantic and evocative picture which Londoners of this generation have had the poignant good fortune to see. To behold the scene of a great tragedy is a tremendous emotional experience. How many of us would not like to go back into the past to witness with immunity to ourselves the marking of the houses and the burial pits of the Great Plague, the high drama of the Great Fire of 1666? Must I not therefore consider myself fortunate to have picked my way, blinded by smoke, through the still fiercely burning wreckage soon after dawn on 30th December 1940.

But I have watched a slow process of metamorphosis taking place gradually over some seventeen years, in which many acres of the most famous city in the world have changed from the feverish hum and activity of man into a desolate area grown over with brightly coloured flowers and mysterious with wild life. And I am not sure that this experience has not been more deeply affecting than that of witnessing the flames and hearing the crashing of masonry during the Second Great Fire of London.

Here on this Easter morning the picture was heightened by a blue sky and a forest of trees and shrubs everywhere breaking out into tender leaf. All this was made more romantic and lovely by the tall tower and blinding white skeleton of the church of St Giles dominating the north-west corner. Fire does not appear able to cast down this jewel of architecture, for though it is officially in ruins yet from a distance it stands out more beautiful than ever. The first church, built just after the Norman Conquest, was replaced by another in 1390. Though a fire during the reign of Henry VIII swept through this one, the walls and tower withstood the flames, as they were again to withstand flames equally fierce when incendiaries gutted the church in 1940. The only important modification of the tower since the fourteenth century took place whilst Wren was rebuilding St Paul's—it was raised some fifteen feet.

Was it to avenge the fact that St Giles's had so miraculously escaped the conflagration of Milton's old age that it was the first church to be hit during the opening stages of the battle of London—24th August 1940? This was only the first of three occasions on which it was subjected to aerial attack. Bombs and incendiaries rained down upon it, though never able to rob it of its exterior shape, its poetic silhouette. While walking slowly toward it, pausing awhile to admire the superb bastion of the Roman Wall, it was hard to believe that the inside of the church was so utterly destroyed. The hot sun brought out the heavy sweet scent from a veritable sea of ragwort whose yellow flowers covered several acres. Here you may see how the Romans built with small stones square on the face, bonded every sixth or seventh row with layers of flat tiles.

Half a dozen boys, with a girl urging them forward, raced up a staircase inside a wrecked building, and began, like medieval soldiers defending an invested city, to hurl boulders from the roof on to the undergrowth below. Their moss-covered stronghold had something of the mysteriousness of a drawing in an Andrew Lang fairy book. Their laughter echoed from St Alphage as far as the overhanging gardens sweet with lilac above the ribbon that had once been Silver Street.

Over against Jewin Street, where Milton had lodged before the Plague, and where he had dictated most of *Paradise Lost*, another group of boys, dressed in their smartest Easter clothes, rode round a wild patch of young bracken and broken tombstones on shining new bicycles.

This name—Jewin Street—was old when Milton lived there, dating from the days when Londoners perpetrated appalling crimes against the Jews, most of whom had come from Rouen at the invitation of William the Conqueror.

Richard Cœur de Lion, whose chivalrous fervour was celebrated in the crusades, allowed a great massacre of the Jews on the day of his coronation. King John, whom we are told lost his crown in the Wash, imprisoned, blinded, and tortured them. Edward I made them wear badges of yellow taffeta as Hitler made them wear a yellow star, so that they could be distinguished in the street. During his reign all the Jews in England were imprisoned in a single night and only released on a fine of £20,000, which he wanted for the building of Caernarvon and Conway castles. This did not satisfy him. In 1290 all the Jews in England, about 16,000 tormented souls, were expelled from the country. Some, through the treachery of sailors, were left behind and savagely murdered. Jewin Street marked their ancient burial ground, and Milton, living here blind and in the fullness of his poetic ardour, could at least rejoice that it was Cromwell who, setting the first great example of toleration in their regard, had allowed them after more than three centuries of exile to come back to England.

Jewin Street, with Jewin Crescent forming a half-circle on its northern side, runs from the garden of St Giles,

Cripplegate, to a point in Aldersgate Street less than three minutes' walk from St Botolph's. As Jewin Street, like the Barbican, a hundred yards farther along, was just outside the City walls, the houses in Milton's day probably had a countrified look about them. He is described as sitting

in warm weather outside his front door with friends coming to talk to him.

Though the youths riding their bicycles about here on Easter morning considered the wilderness of ragwort, elders, and chipped granite as their own particular playground, not one of them, any more than the younger members of the City police force who patrolled this part of London, had ever heard of Jewin Street. How could they have done? They were far too young. Jewin Street, like Jewin Crescent, had been churned up seventeen years earlier and could only now be rediscovered by a careful examination of the terrain. Like an archaeologist exploring a lost civilization, one had to search out where the ancient roads had run.

There was less wild life in this particular stretch of desolation. Parts of it were completely arid, and so many slabs

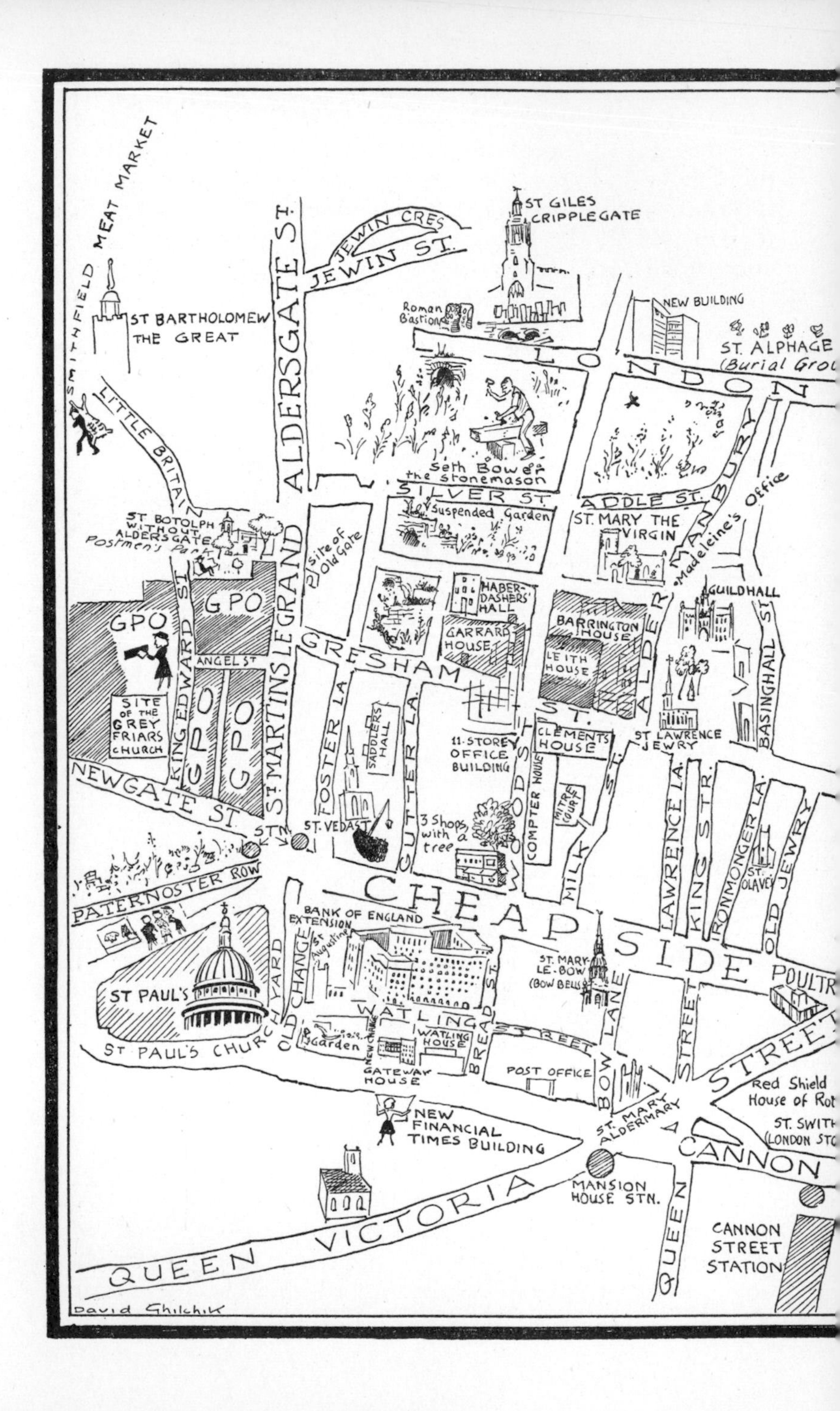
SMITHFIELD MEAT MARKET
ST BARTHOLOMEW THE GREAT
LITTLE BRITAIN
ALDERSGATE ST.
JEWIN CRES
JEWIN ST.
ST GILES CRIPPLEGATE
Roman Bastion
NEW BUILDING
ST. ALPHAGE
(Burial Grou
LONDON
Seth Bower the stonemason
SILVER ST.
Suspended Garden
ADDLE ST.
ST. MARY THE VIRGIN
MANBURY
Madeleine's Office
ST BOTOLPH WITHOUT ALDERSGATE
Postmen's Park
Site of Old Gate
GPO
GPO
ANGEL ST
HABERDASHERS' HALL
GARRARD HOUSE
BARRINGTON HOUSE
LEITH HOUSE
GUILDHALL
GRESHAM ST.
ALDER
SITE OF THE GREY FRIARS CHURCH
KING EDWARD ST
GPO
GPO
ST MARTINS LEGRAND
FOSTER LA
SADDLERS HALL
GUTTER LA.
11-STOREY OFFICE BUILDING
CLEMENTS HOUSE
ST LAWRENCE JEWRY
BASINGHALL ST
NEWGATE ST
STN
ST. VEDAST
3 Shops, with a tree
WOOD ST
COMPTER HOUSE
MITRE COURT
MILK ST.
LAWRENCE LA.
KING STR.
IRONMONGER LA.
ST. OLAVE
OLD JEWRY
PATERNOSTER ROW
CHEAPSIDE
BANK OF ENGLAND EXTENSION
St Augustine
OLD CHANGE
YARD
ST PAUL'S
ST. MARY-LE-BOW (BOW BELLS)
POULTRY
BREAD ST.
WATLING STREET
Garden
NEW CHANGE
WATLING HOUSE
GATEWAY HOUSE
ST PAUL'S CHURCH
POST OFFICE
BOW LANE
QUEEN STREET
STREET
Red Shield House of Rot
NEW FINANCIAL TIMES BUILDING
ST. MARY ALDERMARY
ST. SWITH (LONDON STO
CANNON
MANSION HOUSE STN.
QUEEN VICTORIA
QUEEN
CANNON STREET STATION
David Ghilchik

MOORFIELDS
FINSBURY CIRCUS
WALL
BLOMFIELD ST
LIVERPOOL STREET STATION
LIVERPOOL ST.
MIDDLESEX ST
'PETTICOAT LANE' MARKET
THROGMORTON AVENUE
OLD BROAD STREET
BISHOPSGATE
HOUNDSDITCH
Priory of Holy Trinity, Aldgate, dissolved by Henry VIII in 1531
DUTCH CHURCH
ANGEL COURT
COPTHALL CT.
DRAPERS' HALL
AUSTIN FRIARS
THROGMORTON ST
STOCK EXCHANGE
BARTHOLOMEW LA.
NEEDLE STREET
THREAD
ROYAL EXCHANGE
ST. MICHAEL'S CORNHILL
BANK STATION
CORNHILL
LOMBARD ST.
George & Vulture
Shields of the great banks
KING WILLIAM ST.
GRACECHURCH ST.
LEADENHALL ST.
LLOYD'S
NEW LLOYD'S
Leadenhall Market
LIME ST.
FEN COURT
GLASS BUILDING
BILLITER ST
FENCHURCH ST.
ST. MARY AXE
Madeleine ringing the bell
CUNARD HOUSE
ST ANDREW'S UNDERSHAFT
CREECHURCH LA.
GREAT SYNAGOGUE
ST. CATHARINE CREE
ALDGATE PUMP
ST. BOTOLPH ALDGATE
STN.
British India Steamboat Navigation Co's wonderful new building
MINORIES
Abbey of the nuns of St. Clare, surrendered by Dame Elizabeth Salvage to Henry VIII in 1539
EASTCHEAP
MONUMENT STN

of granite were thrown one against the other, as if by giant ocean waves pounding upon a rocky coast, that one wondered where they could all have come from.

In the centre of this arid desert one came upon two small huts of steel rods clamped together, roofed and protected from the wind on three sides by rusty sheets of corrugated iron, the cracks covered over with jute sacks. A week later, when passing along this way, I discovered that this was the open-air workshop of the mason Seth Bower and his two aides, who were busy pitting, punching, and chiselling kerb-stones taken from City streets such as Jewin Street, Jewin Crescent, Hamsell Street, Citywell, and a hundred others from Barbican to Cheapside and even well beyond. These had been blasted and burned out of recognition so that traffic could no longer go along them and flowers grew and elder-trees flourished.

What a picturesque craft this is! See this man, blue eyed, thoughtful, ochre skinned, remove a pipe from between his lips and hold out in welcome a scarred hand as tough as the stone he works. I asked him about himself and what he was doing.

'That will take a little time to answer,' he said slowly, going over to the side of his home-made shelter and taking a brown coat from a nail. He was hot from his work and experience had taught him to beware of a sudden chill when he was in this condition.

Now he stood before me in the brown jacket, his pipe back in his mouth, his head covered by a battered hat which had such an air about it that I had seldom seen a man with a greater appearance of dignity. His thick boots were covered in white dust, and his trousers had neither shape nor colour.

When he spoke again it was to address me in language almost biblical. How could he tell exactly how long he had been in granite? His father had worked as a lad in the quarries of Dorset. Maybe that was a hundred years ago, seeing that he himself was now sixty-six and had been knocking about England, north to south, east to west, these fifty years. What was he doing here? Re-dressing the kerb-stones, squaring them (that was the correct term) to specification. Some were as tall as a man, some were curved for the corners, some were relatively small. As each length was finished, he dabbed some red paint at the end, and then it was ready to be placed standing upright against one or other of the piles. These would serve for the yet uncharted streets of to-morrow.

I asked him naïvely if the kerb-stones were very old, and he answered with an indulgent smile:

'Millions of years, unless, of course, you are of those who believe that the Garden of Eden is not as old as that.'

I realized then that he was referring to the granite itself, not to the number of years that these pieces had served to protect the sides of a road, and I corrected myself by asking:

'How long, in your opinion, have they been used in City streets?'

'Some have not been in use for more than thirty years,' he answered. 'Others were fashioned more than two hundred years ago.'

'So coaches could have bumped against them? The lumbering coaches of Georgian times?'

'That could have happened,' he conceded.

What puzzled me was to see these piles of re-dressed kerb-stones so neatly packed, with no machinery to move them, and I said to him hesitantly, so that he should not laugh at me again:

'No man alone could move such a weight. They are giant's playthings.'

'I am no giant,' he said, 'and I cannot lift as much as I used to, but I can still move four hundredweight without trouble, and that suffices for most of what you see here.'

'Four hundredweight?' I exclaimed.

'It is not as difficult as it sounds,' he explained modestly. 'We learn the right way to do it. One might almost call it a trick.'

I asked him if all the granite was from the same quarry.

'Come,' he said, 'I will show you. These are two Scottish kerbs, Peterhead and Aberdeen. Here are Leicester, Cornish, Jersey, Guernsey, Norwegian . . .'

'How you seem to love them!' I exclaimed.

'Yes,' he agreed, 'but, mind you, I am not infallible. I remember once my wife and I were on holiday in the Lake District, enjoying the scenery. We are rare ones for walking. Suddenly I looked up at her and said: "I 've made a mistake!" "Oh!" she cried, alarmed. "What have you done?" "It 's not Irish!" I answered. "It 's Shap!" I had been looking at the kerb-stones and felt sure, because of the texture, they must be Irish. Then, for the first time, I realized I could make a mistake. Why, indeed, should they have gone to fetch kerb-stones from across the sea when they could quarry them on their very doorstep in Cumberland!'

Seth Bower's two aides had ceased chipping granite and had now retired to their own hut, where they sat side by side, thoughtfully looking out over the windy plain of Jewin Street. They had arranged three lengths of granite, Stonehenge fashion, in front of them, using the crossbar as a table upon which to place steaming mugs of tea. This scene was primitive, desolate, and timeless.

'Do you see much wild life?' I asked Seth Bower.

'Rats occasionally,' he answered. 'Plenty of birds, and the other day a budgerigar came to perch on my tin box.'

He had been playing with his chisel and started to work on the granite, partly, I think, to occupy his hands, and partly to give me a demonstration of his skill. Pieces of granite flew about and there were sparks.

Instinctively I shielded my eyes, and queried:

'Why don't you wear goggles? Are you not afraid?'

'Not afraid, but I often get pieces of granite in my eyes.'

'You do?'

'A woman doctor happened to be calling on my wife. "Oh, Mr Bower," she said, "what have you got in your eye?"

'"A piece of granite."

'"What are you doing about it? Are you bathing it?"

'"No, I believe my blood is pretty good and that should be enough."

'She looked puzzled. A fortnight later when she again came to visit my wife, she said:

'"Mr Bower, how is the eye? It looks very swollen."

'"I have had a much worse piece in it since then. To-day it's real bad."

'"This time, Mr Bower, I hope you will be more sensible and consult a specialist."

'"I have already taken it to the greatest physician there is," I said to her.

'"Who is that, Mr Bower? Do I know him?"

'"I prayed about it."'

Seth Bower put down his chisel and added:

'When I woke up the next morning, my eye was quite cured.'

'Do you go to church on Sundays?'

'I go to the Baptists just now.'

'Are you a Baptist?'

'No. I don't believe in any "isms." When I was in Cornwall I went to the Methodists in the morning and to the Congregationalists in the evening. Both churches were practically empty. They would have done better to unite. That church over there, for instance'—Seth Bower pointed to St Giles, Cripplegate, standing more beautiful than I had ever seen it, in its medieval splendour—'is merely a lovely picture of the past, and I am not one to be satisfied with tradition without the living flame.'

I looked at him searchingly.

'I mean,' he continued, 'that four or five years ago they went to big expense to repair the tower and the nave. Yet before the war, so they tell me, hardly anybody worshipped there.'

'Where do *you* pray most often?'

'In the open air, while I am at work. I try to live with my Creator.'

'You speak like Milton.'

I was amazed at his wisdom and directness. There was a pause in our conversation and then I asked:

'How did you meet your wife?'

'She is a Kentish girl, and we started courting during the

First World War while I was a drill instructor waiting to be sent to the front. I went occasionally to a chapel in Chatham, and afterwards she would lunch with me and we would go for a stroll. One day I said to her:

'"Your birthday is next week. What would you like me to give you, a nice watch, or a ring?"

'"A ring!" she answered quickly.

'"I expect you would," I said, "but I don't know about getting married. Suppose I were not to come back from France?"

'"I will chance that," she said. "Besides, if you were not to come back and there was a child, I should still have a little of you left."'

The child she so much wanted proved a boy, and what is more, Seth did come back. Under the nail from which Seth hung his coat was a black steel box in which he kept his tools. This had belonged to his son when he had been in India and Burma during the Second World War and across the lid were painted the words: Lance-Corporal S. Bower, Military Police.

'When my son came back from the war,' the mason said reflectively, 'he told me he wanted to lead his own life. "Well," I answered, "that's as it should be, son."'

Seth Bower did not pursue this subject but what impressed me about these words were the deep affection and tolerance with which they were uttered. He had reached the age when men become philosophers. His blue eyes were those of a man who is accustomed to be always in the open air, looking up from his work, at the birds, the flowers, and everything on the landscape. He called my attention to a magnificent piece of carved stone which must have been hurled down from the top of some medieval building and now lay on a piece of low ground half hidden by grass and ferns. Had this come from a religious or secular edifice? The carving was of a dog with its head between its paws, and was the work of some highly skilled and long forgotten craftsman. Now it was cast away on this waste ground for roving bands of thoughtless youths to kick and deface. I would have liked to rescue it but what could I do with a piece of stone weighing three-quarters of a ton?

Seth Bower, who claimed to dislike tradition, was gazing in admiration at the tower and walls of St Giles, Cripplegate. He grudged the money which was being spent on its renovation but he was too good a craftsman not to feel his heart beat faster at the sight of this superb stone-work which loomed up so beautifully across the moor.

'Nobody will ever work like that again!' he murmured.

'Why not?'

'No architect would even dare to suggest such a thing. The cost would be prohibitive. Nowadays they only use stone as a facing; what is out of sight is false.'

'What sort of stone is it?'

'I have often wondered. I think it is mostly Portland with, perhaps, Rag, but not Oxford Rag,[1] between the buttresses. Do you know when it was built?'

'Yes, the stone tower and walls date from 1390 according to Stow. They are substantially unchanged since then.'

Did Seth Bower still believe it had been a waste of money to repair the stone-work? If only he knew how little needed to be done! For a long time people failed to realize that the fire which swept through the church in 1545, during the latter part of Henry VIII's reign, had done no harm whatever to the tower and walls. They survived then as they did on the 29th December 1940 when all this part of London burned. On both occasions, however, the whole of the interior was destroyed.

The first fire has been described in fair detail by residents. It broke out on 12th September 1545, at 5 a.m.

'Sent Gylles was burned, alle hole, save the walles, stepall, and alle, and how it came God knoweth.'

Wriothesley wrote:

'The stone walles onelie saved, which could not burne.'

[1] It is Kentish Rag.

Little wonder, for the walls of the tower represent nearly five feet of solid masonry.

Until several years after this fire these same walls which Seth and I looked upon across the moor echoed to the chanting of mass in the Latin tongue.

The first effects of the new faith began to be felt in 1548, the second year of the reign of Edward VI. The Whitsuntide censing at St Paul's was discontinued, as were also the use of candles on Candlemas Day, ashes on Ash Wednesday, and palms on Palm Sunday, and the watching of the Sepulchre and the Corpus Christi procession.

By March, confession to a priest was to be used 'only by those that would,' but no longer as an indispensable part of preparation for communion. The Latin missal began to be superseded by the English psalter, and English was more widely used in divine service.

There were at this time many houses on what is now so desolate a moor. Goldbeaters, cordwainers, pelterers, pepperers (grocers), tanners, plasterers, and frippeurs (dealers in old clothes) were doubtless still to be found here. Wood Street led to Cripplegate. Between the City Wall and St Giles's Church ran a running stream 'with quantity of good fish taken in it.'

Until this year Morrow Mass had been said very early every morning in nearly all the City churches, including St Giles's, and this had made it possible for every man, however busy, to be present on any day at divine service, and we learn that up till 1538 a 'great multitude of people were accustomed to avail themselves of this privilege.' No wonder that the City churches were then very much alive. But from this year on Morrow Mass, Lady Mass, and Jesus Mass were discontinued.

Throughout the autumn and winter the subject of the mass was a burning one, and evoked great bitterness. In September a boy was sentenced to be whipped in the church of St Mary Woolnoth for having thrown his cap at the Blessed Sacrament at the moment of the Elevation.

On 21st January 1549 the first Prayer Book of Edward VI was issued, and the old church books were ordered to be sold, but the king was soon complaining that the book was not universally accepted and ordered the old ones to be defaced.

Mary I was proclaimed Queen at the Cross in Cheapside on 19th July 1553, and from that place, says Machyn, 'they went into Paul's, and there was the Te Deum Laudamus, with song, and the organ playing, and all the bells ringing through London, and bonfires and tables in every street.'

Within a few weeks of Mary's accession mass was restored in several of the London churches, not by commandment but of the people's devotion. The Latin service was said in St Paul's before the end of August, and by December 1553 the married clergy were being forbidden to minister, or to say mass. Three years later the church of Westminster was restored as a Benedictine abbey with fourteen monks under the rule of Abbot Fechenham, late dean of St Paul's. On Queen Mary's death, in 1558, the faith was again changed, and the reformers who had fled to the Continent returned to England.

Roving bands of children who descend on the moor with their sticks and dogs add to the effect of wilderness. Seth Bower bewailed the fact that they had already twice broken into steel boxes in which he kept the tools of his craft, and this caused him to hang up a notice in his encampment warning pilferers away. Seldom in the heart of London had there been such an eerie, desolate, evocative place to attract wandering children. The bracken covered gaping holes which led by twists and turns into mysterious subterranean caverns, inviting exploration.

In Jewin Street, up and down this staircase exposed to the sun and the wind ran children and dogs, and on the top step someone had planted a flag!

Whence came these children? From Moorgate or Finsbury? Those who had bicycles travelled swiftly between here and the muddy banks of the Thames between Billingsgate and the Tower, and those newly arrived would cry to the others that it was high water, and time to paddle and bathe.

Now I must discover to what extent the interior of St Giles's was being repaired.

Everything in and round the church had already been carefully cleaned, and when I peeped inside I had the impression of looking at the sort of cleanliness that a woman achieves with a broom. In fact, this was no woman's work. Craftsmen were already beginning to make a new floor.

Though tombs had been blasted open, tablets and memorials remained to tell their stories. The monument to Martin Frobisher, who was buried here in 1594, had lost its Elizabethan galleon, but the epitaph remains to Charles Langley, who died in 1602. As there is no vicarage, the Guildhall library now holds the registers, which go back to 1561, the churchwardens' account books, which go back to 1648, and the vestry minute book, which goes back to 1659. The records show that on a single day—18th August 1665—during the Great Plague, there were 263 burials in the churchyard.

The entries of Cromwell's marriage and of Milton's burial may still be read. The blind Milton must often have been seen walking in his coarse grey cloth coat on the very spot in Jewin Street where Seth Bower and I had talked. How strange to think that Milton's religious views had shown, toward the end of his life, a marked sympathy with the way of thinking which later came to be associated with the Quakers—a simplicity and toleration unmistakably similar to the beliefs the stone-mason had just now expressed to me as we stood on the site of the poet's home.

Milton's body, laid to rest under the chancel of St Giles's, was not to be left in peace. Toward the end of the eighteenth century, and again in our own times, while the church lay vacant and damaged, there occurred scenes against his memory of horrible profanation and disrespect.

The very earth hereabouts has been steeped, through the centuries, in tragedy, strife, cruelty, plague, and misery. Small wonder, then, that some may feel that these places are haunted by night.

The first of these happenings took place in the summer of 1790 when minor alterations were being carried out in the church. The contemporary account, preserved in the Guildhall, is written on fifty small sheets sewn together without a cover but with the heading: 'A Narrative of the Disinterment of Milton's Coffin in the Parish Church of St Giles, Cripplegate, on Wednesday 4th August 1790, and of the Treatment of the Corpse during that and the following day. Second Edition. London. Printed for T. and J. Egerton, Whitehall. MDCCXC.'

This is what it says:

Having read in the Public Advertiser, on Saturday 7th August, 1790, that Milton's coffin had been dug up, in the parish church of St Giles, Cripplegate, and was there to be seen, I went immediately to the church, and found the latter part of the information untrue; but, from conversations on that day, on Monday the 9th, and on Tuesday, the 10th of August, with Mr Thomas Strong, Solicitor and F.A.S., Red Cross Street, Vestry-Clerk; Mr John Cole, Barbican, Silversmith, Churchwarden; Mr John Laming, Barbican, Pawnbroker, and Mr Fountain, Beech-Lane, Publican, overseers; Mr Taylor of Stanton, Derbyshire, Surgeon; a friend of Mr Laming, and a visitor in his house; Mr William Ascough, Coffin-maker, Fore Street, Parish Clerk; Benjamin Holmes and Thomas Hawkesworth, journeymen to Mr Ascough; Mrs Hoppey, Fore Street, Sexton; Mr Ellis, No. 9 Lamb's Chapel, comedian of the Royalty Theatre; and John Poole (son of Rowland Poole), watch-spring maker, Jacob's Passage, Barbican; the following facts are established:

It being in the contemplation of some persons to bestow a considerable sum of money, in erecting a monument, in the parish church of St Giles, Cripplegate, to the memory of Milton, and the particular spot of the interment, in that church, having for so many years past, been ascertained only by tradition, several of the principal parishioners have, at their meetings, frequently expressed a wish that his coffin should be dug-for, that incontestable evidence of its exact situation might be established, before the said monument should be erected. The entry, among the burials, in the register-book, 12th of November 1674, is: 'John Milton, Gentleman, consumpcon, chancell.'

The church of St Giles, Cripplegate, was built in 1030; was burnt down (except the steeple) and rebuilt in 1545; was repaired in 1682; and again in 1710. In the repair of 1682, an alteration took place in the disposition of the inside of the church; the pulpit was removed from the second pillar, against which it stood, north of the chancel, to the south side of the present chancel, which was then formed, and pews were built over the old chancel. The tradition has always been, that Milton was buried in the chancel, under the clerk's desk; but, the circumstance of the alteration in the church not having of late years been attended to, the clerk, sexton, and other officers of the parish have misguided enquirers, by shewing the spot under the clerk's desk, in the present chancel, as the place of Milton's interment. I have twice, at different periods, been shewn that spot, as the place where Milton lay. Even Mr Baskerville, who died a few years ago, and who had requested in his will to be buried by Milton, was deposited in the above-mentioned spot of the present chancel, in pious intention of compliance with his request. . . . Mr Strong, Mr Cole, and other parishioners, having prudently judged that the search would be made with much less inconvenience to the parish at this time, when the church is under repair, than at any period after the said repair should be completed, Mr Cole, in the last days of July, ordered the workmen to dig in search of the coffin. Mr Ascough, his father, and grandfather, have been parish-clerks of St Giles for upwards of ninety years past. . . .

On Tuesday afternoon, August 3rd, notice was brought to Messrs Strong and Cole that the coffin was discovered. They went immediately to the church; and, by the help of a candle, proceeded under the common-council-men's pew, to the place where the coffin lay. It was in a chalky soil, and directly over a wooden coffin, supposed to be that of Milton's father; tradition having always reported that Milton was buried next to his father. . . .

When he and Mr Cole had examined the coffin, they ordered water and a brush to be brought, that they might wash it, in search of an inscription, or initials, or date; but upon its being carefully cleansed, none was found. The following particulars were given to me in writing, by Mr Strong, and they contain the admeasurement of the coffin, as taken by him with a rule.

'A leaden coffin, found under the common-council-men's pew, on the north side of the chancel, nearly under the place, where the old pulpit and clerk's-desk stood. The coffin appeared to be old, much corroded and without any inscription or plate upon it. It was in length five feet ten inches, and in width, at the broadest part, over the shoulders, one foot four inches.' . . .

On Tuesday evening, the 3rd, Mr Cole, Messrs Laming and Taylor, Holmes &c. had a merry meeting, as Mr Cole expresses himself, at Fountain's house: the conversation there turned upon Milton's coffin having been discovered; and in the course of the evening, several of those present expressing a desire to see it, Mr Cole assented, that if the ground was not already closed, the closing of it should be deferred until they should have satisfied their curiosity. Between 8 and 9 o'clock on Wednesday morning, the 4th, the two overseers (Laming and Fountain) and Mr Taylor went to the house of Ascough, the clerk, which leads into the churchyard, and asked for Holmes; they then went with Holmes into the church, and pulled the coffin, which lay deep in the ground, from its original station to the edge of the excavation, into daylight. Mr Laming told me that to assist in thus removing it, he put his hand into a corroded hole, which he saw in the lead, of the coffin foot. When they had thus removed it, the overseers asked Holmes if he could open it, that they might see the body. Holmes immediately fetched a mallet and chisel, and cut open the top of the coffin, slantwise from the head, as low as the breast; so that, the top being doubled backward, they could see the corpse: he cut it open also at the foot. Upon first view of the body, it appeared perfect, and completely enveloped in the shroud, which was of many folds; the ribs standing up regularly. When they disturbed the shroud, the ribs fell. Mr Fountain told me, that he pulled hard at the teeth, which resisted, until some one hit them a knock with a stone, when they easily came out. There were but five in the upper-jaw, which were all perfectly sound and white, and all taken by Mr Fountain; he gave one of them to Mr Laming. Mr Laming also took one from the lower-jaw; and Mr Taylor took two from it. Mr Laming told me, that he had at one time a mind to bring away the whole under-jaw with the teeth in it; he had it in his hand, but tossed it back again. Also, that he lifted up the head, and saw a great quantity of hair, which lay strait and even, behind the head, and in the state of hair, which had been combed and tied-together before interment; but it was wet; the coffin having considerable corroded holes, both at the head and foot, and a great part of the water, with which it had been washed, on the Tuesday afternoon, having run into it.

The Overseers and Mr Taylor went away soon afterwards; and Messrs Laming and Taylor went home to get scissors to cut off some of the hair: they returned about ten: when Mr Laming poked his stick against the head, and brought some of the hair over the forehead; but as they saw the scissors were not necessary, Mr Taylor took up the hair, as it laid over the forehead, and carried it home. The water, which had got into the coffin, on the Tuesday afternoon, had made a sludge at the bottom of it, emitting a nauseous smell, and which occasioned Mr Laming to use his stick to procure the hair, and not to lift up the head a second time. Mr Laming also took out one of the leg bones, but threw it in again. . . . Elizabeth Grant, the gravedigger, and who is servant to Mrs Hoppey, therefore now took possession of the coffin; and, as its situation, under the common-council-men's pew, would not admit of its being seen without the help of a candle, she kept a tinder-box in the excavation, and, when any persons came, struck a light, and conducted them under the pew; where, by reversing the part of the lid which had been cut, she exhibited the body, at first for sixpence and afterwards for threepence and twopence each person. The workmen in the church kept the doors locked to all those who would not pay the price of a pot of beer for entrance, and many, to avoid that payment, got in at the window at the west end of the church, near to Mr Ascough's counting-house. . . .

Furnival's Inn,
14th of August, 1790. PHILIP NEVE

Though Philip Neve's narrative is not mentioned in the vestry minute book, one finds the names of the chief persons who took part in it fulfilling their usual functions in connection with church business. Neve's story excited bitter resentment and many people, in their efforts to discredit him, claimed that the body was not that of a man but of a woman. In the second edition of his narrative, dated 8th September 1790, Neve adds in a postscript:

On Monday 16th I called upon the Overseer, Mr Fountain, when he told me that the parish-officers had seen a Surgeon who on Wednesday 4th had got through a window into the church and who had, upon inspection, pronounced the corpse to be that of a woman. I thought it very improbable, that a surgeon should creep through a window, who could go through a door for a few halfpence; but I no otherwise expressed my doubts of the truth of the information, than by asking for the Surgeon's address. I was answered, 'that the gentleman begged not to have it known, that he might not be interrupted by enquiries.'

Will Cowper, who was then approaching his sixtieth year, wrote in horror:

> Ill fare the hands that heaved the stones
> Where Milton's ashes lay,
> That trembled not to grasp his bones,
> And steal his dust away.

Those bones long since turned to dust knew, as everything else had done in this historic church, the inferno that raged inside during the night of 29th December 1940. The coffin had been eventually nailed up again and put back in its original place in the chancel. This custom of burying any parishioner who so desired it in the nave went on for some time. For a trifling extra sum of money the deceased could be interred under the very pew where in his lifetime he had been accustomed to worship. Thus when relatives went to church on Sundays they had the consolation of offering their prayers close to the body of their dear one.

As the grave-digger in those days merely made a hole in the floor deep enough to entomb the coffin, the surface of the floor became uneven. After the great fire of 1940, it was decided to put down a new floor. This is what I had perceived when I peeped through the window.

Though Milton's resting place was roasted and scorched, it was not otherwise disturbed. The bronze statue of the poet in the garden, however, was hurled by a high explosive face downward in the grass. The authorities, believing that it would be safer inside the church, stored it in the chamber under the tower. All went well as long as the raids continued, but after the war, when there was no longer any danger from the sky, roving bands of youths came by night across the lonely moor, and breaking into the damaged church, collected bricks, pieces of jagged stone, and fragments from the various monuments, and hurled these missiles at Milton's statue as if it had been an Aunt Sally. Other things, too, these youths did of an even worse kind.

The Rev. Everett George Turner has been vicar—he is now called rector—of St Giles, Cripplegate, for twenty-three years. If Oliver Goldsmith were still alive he might be tempted to write, with gentle wisdom and understanding, about the tribulations of a rector whose beautiful medieval church is there, and yet not there. For this parish underwent a metamorphosis in the space of a single night, when it changed from one of the most congested areas on the face of the globe to a wild, bleak desolation where, later, weeds and wild trees were to flourish.

This good and learned man, educated at Lincoln College, Oxford, has heavy white eyebrows, hornrimmed spectacles, a small moustache, and a tiny pointed beard. Utterly modest, a wanderer without a home in his own parish, he has been called upon to hold office during one of the most poignant periods in English history.

How full of promise must the future have seemed when, in December 1934, he first entered the vicarage that was to be his, and is now but a place where daisies push up their heads in spring!

'My study overlooked the buttress of the Roman Wall which was in my garden,' he says with such nostalgic simplicity that one is drawn into immediate interest. 'The vicarage, which stood in the churchyard, with its pretty garden, was divided from the church by a path, but at night the whole area was enclosed by gates of which only the police and I had the keys.

'My drawing-room and dining-room, with a view across the garden and the church path, faced the west door. Milton's magnificent bronze statue stood on its plinth on the north side of the church facing Fore Street, on ground which belonged, as did the statue, to Cripplegate Foundation. Every three hours during the night, from dusk to dawn, police, always two at a time, having unlocked the iron gate in Fore Street, would patrol slowly along the path, later unlocking other gates that gave them access both to the lane round the church and to the garden in which was my vicarage. They came two at a time because, as I have always heard tell, a policeman was once murdered there. When I was working at night, or turning in bed unable to sleep, I would hear at regular intervals the tread of these policemen as they patrolled the churchyard, and their heavy footsteps would give me a feeling of peace and security.'

Milton's statue, which was discovered face downward on the grass when the church was hit near the north door on the night of 24th August 1940, was not left in that position for long. A place was found for it inside the church at the base of the tower. The damage to the edifice was relatively unimportant, for the wall was so strong that the bomb merely succeeded in making a hole in it. Mr Turner had made arrangements to reopen the church for divine service on New Year's Day. The great fire of 29th December frustrated this plan. The roof collapsed and everything inside the church was completely burnt. Some idea of the terrific heat of the fire may be imagined by the fact that the stone piers in the corner by the organ were calcined. The vestry, separated from the church by a wall four feet six inches thick, was saved.

Mr Turner said to me:

'During the rest of the war the wrecked church remained more or less unmolested. The danger which threatened from the sky by night, and later by day also when guided weapons came into action, kept marauders away, but when peace came and morals were relaxed, hordes of youths, more dangerous than children with dogs, roamed the heath at night, clambered into the church, and desecrated all that was most holy.

'Bricks hurled at Milton's statue injured an arm and broke off a hand. Lawless lads and hooligans from Old Street and Finsbury vied against one another to spoil and to loot. The church vestry, which escaped the fire, was destroyed by arson. I who had been a wanderer for all these years was seeking refuge here. The police arrived one night about 9 p.m. to say that the vestry was on fire. Afterwards even the lead was stolen from the roof.'

Thus spoke the rector, who by then had found a temporary home elsewhere, but is still frequently to be found at the Cripplegate Foundation in Redcross Street (known in the twelfth century as La Red Crosse Street, *une crosse* being French for a bishop's crook) at the extreme north of his parish against Barbican.

Here in the entrance hall of the Foundation was the magnificent bronze statue of the poet, restored by experts to its former glory.

'It will not go back to the site outside the north porch till we think it safe,' added the rector. 'There used to be plaques on the plinth, representing incidents from Milton's poetic works, but we do not know where they are. There has been so much vandalism.'

The fire revealed traces of a superb fourteenth-century east window with some of the most beautiful traceries to be seen in any church of the period. 'We agreed to put all the war damage compensation into stained glass for it, and I had the privilege of choosing the subjects,' said the rector.

'These are they: the Crucifixion in the centre, with St John on the right and the Virgin Mary on the left; St Giles on the extreme left, and on the extreme right St Paul because, since medieval times, this living has been in the gift of the Dean and Chapter of St Paul's.

'For the five lights underneath—St George, because he is the patron saint of England, but also because George is my second name; St Alphage, whose church is now combined with ours; St Anselm, archbishop when the first Norman church was built; Bishop Lancelot Andrewes, and St Bartholomew.'

Now, almost in the centre of this lonely heathland, there has suddenly arisen a tall new building, virginally white, its thousand windows shimmering in the midday sun. One looks on it in wonder, though not without apprehension, for it is the first of a hundred others, no less gigantic and smooth of line.

This building was obviously designed to incorporate

everything commodious and hygienic that will make the lives of those who are to spend their working hours in it more pleasant. It is a beautiful, clean, airy apparition which rides as if at anchor against the end of London Wall. Truly this simile is the most apt. The buildings of the City of to-morrow have little in common with those that characterize the sky-line of New York City. They bear a much closer resemblance to those gigantic liners that, in spite of increasing competition from the air, speed between Europe and America, with their curved lines and thousand lights, their cabins, their restaurants, and their recreation decks, their complicated heating and lighting equipment, and their telephone exchanges.

What surprises me is that I find nothing incongruous in the presence of this sleek monster, which is the very essence of all that we look for to-day, in the middle of this fenland so steeped in English history since before the birth of Christ. We have become inured to the incredible. One accepts, almost without a tremor, such apparent contradictions as medieval mystery and solitude and a conception of life so new to us that we cannot yet comprehend all its stupendous wonders and potentialities.

The vicar of St Giles, Cripplegate, is so afraid of marauding youths that he does not yet dare to expose the blinding beauty of the stained glass in his miraculously rediscovered fourteenth-century east window. So it is hidden from sight by heavy boards. Nocturnal gangs cannot shatter the figure of Christ on the crucifix with stones and pieces of broken tombstone. Yet, facing the east window, less than two hundred yards south-west of it, rides the sheet-glass city of to-morrow.

Against the flank of this monster, and in the shelter of London Wall, there sleeps a little garden that is heavy with the scent of forget-me-nots, tulips, and red and yellow wallflowers. This happy combination of flowers, so often admired at Hampton Court in the borders which run parallel to King Henry VIII's tennis-court, has added great fragrance to the City this spring. For those who have a love of history, the scent of certain flowers is as evocative as a glimpse of some period costume, or the lines of a well-loved poet.

Until the reign of Henry VIII the church of St Alphage was on this north side of the road against that part of the Roman Wall a fragment of which is now adorned with climbing roses. When the Norman church was pulled down, another was built on the opposite side of the road on the side of the priory of St Mary the Virgin, originally founded in 1329 by William Elsing, a London mercer, for a hundred blind men. The new St Alphage escaped the Great Fire of 1666, but in Georgian times it was mostly rebuilt. That is why some thirty-five years ago people thought so little of it that the church, all except the steeple, the vestry, and a new porch, was pulled down, and the parish was merged with that of St Mary the Virgin, Aldermanbury, which lies at the corner of Aldermanbury and Little Love Lane to the south.

I once asked a man who, when this part of the City was at its most desolate after the great fire of 1940, had taken up his abode in a cavern hereabouts, why the whole of St Alphage had not been pulled down before the war. He answered:

'St Alphage came under the tithe rate and St Mary did not. The rector received some £1,200 a year from the warehouses in the vicinity, and so the porch and the vestry were left standing. Otherwise the rector would have had no stipend. They fixed up a little piece that was left very nicely with chairs and an altar. All sorts of folk came to pray during the lunch hour. In winter tea was served in the vestry at one penny a cup, and in summer lemonade at the same price. It was a church, and it was not a church. Incidentally, St Mary the Virgin, Aldermanbury, the one that was no good for a salary, is wrecked also.'

In 1948 tithes were abolished, and the parish of St Alphage was divorced from St Mary the Virgin and amalgamated, as Mr E. G. Turner pointed out when discussing his east window, with the church of St Giles. This is now officially known as St Giles without Cripplegate and St Alphage, London Wall.

What a dwarfed object will this fourteenth-century church appear in the London of to-morrow! How ridiculous its sturdy tower! Who will ever believe, looking down on it from so high, that it withstood the two greatest fires in English history? Was it possible that those same stones listened to the joyous bells of Cromwell's wedding and to the slow tolling for Milton's funeral?

Will typists working in the myriad-windowed palaces of the future only use its gardens, where hundreds of victims of the Great Plague lie buried, as a place in which to munch their sandwiches at lunch-time?

Or will the church be able to shake itself alive, and make people count it a privilege to worship Almighty God before beginning their day's work, as in the days when Morrow Mass was sung there?

## 2

WHEN WE look back on what we have chosen to call moorland, because it is so desolate and dotted about with wild flowers and bushes, we see little in the middle of it but the bastion of the Roman Wall, the stone tower and walls of St Giles, Cripplegate, and that solitary new building anchored like a liner against London Wall and the burial ground of St Alphage.

Barbican lies to the north; to the west is Aldersgate with St Botolph's; to the east is Basinghall Street, which flanks the Guildhall; to the south are Silver Street and Addle Street.

These two narrow medieval streets, though virtually wiped out and quite useless for traffic, had enough half-wrecked buildings to the south of them to give the impression of bringing our moorland to an end.

Between here and the Thames, always hidden from view by a line of warehouses, were areas of almost equal desolation, but from the very beginning they presented a different aspect. They never gave one that feeling of moorland in the heart of the town. Traffic continued to flow through their main west-to-east arteries—Gresham Street, Cheapside, Cannon Street, Queen Victoria Street. The golden cross at the top of St Paul's imparted its special protection. Omnibuses, lorries, and cars, City police on point duty, shops, offices, and restaurants, combined to give a picture of normality in contrast to the stillness of our moorland. Through these great arteries passed the traffic eastwards to the Bank of England, the Mansion House, Throgmorton Street; westwards to Fleet Street and the Strand. No wonder that this area began to be redeveloped, while hooligans, armed with sticks and stones, were still roaming the wilds of Cripplegate and London Wall.

When my father-in-law was curate at St Botolph's, Aldersgate, his delight, so he used to tell us, was to visit the small shops under the plane-tree at the corner of Wood Street and Cheapside. Cheapside, for the young curate, was the most exciting street in the City, crowded, amusing, dignified, pulsating with life and energy, a picturesque and proud reflection of the ever expanding commerce which a wealthy empire was bringing to the citizens of London.

Pleasant indeed it must have been on a summer's day with the wind rustling amongst the leaves of the famous plane-tree, the omnibuses dashing past crowded with young men on their way to Lombard Street, the bells of St Mary-le-Bow ringing gaily out, the laughter of cheeky office boys—the irrepressible 'children of the Chepe.'

How satisfying it is to walk the very ground where nearly two thousand years of vital, picturesque happenings have taken place. Here ran a Roman causeway of rough stone, close and well rammed, with brick and rubbish for a foundation, all firmly cemented, four feet thick and over natural clay. To the east was the Roman Forum. The Saxons made this their High Street. The Normans lodged here and built a church which was to be the first St Mary-le-Bow. Early in the twelfth century Thomas à Becket was born here in his father's house in Cheap. In medieval times it became the centre round which grew up the famous City guilds. The candle-makers, the hatters, the haberdashers, the makers of fish panniers and wine measures all shouted and cheated and fought. When Edward II's Queen Isabel, in 1312, gave birth to a son, the future Edward III, the conduit at Chepe ran with nothing but wine for a whole day, and did not Chaucer, in the *Coke's Tale*, sing of the prentice of Cheap who preferred the tavern to the shop!

There stood here in the centre of the road, opposite what is now Wood Street, the famous Cheapside Cross, one of the nine crosses erected by Edward I to mark the resting places of the body of his beloved queen, Eleanor of Castile, on its way from Lincoln to Westminster Abbey. Built by Master Michael, a mason of Canterbury, in 1290, there was an effigy in a niche of the Pope; round the base were four apostles, each with a nimbus; and above them sat the Virgin, with the infant Jesus in her arms. At the top was a cross surmounted by a dove. The cross was somewhat altered and combined with a drinking fountain during the reign of Henry VII, not long after which Wood Street is thought to have been named after Thomas Wood, a sheriff.

Cheapside was still a street of lively commerce. Tavern signs and shop signs hung outside the houses; carts brought water up from the river; fish caught in the Thames west of London Bridge was sold near the conduit in Chepe, and Friday, of course, was the busiest day.

The bell of St Mary-le-Bow rang gaily for mass, echoed by that of St Mildred in Bread Street; passers-by knelt before the Virgin of Cheapside Cross and prayed a moment; but soon after Elizabeth I's accession the puritans who had fled to the Continent flocked back to England, and in their professed horror of 'image-worship' began to take exception to the 'idolatrous cross of Chepe.' During the night of 21st June 1581 an attack was made on the lower tier of images, and the 'Virgin was robbed of her Son, and the arms broken by which she stayed Him on her knees, her whole body also haled by ropes and left ready to fall.'

Elizabeth, indignant at this vandalism, believing that a plain cross, a symbol of the faith of our country, ought not to give scandal, ordered a gilded one to be placed on the summit. The Virgin also was restored, but twelve nights afterwards she was again attacked, 'her crown being plucked off, and almost her head, taking away her naked child, and stabbing her in the breast.' This deplorable behaviour continued throughout Elizabeth's reign. John Milton, the poet's father, living across the way in Bread Street, at the sign of the Spread Eagle, in opposition to his own father, accepted the new faith and soon (9th December 1608) his son was to be born here and he would be calling at the church of Allhallows next door to arrange about the baptism.

On 2nd May 1643, by order of Parliament, the cross in Cheapside was finally pulled down.

'At the fall of the top cross, drums beat, trumpets blew, and multitudes of caps were thrown into the air.'

What my father-in-law liked best about Cheapside were the small shops in front of the tree at the corner of Wood Street. At one time rooks built their nests in the topmost branches, but I think the birds had gone before his curate days.

There used to be four little shops; now there are three. The general effect cannot have changed much, however, since they were first put up in 1687 during the reign of James II. Wren had already rebuilt many of the City churches, mostly dating from the eleventh and twelfth centuries, which after the Great Fire of 1666 lay in ruins. What irony that the day would come when nearly all his churches, except St Paul's, would suffer a similar fate.

Some, of course, were not rebuilt at all. St Peter in Chepe was an example. The damage was too great. This church, which probably dated from the early part of the twelfth century, was famous for the fact that Nicholas Farindon, the celebrated goldsmith appointed by Edward II to be Mayor of London for 'as long as it pleased him,' was buried there. Farindon gave the name to that part of the City known as Farringdon Ward, which had been in his family for eighty-two years, and, good Catholic that he was, left money for a light to burn before Our Lady the Virgin in the church of St Peter in Chepe for ever.

Meanwhile, in the year 1401, early in the reign of Henry IV, licence was granted to the inhabitants of the parish to erect a shed or shop in Chepe in front of the church. This became known as the Long Shop and was burned down at the same time as the church during the Great Fire of 1666.

Doubtless shrubs and young trees began to grow amongst the rubble. In 1687 the shops were rebuilt 'at ye sole costs and charges of the Parish.' This we learn from the original stone slab set into the back of the houses and which

*The corner of Wood Street*

gives the names of the two churchwardens, William Howard and Jeremiah Taverner.

Nicholas Farindon's light in front of Our Lady the Virgin had gone out. The statue of the Virgin had gone. Eventually, however, something quite as bright as a lamp, and much more wonderful, rose up as a memorial to Our

Lady. Shrubs and trees gave green foliage. Then in 1821 three churchwardens planted a sapling at the cost of sixpence where the medieval church had stood. This is the tree that has by now grown so mighty that it not only occupies the whole site of St Peter in Chepe but its topmost branches, taller than many a church spire, spread themselves over the three little shops.

A very pretty drawing made in the eighties portrays them as they must have been just before my father-in-law knew them, two-storeyed as they still are, with the great plane-tree looming up very tall and magnificent behind them. Delicate brick chimneys rose above the flat roofs. A. W. Kibble, later Ive, owned the first shop; Raymond owned the second; F. Passmore, stationer and printer (under the tree) owned the third; and the fourth was the so-called music warehouse of one Joseph Williams, a maker of pianofortes. The tree had two nests in it, though the rooks had probably gone by then. Women could be seen looking into the shop-windows. They were wearing bonnets, shawls, and bustles, their skirts sweeping the pavement. A covered wagon drawn by two horses was turning into Cheapside from Wood Street.

F. Passmore, the stationer, and Joseph Williams, the pianoforte maker, disposed of their leases in 1894 to two brothers, Llewellyn and Robert Wooderson, shirtmakers, who knocked the two shops into one. Llewellyn emigrated later to New Zealand but Robert continued the business, and having now reached the age of eighty-two has made his son Thomas the active partner.

The music warehouse disappeared altogether but Passmore, the stationer, who also sold toys, played a sort of musical chairs. Having abandoned the shop next to the corner, he opened up again in the first one in the row, which had by then become vacant. He was not to remain there for long. Sweets were sold there for a time, then gowns, and much more lately it has become a florist's, and Mrs Carrie Miller, its owner, supplies flowers on occasion to the Guildhall and to various City companies.

Nobody lives any longer in the rooms on the first floor.

The era of the shopkeeper who lived with his family above his shop has passed for ever. Thomas Wooderson uses his first floor, which is both light and airy, in part as an office, in part as a cutting room for the men's shirts he makes. The cellars formed part of the crypt of St Peter in Chepe.

'My father at eighty-two,' said Mr Thomas Wooderson to me one day, 'deserves to take things more easily. He lives at Clapham Park. When my Uncle Llewellyn and he first opened the shop, they both wore bob-tailed coats, and they never went out without a tall silk hat and gloves; my father had waxed moustaches. All the smart City gentry came to us.'

'Do men spend less on their clothes?'

'Certainly. In my father's day, and indeed when I was younger, a man's pride was to be well dressed. What matters to him to-day is the date of his car. Good dressing disappeared with the change in the observance of the Sabbath. In the old days a man put on his best clothes on Sunday; to-day he puts on his worst. Yes, indeed; men used to take a pride in dressing tastefully. Edward VII, when Prince of Wales, used to send to my father for silk for his ties and cravats.'

'Did your father worship in the City?'

'Not on Sundays. We are dissenters, Baptists; but my father held the office of treasurer churchwarden at St Vedast, Foster Lane, which they are now in the process of rebuilding.'

'What happened to your uncle?'

'My Uncle Llewellyn died, but one of his sons, who is farming very successfully in New Zealand, came over to visit us two years ago.'

A walk down Wood Street provides a glimpse of the City of to-morrow. These great buildings on the verge of completion will perhaps in fifty years' time be dwarfed by many others of the same kind, and their façades which just now are so virginally clean may have turned black with London grime, but this Easter they are beautiful. The new Compter House gives the impression of a liner at anchor even more than the building at London Wall. The upper floors curve slightly inwards as if to the prow, so that one has the illusion that the people inside must be able to promenade along sunny covered decks. The letter-boxes at the entrance are decorated with flowers, and there is a plaque which says that it was placed there by Sir Rupert de la Bere, Lord Mayor, on 25th September 1953.

A narrow passage leads into Mitre Court with the Mitre at the north-west corner. Of this old tavern in Wood Street, Pepys wrote, on 31st July 1665: 'Proctor, the vintner of the "Miter," in Wood Street, and his son, are dead this morning of the plague; he having laid out abundance of money there, and was the greatest vintner for some time in London for great entertainments.'

A century-old canopy in the centre of the court covers the entrance to the cellars of Norton & Langridge Ltd, beneath the flagstones of Mitre Court. These are the original underground dungeons of the old Wood Street City Comptor, a debtors' prison, under the control of the sheriffs; it was first established in 1555, later burned down in the Great Fire and rebuilt in 1670, and finally closed in 1790.

More than ever the City of this transient stage provides us with a strange mixture of old and new. A wax mannequin in a showroom window wears a red velvet cloak over a cotton dress as she languidly looks upon the scene with plastic eyes.

Milk Street, into which we could go if we pleased, through another passage from Mitre Court, is just at this moment in a turmoil owing to the presence of one of the largest travelling cranes I have ever seen. The lumbering creature has a neck about seventy feet long at the top of which is its narrow head and dangling tongue of clinking chain. The driver tells us that he is on his way to the new Bank of England building on the other side of Cheapside.

Back in Wood Street, a beautifully cool breeze blows from the still empty site between here and Gutter Lane. Beyond, and just far enough away to make it particularly effective, lies the new Saddlers' Hall, and just to the left of it what remains of the tower and walls of St Vedast, Foster Lane.

What a pity that some of these bombed sites cannot be turned into permanent gardens so that at every turn one would be faced with unexpected and poetic vistas! Farther along Wood Street, on the same side as the new Compter House, is an even bigger one called Clements House, which has deep blue tiles at eye level, with mosaic work above it, and windows edged with green and blue, all the changing colours of the sea. If only these vivid colours remain clean, then our architects will have made a big step forward into the future. Dazzling whiteness soon turns to black, but if our city of to-morrow can dazzle us with lovely colours to refresh our tired eyes the City will indeed be a lovely place to work in.

Gresham Street is very quiet, almost like a country lane, at this point. That is because none of these monster buildings is quite finished. How exciting it is to lift the curtain on a new age. The players, of course, are not yet on the stage. The orchestra pit and the stalls are empty. All the better. Anybody can go to the theatre when the play is on. I much prefer the preliminary hopes and fears. Between Wood Street and Gutter Lane an eleven-storey office building is starting to go up; on the opposite side of Gresham Street, between Wood Street and Staining Lane, Garrard House with its beautiful glass entrance doors, like the glass doors to a fairy palace, is nearly ready to be lived in. On the other side of Staining Lane are the most beautiful gardens, trees, shrubs, wallflowers growing as their name denotes against half demolished red brick walls, with hanging geraniums of every colour from deep red to white, forget-me-nots, and tulips. How good it smells! How beautifully quiet. Who would guess that over by the Mansion House the City throbs and vibrates. Here, against the side of Garrard House, is the new Haberdashers' Hall, with a plaque which reads:

1448–1954
Haberdashers' Hall

This stone was laid by the Rt Hon. Lord Mayor of London, Alderman H. W. Seymour Howard, on the Feast of St Catherine, the Virgin, 25 Nov. 1954.

Beyond this, there is still not a soul in sight. Here I discover two gardens more beautiful than any I have seen so far, even more lovely than the one I came across at the beginning of Staining Lane. The one to the left has flowers and plants growing against tiers and tiers of broken wall, so that one really has the impression of a fabulous garden of four thousand years ago. The leafy garden to the right is up three or four mossy steps, an Elizabethan garden with herbs and lilies of the valley, entwined roses, marigolds like those one sees on the Mediterranean coast, and tulips in profusion. A rock garden has been made with pieces of broken sixteenth-century gravestones. A tiny lawn is smooth and green. This is truly like a little corner of paradise! We are high above Silver Street looking down on its dusty, silent track, and in the distance, across the fen, is the church of St Giles, Cripplegate, and the bastion of the Roman Wall.

A temporary door nailed across one of the entrances to the church of St Lawrence Jewry says: KEEP OUT. From inside may be heard the voices of craftsmen at work, repairing, or rather rebuilding, this famous church. Let us look farther at what they are doing.

Before we seek out and talk to these twentieth-century craftsmen, however, it is vital to remind ourselves of certain facts.

The greatness of our land has, from the time of the Romans—which is almost the same as saying from the time of Christ—centred on this square mile. The Romans built their temples here. On occasion we find traces of them, and then the public, always avid for what is picturesque, becomes wildly excited. Modern commercial buildings, however, cost millions of pounds to erect and so the public is made to understand that neither the owners of the ground, nor the contractors, can afford to postpone their work. The best example of this was when the temple of Mithras was discovered in September 1954 on a site being cleared for

Bucklersbury House, one of the giants of the London of to-morrow.

The area that was once encompassed within the Roman Wall is far too valuable to allow of anything which no longer serves a vital need. When, in 653, Sigebert, King of the East Saxons, became a Christian, London was recovered from heathenism. A need arose for Christian churches. Peter of Blois, Archdeacon of London, was able to write to the Pope at the end of the twelfth century that there were 120 parish churches in London. You may be sure that all of them were fully used.

Before the Great Fire of 1666 the City had 97 churches within the walls, and 10 without. Some were Saxon; most were Norman. Generally they had small towers with Norman arches and fonts. St Olave, Hart Street, was an example. There were few spires to be seen, not more than two or three.

In the Great Fire of 1666 no fewer than 86 parish churches were gutted, and of these Sir Christopher Wren rebuilt 51.

The money was raised with comparative ease owing to the deep underlying sense of religion which had survived the Commonwealth. The Restoration, in spite of the licentiousness of the court and the ribaldry of the theatre, was a time of faith. The City was crowded with shopkeepers who lived over their rebuilt shops, and merchants who lived over their merchandise. All these people were anxious to see their churches rise again from the ashes, but it is important to note that Wren, when rebuilding them, no longer left room, as in medieval churches, for the processions which formed such an important role in the life of Roman Catholic Londoners. Wren's churches were framed for the new Faith.

The rebuilding of the City churches was greatly helped by a tax of three shillings on every ton of coal entering the Port of London. Many accounts are preserved at the Bodleian, together with the names of the principal craftsmen employed in building the churches. Londoners were so impatient to see them rebuilt that many parishioners openly offered bribes to Wren, or to those working under him, in the hope of getting preferential treatment. They longed for their Sunday services again. Some were astute enough to offer gifts to Wren's wife and we are told that she received a pair of fine silver candlesticks. Londoners also remembered to be grateful when their particular church was finally ready, and gifts of gratitude include several hogsheads of claret.

The nineteenth century saw the appearance of a new and mightier City of London. Queen Victoria was on the throne and the Empire was being made. Banks, insurance companies, and splendid commercial buildings were going up everywhere. Already the churches were crowded out. St Benet Fink, which Wren had rebuilt in 1673 on the site of a medieval church destroyed during the Great Fire, was ruthlessly pulled down toward the end of 1843 in order to build the Royal Exchange. Threadneedle Street stands in the centre of Roman London, and while the site was being excavated, workmen brought to light from under the foundations of the first church valuable Roman tiles, glass, and fragments of black, pale, and red Samian pottery.

By 1870 the voluntary destruction of the Wren City churches was going on apace. As the call of money became greater, so the pickaxe became busier. Here are some of the casualties: St Mildred, Poultry (1873); St Antholin, Watling Street (1875); St Michael, Queenhithe (1876); St Dionis Backchurch (1876); St Michael, Wood Street (1876); St Michael, Bassieshaw (1876).

Now came the demolition of one of the first two churches that Wren rebuilt after the Great Fire. In 1671 Wren built both St Mary-le-Bow and St Christopher-le-Stocks. St Mary-le-Bow in Cheapside was to benefit by the sentimental value which Londoners attached to its connection with Dick Whittington and the cockneys born within the sound of its bells, but in 1881 his church of St Christopher-le-Stocks in Threadneedle Street was pulled down to make way for the Bank of England, pride of the Victorian reign.

By 1939 the number of City churches had fallen to 46, of which 35 were built by Wren, but the resident population was no more than 9,180. So few people attended Sunday morning services that many rectors did not even bother to unlock the church door. They said that if any strangers did wander into the City they were bound to go to St Paul's.

The Great Fire of 1940 and the heavy night raids during the Battle of Britain once again gutted nearly all the City churches. The only difference from the Great Fire of 1666 was that St Paul's did not need, on this occasion, to be entirely rebuilt.

As the Bishop of London looked upon his wrecked and ruined City churches, he was obliged to reflect that the resident population had dropped to fewer than half what it had been before the war. The figure, at its most optimistic, was a miserable five thousand. If nobody had attended divine service before the war, how many would attend now? Had the City churches become as superfluous to modern Londoners as the temple of Mithras?

The Bishop of London and the Diocesan Reorganization Committee presented, in July 1951, their revised and final proposals for the reorganization of the City parishes and the rebuilding of the City churches. They wanted 'to make better use of the Church's manpower, money, buildings, and the great spiritual opportunities in the City; to make good, for the most part, the destruction and damage caused in the war; to strengthen the links with the civic life; and to make better pastoral provision for the large non-resident day-time population.'

This day-time population, incidentally, already crowding some 400,000 people within the square mile, might easily become astronomical when all the giant new buildings were put up.

The 46 parish churches, said the committee, would be reduced to 24 as follows:

| | |
|---|---|
| All Hallows-by-the-Tower | St Helen, Bishopsgate |
| St Dunstan in the East | St James Garlickhythe |
| St Andrew Undershaft | St Margaret, Lothbury |

St Andrew by the Wardrobe
St Bartholomew the Great
St Botolph, Aldgate
St Botolph, Bishopsgate
St Bride, Fleet Street
St Clement, Eastcheap
St Magnus the Martyr
St Edmund the King
St Giles, Cripplegate
St Mary at Hill
St Mary-le-Bow
St Michael, Cornhill
St Peter, Cornhill
St Olave, Hart Street
St Sepulchre, Holborn
St Stephen Walbrook
St Vedast, Foster Lane

All these churches would be rebuilt or restored, together with St Lawrence Jewry, which was to become the official church of the City Corporation.

Fifteen more churches were to be rebuilt or restored as Guild Churches. This was the list:

St Mary Woolnoth
St Mary Aldermary
All Hallows, London Wall
St Margaret Pattens
St Nicholas, Cole Abbey
St Martin, Ludgate
St Katherine Cree
St Michael, Paternoster Row
St Andrew, Holborn
St Botolph, Aldersgate
St Dunstan in the West
St Ethelburga, Bishopsgate
St Mary the Virgin, Aldermanbury
St Mary Abchurch
St Benet, Paul's Wharf

Five churches were not considered worth restoring:

St Stephen, Coleman Street
St Alban, Wood Street
St Alphage, London Wall
St Mildred, Broad Street
St Swithin, London Stone

The fate of two remained uncertain:

Christ Church, Greyfriars
St Anne and St Agnes, Gresham Street

The chief innovation were the so-called Guild Churches. Their creation and constitution were without precedent. Baptisms and marriages could be solemnized in them, but they would have no parochial responsibilities, and they would not be obliged to hold Sunday services, their chief function being to serve the growing Monday to Friday day-time office population, those 400,000 men and women who poured into the City every morning from the outer suburbs and left it every evening as soon as the offices closed.

This is how the Bishop of London and his committee describe the innovation:

'The name Guild Churches has been chosen because these are intended primarily for City workers, both employers and employees, many of whom are the present-day successors of the ancient craft guilds who comprised masters, journeymen (employees), and apprentices.'

What a fine thing that so many historic churches were to be rebuilt.

Where was the money to come from? In part, of course, from war damage compensation, but it was generally supposed that this would only cover a fraction of the cost. The rest, it was hoped, would be subscribed by commercial firms in the immediate area. St Giles, Cripplegate, however, needed another £40,000, but to whom could the rector appeal when more than nine-tenths of his parish, one of the largest in the City, had entirely disappeared from the face of the earth. Meanwhile his resident population scarcely reached half a dozen souls.

The Corporation of London undoubtedly came to the help of St Lawrence Jewry, and the Lord Mayor made a personal appeal for St Mary-le-Bow though some other rectors secretly accused him of discrimination. All this was not nearly so comfortable as the tax on coal which provided the money for Wren's 51 churches 300 years earlier.

St Lawrence Jewry, in case the reader cannot immediately bring it to mind, is the corner church with the square tower and lead spire, on the left as one enters the courtyard of the Guildhall. Its south wall flanks Gresham Street; its north wall, with the north entrance and the vicarage door, is shaded by two beautiful plane-trees which grow so happily in the quiet retreat known as Church Passage.

St Lawrence Jewry, which Wren began in 1676, was richly decorated, and proved, after St Mary-le-Bow, the most costly to build.

On the morning after the Great Fire of 29th December

*The courtyard of St Lawrence Jewry*

1940, when the City was still in flames, Mr Douglas Clarke, churchwarden of St Michael Bassishaw (a parish united with St Lawrence), found that although the walls and the tower had withstood the flames, the roof had collapsed and the church was knee deep in smouldering ruins. Valuable plate and vessels, much of it belonging to churches which had not been rebuilt after 1666, were found intact when the church beadle and the then rector, helped by firemen with hoses, were able to open the strong-room.

Let us now, seventeen years after the fire, pass under the plane-trees and enter. Plaster walls gleam white. A carpenter is planing a piece of wood. A door in natural oak, a lovely thing to look upon and obviously freshly put up, is ajar to the right, and leads into a room which eventually will be the vestry but which, for the moment, in its stark severity, save for some panelling by the door, is the office of Mr William George, the general foreman not only of this church but of St Mary-le-Bow, Wren's other costly masterpiece. William George is on the telephone. Let us study the man whose name must be given a place in the history of London.

He is of middle height, clean shaven, short hair parted on the left, and having a few rebellious wisps falling over his right temple. Born in Norfolk fifty-two years ago, he joined Dove Brothers during the economic slump of the late twenties. 'Because,' he says, 'I was in need not so much of a well-paid job as of one that would last.' The spectre of unemployment was becoming serious in the building trade.

His first big job, though his own situation was still modest, was in 1929 at the City's oldest and most beautiful church, St Bartholomew the Great (the present church is the choir of the ancient priory), where the roof was attacked by death-watch beetle. That proved for William George the beginning of a career devoted to the repairing and rebuilding of old churches. 'The work at St Bartholomew the Great lasted two years,' he says, 'and I picked up the business as I went along.'

His office is most fascinating. An unshaded electric bulb hangs down from the plaster ceiling and there are two narrow tables with drawing-boards against opposite walls. Hanging on one wall, between sheaves of builders' requirements and head-office memos fastened with bulldog clips, is a photograph of St Lawrence Jewry as it was before the war. The church externally is being rebuilt exactly as it was, and every now and again Mr George goes over to look at the photograph to refresh himself about some detail. Next to this is a pre-war picture of St Olave, Hart Street, that priceless fifteenth-century gem built above an early thirteenth-century crypt, in which Samuel Pepys and his twenty-nine-year-old wife are buried. The rebuilding of this church, exact to every detail (it had been reduced to a shell), is William George's masterpiece.

'Roof, walls, bells, and all,' he says contentedly. 'We even put the spikes back on the entrance gates—yes, everything precisely as it was in 1450.'

It is a pleasure to see him, for he has the face of a true English craftsman.

A moment later he returns to his youthful beginnings at St Bartholomew the Great.

'I want to show you something I found under the floorboards there,' he says.

He opens a drawer and pulls out a plastic envelope in which he keeps this delicate fragment of a letter dated 18th June 1735. He found this treasure himself. It constituted for him an element of romance which made his work different from all other. It was a letter two hundred years old, discovered in a secret hiding-place under the floorboards of one of the most awe-inspiring Norman priories to be seen anywhere. For a young man so minded there is romance and tragedy to be dreamed up out of this.

He takes up a magnifying-glass, though he must have done this a thousand times before, and reads aloud what he is able to decipher. 'See,' he says, 'it was written in Malaya to "my friend and benefactor."'

From St Bartholomew the Great, Mr George went to repair the tower at St Sepulchre, High Holborn. I broke into his narrative to ask a question.

'You love your work so much, don't you? Are you a churchman?'

'In a sense I am, though not a regular churchman,' he

answers. 'We have a six-year-old daughter, Patricia, and a ten-year-old daughter, Marian, and once a month I take them to church on Sunday morning.'

'Where do you live?'

'Blackfriars.'

He came to St Lawrence Jewry from All Hallows, Barking, which was now almost ready to be opened by the Queen Mother. I asked him what, in his opinion, was the biggest difference in building and motive methods in Wren's time and our own.

'A difference which comes from the trouble they had in cartage,' he answered immediately. 'The Normans built their churches of Caen stone not only because presumably they had greater facilities for quarrying it in their own country but because they could bring it right up to where they needed it by water. Wren used Portland stone and so do we, but though on occasion Wren, judging by what we see at St Paul's, brought from Portland individual blocks weighing up to three tons—I cannot imagine how he lifted them—he was obliged in a general way to be extremely economical. Consider the amount of stone he needed not merely to build St Paul's but also his fifty-one City churches. Our problems of cartage are nothing compared with his. We merely bring the stone by road to our yard in Islington where, except for some work done inside the church or by the porch, it is cut up according to what we need.

'Wren was able to effect his chief economy in this way. When building the walls of a church, instead of using solid blocks of Portland stone, he merely put a stone skin on the outside and another on the inside of the wall, and then filled in the centre with rubble. When we were pulling down the spire of St Dunstan in the East, for example, we discovered that the pinnacles, which at least one would have expected to have been made of solid stone, were hollow and filled in with gravestones most of which bore dates of 1540 and earlier. Little could the relatives of those people who died during the reigns of Henry VIII, or even Henry VII, have guessed, when they gathered round the grave, that one day the names of their loved ones, stone and all, would climb so high over London!'

'Do filled-in pinnacles last as long as solid ones?'

'How can one tell? At least they stood firm for three hundred years, and for all we know they might have lasted for another three hundred years. Traffic, of course, was less heavy when they were first put up. They would have had less vibration, but the fact is that the pinnacles were built by Wren in a way that, according to present standards, would not be allowed—and yet they did their job magnificently!'

'Are the walls of this church also filled with rubble inside?'

'Yes, indeed they are.'

'Yet they stood up to the fierce fire of that night in December 1940?'

'Yes, that is amazing, because stone is much more vulnerable to fire than most people think. These walls are, of course, much thicker than modern ones would need to be. The stone skin on either side might be from nine to twelve inches thick, but the whole wall might measure as much as four feet across. If we were to replace them with solid stone, the walls would not need to be so thick—at least, that is what modern architects believe. But who knows for certain?'

'Did you find anything curious in the walls of St Lawrence Jewry?'

'Indeed I did, but not on the ground—way up when we were cutting away to fix the bell frames sixty feet up. Look!'

Mr George had opened a deed box, and from this he brought out part of a human jaw.

'Here is the sort of thing one finds in rubble, even sixty feet high. The molars of an unknown man or woman in the days of Henry VIII, or even earlier, perhaps.'

'How did they get there?'

'I have already told you that at St Dunstan in the East we found pieces of gravestone inside the pinnacles. Everything was grist to the builder of Wren's walls. In this case,

I expect they just tilted in what they found in the churchyard or under the floor of the previous church.'

'Did you find anything else?'

'I found a quill ink-well in another place.'

'Do you ever come across any bodies?'

Mr George laughed.

'Oh dear, yes. When I broke into part of the crypt under St Mary-le-Bow, a vaulted chamber which had been sealed up for about 150 years, I found at least a thousand coffins stacked from floor to ceiling. More than half were lead coffins, and we were obliged to cut through the lead so that the bodies could be removed.'

'Why?'

'Because the crematoriums will not accept lead coffins. Lead does not burn.'

'What do the bodies look like inside?'

'They look almost lifelike! Well, no, that is not quite true. I mean they are all in one piece, with hair and teeth, and I think one might be able to recognize a face, though the features are sallow and ghoulish. I can't describe them very well, but I have dug them up at least five hundred years old. Wooden coffins disintegrate, of course. One merely finds the metal plates, when there are any.'

'Where did all these coffins come from in the sealed crypt under St Mary-le-Bow?'

'From adjoining churchyards, I expect, when the City was being built up at the beginning of the last century. We will walk over to St Mary-le-Bow later, if you like, and I will take you down into the crypt so that you can see for yourself where I found them.'

'Did you find any coffins here?'

'Yes, about two hundred. If they are not in the way, we leave them where they are. Otherwise they are sent to the crematorium.'

The craftsmen were having their lunch at three long tables outside the entrance to the vestry. Remembering how the names of the men who had built this church and that of St Mary-le-Bow, in Wren's time, had been handed down in documents now to be seen at the Bodleian, I asked Mr George to tell me how many men he had working under him.

Frank Martin, aged about sixty, was the foreman mason, with four or five men under him. Billy Webster, aged about forty-six, was the foreman carpenter, with about four or five men under him. Harry Henning, aged about fifty-three, was the foreman bricklayer, with about two men under him. There were six to eight general labourers.

We went into the church.

What a strange sensation to find oneself in a Wren church in which everything is absolutely new—the blinding white ceiling and walls, the heavy gold leaf, warm and rich, on the ceiling designs and on the tops of the Corinthian pillars, and everywhere this stained and polished oak which was such a feature of the Wren church. The stained and polished oak reredos, almost black, with the angels and lifted trumpets on either side, had a dust-sheet covering the centrepiece, which must await the unveiling ceremony. The two altar tables have just been brought in by the carpenters; long and narrow, they are of natural oak, and I admit that I find them more beautiful than the dark stain which Wren used with undoubted effect. Soon, of course, the altar tables will be covered with rich embroideries, and the silver cross and the candlesticks will stand upon them.

I am surprised by the relative silence in the church. A man is passing a heavy electric sweeper over the tiled floor in front of the altar. Mr George says: 'We have to keep on sweeping because of the dust, not to allow it to settle on the gold leaf or the paint.'

One hears the sound of chisels against Portland stone underneath the tower, but there is no shouting. While I was with Mr George in the vestry, I did once hear a man's voice breaking out into a few bars of a popular song, but the sound died away almost immediately, and merely remained in my mind as something rather lovely to remember.

Only the stained-glass windows are different. High in the east wall, to the left of the altar screen, is St Paul and, in a light underneath, an angel holding the burnt-out church. To the left is St Catherine with, in a light underneath, another angel showing it built up again, triumphant.

Along the south wall are St Mary Magdalene, St Michael, and St Lawrence, saints of the combined parishes.

I cannot attune myself to the modern idea of having colour only in the centre of a stained-glass window. Is this a matter of saving money, or is it to capture more light? I do not suppose that in this case it was a question of money. The architect was anxious to see St Lawrence Jewry on summer mornings filled with sunshine. This conception is quite new. Medieval builders were wiser, I think, to work for dark, mysterious half lights, shafts of heavenly tints, so conducive to contemplation and prayer.

Seeing a carpenter planing the side of a stained door, I put a finger on the wood, saying:

'I do love oak.'

That is true. I love oak, for I have so often seen my own oak-trees brought down and turned into bookshelves and furniture in Normandy, and I hold this superb tree in reverence, though I do not think it should be stained.

The young, dark-haired carpenter, without noticing my remark, looked round and said:

'The place is getting to look beautiful, isn't it?'

'The place?'

'The church.'

'Yes, I thought you meant the church, but I was not sure. Do you feel any affection for it?'

'Yes,' he answered with unexpected simplicity. 'It could not be otherwise.'

'Come along,' said Mr George. 'I will take you to St Mary-le-Bow.'

'Yes, I would like that.'

We went out into the spring air, and across Gresham Street. Mr George then stopped, turned round, and pointed up to the lead and oak spire above the tower, and to the deal and lead roof.

'Looks nice, doesn't it?' he said. 'Can you see where we retained the original stone and, farther along, where we were obliged, for some reason or other, to replace it? The first is darker than the second.'

Turning, he led me in the direction of Cheapside. New buildings were going up on every side of us, some original and bold in design, with plenty of colour; others little changed in aspect from the less imaginative pre-war designs.

I already knew a little about the situation at St Mary-le-Bow, having by a fortunate coincidence been to church there the previous Sunday: not in the church itself of course, which was entirely demolished, except for the walls which stood up grimly in all their charred nakedness, but in a temporary chapel erected on the side of the old vestry. A warm, friendly chapel, I had found it, with the interior distempered, half in pink, half in canary yellow, these contrasting colours one above the other and divided by a deep-blue line which ran all round the building.

The east windows were made in the form of small opaque squares with a semicircle effect at the top. A gold cross and some vases of yellow and blue irises stood on the altar table, round which ran an old and beautifully embroidered cloth. In the north-east corner of the chapel was an organ at which sat a spectacled young woman wearing a yellow beret. There a lectern was in the familiar form of a bronze eagle with outstretched wings, and there was a loudly ticking square clock; at the south-east corner was a stall for the rector. A reproduction of a Madonna and Child by Raphael in an oval gilt frame hung from the wall.

The rector, the Rev. Hugh Evan Hopkins, young, spectacled, a Cambridge man, wears preaching bands when in church—the old academic dress which lawyers still cling to—and the two white linen strips augment the ordinary clerical collar with striking effect. He is exactly the sort of man whom the Church of England is so anxious to see in the

City. Going first as a missionary to India—Dohnavar in the province of Madras—he became later, during the Mau Mau troubles, provost and archdeacon at Nairobi Cathedral (1947–55). He took up the rectorship of St Mary-le-Bow because it presented a challenge. He found himself with some fifty resident parishioners, few of whom came to church, and, towering over all the other commercial buildings in his parish, some new giants, as large as anything yet seen in England, such as Gateway House, the new offices of Wiggins Teape paper group, in Cannon Street, immediately to the east of the gardens of St Paul's Cathedral; and the enormous new offices of the Bank of England that will shortly dominate Cheapside. Here then was an ample challenge for the man from Emmanuel College, Cambridge, who had found Nairobi an exhilarating experience. What would he be able to accomplish in the City of to-morrow?

Twenty-four people were present at the Sunday morning service at which I heard him preach. Most conspicuous were nurses from St Bartholomew's, St Thomas's, and London University Hospitals. There were also two or three people who had been converted during week-day lunch-time services and who, though they lived a long way out of London, came to him on Sunday mornings because they considered the church their spiritual home.

The young rector had no illusions about the difficulties he would soon have to face. He had one thousand firms in his parish. Of these the new Bank of England was expected to employ 2,000 people; Wiggins Teape about 600; the new Sun Life building, exactly opposite his church, about 500. How would it ever be possible to establish personal contact with so immense a day-time population?

The task that faced Mr William George appeared to me even more titanic than the one which worried the young cleric. The space within the charred walls of the famous church was flat, arid, and utterly disheartening. I think I might even have welcomed the sight of a solitary dandelion.

One is tempted, when faced with such an overwhelming feeling of emptiness, to ask oneself if there is any sense in rebuilding a dream. What will be left of the original Wren church? Is it all a game to see if we are able to rival him? Are we to conjure up out of nothing, something that once had life, and no longer exists, in order that we may transport ourselves back in thought to the past.

In spite of my misgivings I know that it can be done. Have I not seen, a moment ago, another Wren church, superb in every detail, which like this one had been reduced to absolutely nothing? It was, was not, and is.

The sunshine pours into this empty walled space but it also shines outside on a dozen carpenters putting up a wooden construction which, Mr George tells me, is going to be a temporary chapel to replace the one in which I worshipped the previous Sunday. The old one is to be pulled down. Next week they are going to start the rebuilding in earnest.

A hundred yards beyond the new chapel are great piles of weather-blackened Portland stone. Every piece has a number painted on it, and I suddenly realize that I am looking at the spire, which has been brought carefully down, stone by stone, and numbered.

'So it will be Wren's spire exactly?'

'We shall replace the pieces that have been burnt by the north wind. Some of the stone is beginning to crumble. There will be quite a lot to replace, but all the same it will be Wren's spire.'

'Is this going to be a difficult job?'

'Extremely difficult. The Norman crypt is in a pretty bad way. Let us go down and see it.'

The top of a ladder emerged from what looked like a very deep hole in front of us, which must have been at a point about half-way up the north aisle.

The effect of this ladder rising from out of the ground was rather curious. What could there be so wonderful at the bottom of the hole? Watching Mr George clambering down, I found myself recalling the Hans Andersen story about the soldier coming back from the wars, and meeting a witch who said to him: 'Soldier, I shall make you rich. The big tree over there is quite hollow. Let yourself into the hole and slide down till you get to the bottom. You will see a dog with eyes as big as saucers. . . .'

The Norman crypt under St Mary-le-Bow had become quite a fable. Should I discover inside it the equivalent to the old witch's tinder-box? Was it so very fabulous? True enough, Mr George confessed that he had discovered a chamber not opened for at least 150 years—from which he had brought out more than 1,000 coffins!

The crypt in which we soon found ourselves consisted of a number of vaults leading one into the other. The ceilings were vaulted and comfortably high and therefore not oppressive, and when one lost the light of the hole down which we had come there were electric lamps at the end of trailer wires.

When, according to Hans Andersen, the soldier got down to the bottom of the hole in the tree, he filled his pockets first with copper, then with silver, then with gold. Mr George's treasures, metaphorically, were Tudor brick, Norman stone from Caen, Saxon small stones, and Roman tiles. I had asked him on our way over from St Lawrence in Jewry what gave Tudor bricks their beautiful warm red colour. Had we lost the secret of making them? Who has not looked with wonder at the peculiar tint of the clock tower at St James's Palace or the Tudor warmth of Hampton Court? Mr George claimed that the bricks made to-day were much better than those made in olden days. He said that they could be pressed together so much tighter, which would make them last longer. 'As for the colour, perhaps that particular source of clay is no longer available to us. If it was near London, for instance, it may have become built over as the suburbs were extended. I am not sure about that.' Roman tiles, on the other hand, Mr George said, appeared to last indefinitely. They showed no signs of turning to powder after nearly two thousand years. Presumably, therefore, the Romans had a secret for building bricks which even we do not possess to-day.

As we passed from vault to vault, Mr George must have remembered our talk, for he exclaimed:

'There is some Tudor brick!'

The deep red colour was just as I love it but the general foreman, taking up a stick, began to scratch the surface. Sometimes it turned to powder, at other times little pieces fell off. I picked up a piece the size of a walnut and hesitated whether to take it home, but it was cold and damp, and I decided that I was not sufficiently interested.

The Norman pillars, when rubbed, became gloriously white and new, their surface being quite different from Portland. There were patches of Saxon stones, like pebbles, and a great many Roman tiles which, according to Mr George, had been picked up by the Norman builders, and used as rubble, just as Wren filled in his seventeenth-century walls with fifteenth- and sixteenth-century gravestones, and anything else he found handy.

'I shall do the same sort of thing when I rebuild this church,' said Mr George. 'Though much of the stone will be new, I shall use everything I can from Wren's building, and in the process probably pick up quite a lot which he picked up when he was building it.'

We went to inspect the vault he had unsealed—a long, tall room, with fine Norman pillars, often half hidden behind brickwork which Wren had put in to bolster them up, and I asked if there had been emanations when he had broken in.

'Just what one always meets with in a charnel-house,' he answered.

We were out in the sunshine again, and I took leave of Mr George on the pavement of Cheapside. That Sunday morning, after I had attended service in the temporary building which was now to come down, I had stood for a few moments on this pavement, talking to a young woman who had come out at the same time as myself. I had wondered what had brought her there. Did she live in the City?

'No,' she answered. 'I do not even live in London. My home is in Kent but I am the head of a typing pool in

Gresham Street, and so St Mary-le-Bow is my week-day church.'

'Do you love the City?'

'I loved it when I first came here after the war. We had a lovely view from our office, the Guildhall on one side, and right across the tower of this church to St Paul's Cathedral on this side. And there were the daisies in summer, and the fireweed in the autumn. The City had a strange loveliness. But now our view is blocked by that huge new building across the road.'

I looked in the direction in which she pointed, and saw, written in large letters on a contractor's board, that the building, when finished, was to be the headquarters of a famous life insurance company. Yes, but this company, which promises security to all those who take up its policies, has unwittingly robbed my friend and her colleagues of light and air, and the view across her favourite church to the dome of St Paul's.

'Where do you do your shopping?' I asked her.

'Mostly round St Paul's Churchyard and in Ludgate Circus,' she answered, 'but if we have a little more time, we go as far as Gamages. We only have an hour for lunch and there are queues in all the shops.'

'Do you use the lunch hour for eating or for shopping?'

'For shopping. The men have time to lunch, and often, if the weather is fine, to sit out in the sunshine. We women must do the shopping for our families. Otherwise they would have nothing to eat when we come home in the evenings.'

'It must be a nuisance bringing back foodstuffs to the office?'

'Yes, especially fish. We could buy good fish near Billingsgate but what can we do with it on a warm afternoon? These great new buildings have put up canteens, but canteens do not solve the problem of what we are to do about our shopping. Everything is closed by the time we get home. The truth is that the men eat at lunch-time and the women do not. If the companies who put up these giant buildings really kept abreast of the needs of to-day, they would supply refrigeration for the meat and fish their women employees buy during the lunch hour.'

'Do you like being at work?'

'Yes, for I have a grown-up son who has left home, and so this new interest has given me a second youth.'

## 3

SKIRTING St Lawrence Jewry and the Guildhall is Aldermanbury, running, like Wood Street and Staining Lane, due north toward the wilder neighbourhood of London Wall. The busy part of Aldermanbury is very short, for just as soon as it reaches Addle Street, which, still impassable to traffic, crosses it at right angles, the fens begin.

I come on a pilgrimage because, at the age of seventeen, I worked as a shorthand-typist here, a position which entailed the answering of the telephone, the making of tea, and the posting of letters. My employer was a manufacturers' agent whose small, dim office in this narrow street, where one heard the clatter of horse-drawn vans and the cooing of pigeons, was probably typical of one aspect of City life which soon will have faded into the past like the London of Thackeray and Dickens.

I doubt if one ever has a feel for the City until one has worked in it, and it is a mistake to believe that only stockbrokers, bankers, aldermen, clergymen, or even men in general have this privilege. A girl of seventeen, even though her mind be full of romance and dancing, may well be marked by it for the rest of her life.

What a transformation meets my anxious eyes! Most of the block between Gresham Street and Little Love Lane has been metamorphosed by the twin fairies of annihilation and reconstruction. The gigantic newcomer, with an inner courtyard, is called Barrington House, and I am brought to a sudden halt by the sight of a coal-black West Indian, dressed all in white except for a green visor cap, splashing white paint on some posts in Little Love Lane. I smile at him but he looks suspicious. These swarthy new British settlers in London appear to take life very seriously.

By a miracle this tiny corner dear to my memories remains, if not what it was, at least from a distance recognizable. The old-fashioned building in which my employer had his office was now once again looking very much as it did in my time, and immediately opposite was the quiet garden of the church of St Mary the Virgin with its lime-tree in tender leaf.

Anybody, I think, would cry out in wonder at this evocative piece of London as so many of us knew and loved it. The garden, just now full of red and yellow tulips, gay with chirruping birds darting about amongst the leaves of the lime-tree, is full of Elizabethan memories, for Shakespeare used to come here to visit his two actor friends, Heminge and Condell, who lived in the parish, and who were responsible for collecting his dramatic writings and giving them to the world.

The church garden in which Shakespeare and his friends so often lingered may not have changed so much. English trees and flowers are much the same throughout the ages. The church, however, was destroyed in the Great Fire of 1666 and Wren did not start to rebuild it until eleven years later when he was simultaneously engaged in rebuilding St James, Garlickhithe.

I had stood in Aldermanbury just after the Great Fire of December 1940, and I knew that my church, the Wren church, had been gutted, but now, with the garden in full flower, and the tree so green, I could hardly believe that there was nothing but rubble beyond the walls. I had also hoped, unreasonably perhaps, that just because it was the church of my young womanhood, I should already be seeing the stonecutters at work, repairing the walls and the tower, the carpenters making a new roof, the polishers rubbing down newly made pews and a fine pulpit, and even the electricians wiring new brass chandeliers.

But beyond the flowering garden the gutted church smelled dank.

I also made a discovery that filled me with apprehension.

The small carved figure of the Virgin of Aldermanbury, which stood in a niche above the church door and upon which I had gazed so often as a young woman in my moments of happiness or trouble, was gone.

She had passed unscathed through the great fire of December 1940, and now, suddenly, she was gone.

How did it happen that at the age of seventeen I had come to work in this corner of the City, spending more than a year here, often stealing my lunch hour to come and dream in the garden?

A girl of my own age whom I had met one Saturday afternoon at a chemist's shop at the corner of Greek Street and Old Compton Street, Soho—the corner next to the one now occupied by the London Casino—knowing that I wanted to make use of my recently acquired shorthand and typing, advised me to apply to the French Chamber of Commerce, through which, though she had only recently arrived in London, she had found herself a wonderful situation.

On the Monday, therefore, I hurried to their offices in Queen Victoria Street, where I filled in a form, giving my name and address, and the speeds of my shorthand and typing, both of which were so far below the normal requirements of a good firm that the employee, glancing down the form I handed back to him, said:

'I hardly think we shall find it easy to fix you up in a hurry if these are your maximum speeds. There is something else. Have you no references?'

'Surely one is not expected to have many references at seventeen?' I objected.

'That is true,' he conceded, laughing. 'There must always be a beginning. Well, I will see what I can do for you, and as soon as I hear of anything at all suitable I will send you a postcard.'

I paid him five shillings and started to walk home. Soon, finding myself in the shadow of St Paul's, and never having penetrated inside, I decided to pass through one of the huge doors and offer up a short prayer for the success of my undertaking. I was in no particular hurry to go home, for my mother could easily be prevailed upon to believe that I had been kept waiting at the Chamber of Commerce.

Once inside the cathedral, what surprised me was to find it so full of sightseers, and apparently so empty of worshippers. I had expected to see people continually coming in from the hum of the streets, moving silently in the direction of the altar before kneeling down to pray on the stone floor. The people all about me were sightseers staring around vacantly and open-mouthed. Many were foreigners. A guide inquired if I would care to join the party which he was on the point of escorting up the stairs to the Whispering Gallery. The charge was threepence. I was still anxious to carry out my original intention of moving quietly up the body of the cathedral to pray, but I was appalled by the cold vastness of the place and the complete lack of people doing what I would have so much liked to do myself. I was intimidated by the guide who was waiting for me to give him threepence. I paid the money, and found myself moving off with the others.

When, half an hour later, the guide released us, and I emerged into the brilliant sunshine outside, my heart beat with excitement at this piece of London glittering at my feet. Red omnibuses, so many of which still had open tops, splashed Ludgate Circus with vivid colour. Women wore large, almost cumbersome, hats. A moustached policeman, in front of the Queen Anne statue, put out an arm, and the traffic stopped. Drivers of railway vans reined in their powerful horses, whose hoofs slithered on the smooth surface of the road, sending sparks flying. How stacked they were with merchandise. Behind them, a boy gripping a knotted rope swung precariously.

The dense, slow traffic, producing a picture of solid wealth amassed over the centuries, evoked in my youthful mind a feeling of admiration, envy, and fear. How should I, who had no protection save from a mother weaker than myself, no father, no money, set about to earn a livelihood in this maze of streets about which, for the moment, I knew absolutely nothing? I was inquisitive about these romantic City lanes, jammed with traffic, dark with Victorian office buildings, and warehouses piled high with riches still beyond the powers of my imagination. Was I brave enough to explore these many tributaries on either side of the main flow of Ludgate Hill, on one side toward Newgate and Holborn; on the other side down to the dark flowing Thames?

Slowly I descended the steps of St Paul's. Newsboys were already shouting the evening papers, the vivid contents sheets flapping up against their long trousers. How they yelled the news! The noise of the cart-horses, the shriek of newspaper vans, the honking of taxi-cabs deafened and bewildered me. London had many faces, but this was so different from the others, so entirely a place apart, that it was like walking through another land. The noise of the streets and the smell of the air one breathed were of a special kind. There was everywhere a ponderous slowness. Even the people had different expressions and peculiar ways of dressing. The men, especially, with their bowler hats, striped trousers, freshly cut rose in the buttonhole, attaché-cases, and rolled up umbrellas, were, I felt, a race apart. A pigeon, seeing that the policeman had held up the traffic again, flew down from a grimy cornice to peck at what fell from a horse's nosebag. The bells of the City chimed, and a tug hooted on the Thames.

I thought all this frightening and strange, grimy and dark, and yet colourful because of the trees and the red omnibuses, fantastic, ugly, extraordinary, and magnificent. No human brain could ever have invented this lumbering, sprawling, medieval, modern, oppressive, mysterious City. If I were not to be allowed to come and work here, I would be prevented from living in the way I was determined to live. To work here must be the strangest experience that the world had to offer.

I began to weave a story which I could recount to my mother when finally I reached home, for I not only wanted to explain the fact that I was late but I also wanted to implant in her mind more hope about my ability to find work in the City than my interview warranted. She would be anxious, and very happy to believe anything I cared to tell her, for she was only too aware that as yet I knew very little about life, and my youthfulness frightened her. She had, alas, not by any means made the best of her own youth, and that preyed on her mind. Our resources in experience and intellect, even when pooled, did not amount to much. I had the impression that I was walking very slowly, and I was ashamed not to be able to go faster. All the people I looked at seemed to be in such a hurry. I envied them, and as I was still young enough to play make-believe, I pretended that I had already been engaged as a shorthand-typist, and that I had just been released from one of these important looking offices to go on an errand. From time to time I looked at the front of the buildings, and I marvelled at the frivolities which were dealt with in the vicinity of the cathedral—artificial flowers, straw hats, blouses, veils, and other charming, useless things that I had not expected to discover behind such solemn façades.

Sometimes I turned off to explore narrow streets, or a cul-de-sac which ended up with three solid posts planted in the centre of the carriage-way. Office boys, pushing stout trolleys filled with rolls of material, came upon others of their own age, proud to have left school, awkward but happy, and whistling shrilly as they walked. I pretended that I had suddenly stumbled upon an Eastern bazaar. Perhaps it was like this in Shanghai or in Bombay where, as in London, merchandise arrived from foreign ports in ships.

I wore a hat with a wide brim, which mother had made me, and it prevented me from seeing the tops of the houses, but I could enjoy the occasional streaked gold of the sunshine against the sides of the dark houses.

I must have walked in the sunshine for over an hour, at the end of which time I found myself recognizing streets and buildings and overcoming to a certain extent that feeling of fear which the strangeness of these surroundings had at first instilled in me. When, having retraced my steps, I jumped on a bus in Cheapside, I felt as if I had planted a flag, though perhaps a very small one, in the heart of this territory which I planned to conquer.

One morning a week later I ran down in my dressing-gown to the street door to fetch the letters which the postman had just slipped through the letter-box after beating the usual rat-tat-tat on the knocker. There I found one addressed to me from the Chamber of Commerce. Mr Meller of Aldermanbury, E.C., in need of a shorthand-typist, suggested that I should call on him at ten o'clock to see if I were capable of filling the post. Racing upstairs, I breathlessly imparted the good news to my mother, and dressing with great care to give the right impression, and hardly waiting to swallow my breakfast, I ran out into the narrow passage which, skirting St Giles, Soho, led into New Oxford Street, where a policeman, having examined the address on the letter, told me which bus to take.

I must, I think, have got out near St Mary-le-Bow in Cheapside, and walked down Milk Street as far as St Lawrence Jewry. I remember the panic that I fell into when I discovered that I was half an hour too early, and the excitement I felt when turning past the Guildhall I suddenly looked up to read the name Aldermanbury on the side of a building. The number I was looking for faced Little Love Lane and the garden of St Mary the Virgin. The houses here formed a slight curve. Bronze and painted plaques were attached to the tall doors, giving the names and the floors of the occupants. I read: Manufacturers' Agent—First Floor.

The wooden staircase was wide, dusty, and dark. A frosted glass door on the first landing repeated the name of my prospective employer. I pushed it open and found myself in an office built in the form of a corridor with a long counter under big grimy windows through which could be seen the spreading branches of the lime-tree in the garden of St Mary the Virgin. A small dark man, dressed in navy blue serge, busying himself behind the counter, received me with a great show of politeness, and invited me to take a seat in front of the typewriter, in which position, he amiably pointed out, I would make a good impression when the boss arrived. He then began to open the firm's letters, and as he was so small, the long counter behind which he stood seemed more impressive than it might otherwise have done. I began to look about me, taking in the details—a gas-fire, also a ring on which reposed a rusty kettle; an old-fashioned telephone, to which were attached a note-book and pencil, stood on the counter. I stared at the telephone stupidly until, in my imagination, it had turned into a fantastic black person with a single arm.

'Do you live far away?' asked the young man behind the counter.

'Just a minute from New Oxford Street,' I answered.

'You mean, by Henry Glave. They are customers of ours!'

There was distinct commercial pride in his voice. Did he think of London in terms of his employer's customers? He was friendly and, I decided, amusing and kind.

'They call me Arthur,' he said. Then, putting on his bowler hat, he released himself from behind the counter, and added: 'Stay here. You'll be all right. I have to go out.'

Well, at any rate, Arthur trusted me. Though I was not yet engaged, I was left in charge of the firm. What should I do if the telephone rang?

Five minutes later the door opened, and a tall, blond man arrived. He also wore a bowler hat, which he took off and carefully placed on a shelf before going over to the counter, where he inspected the letters which Arthur had left there.

'Good morning,' he said, suddenly deigning to notice me. 'Are you waiting for Mr Meller?'

'Yes.'

'Do you come from far?'

'From New Oxford Street.'

'That is not far by tube. How long have you been in England?'

'Oh, a long time!'

This answer put him in a hilarious mood.

'In that case,' he said, 'you must have come over as a baby in your mother's arms!'

He opened his sample case, unhitched the telephone receiver, and asked for a number. Meanwhile, Arthur, having come back from his errand, stood on tiptoe in front of the shelf to place his bowler hat next to the one belonging to the man talking on the telephone. A third man now entered, and having bade us all good morning, went to sit by himself in a corner where, after removing the cover from a portable Corona typewriter, and balancing the little machine on his knees, he proceeded to type busily, without bothering to remove his grey soft hat.

Soon new steps became audible on the stairs. People had been coming and going all the time, but the sound of these steps had an immediate effect on Arthur, who straightened himself and called out:

'Careful, all of you! Here he comes!'

The door opened noisily, and Mr Meller burst into his outer office, which he traversed rapidly, crying out a cheery good morning before disappearing into an inner room. I was left with a passing vision of a man still relatively young, with a beige homberg, a small moustache, and a flower in the buttonhole of his grey suit.

'Arthur!' he called from the inner room. 'Arthur!'

Arthur, who had obviously been expecting this summons, snatched up the letters from the counter and disappeared. Two minutes later he was back again and, bending over me, said in a confidential whisper:

'He won't keep you long, mademoiselle.'

I had lost my nervousness. All these men who came and went intrigued me immensely. Arthur and his two companions had, in a sense, become my allies, in addition to which I found the atmosphere congenial. Long show-cards had tiny pieces of coloured silk attached to them like the fluttering wings of butterflies. I decided that any work to do with silk must be less irksome than other kinds. My mother had taught me from earliest girlhood a love and respect for *crêpes de Chine* and satins of natural silk, most of which, at that time, came from Lyons.

Could I not just as easily have fallen upon a dealer in tin cans? The sight of these beautiful materials made me doubly anxious to get the job.

Soon the tall blond traveller was called in to the boss, and on his return I watched him gather up his samples and take his hat down from the shelf. How could he be certain, I wondered, which hat was his? The two bowlers, as they lay side by side, were identical.

'So long!' he called, and a moment later we heard him running down the wooden stairs.

Now Arthur came up to me and whispered:

'Come, mademoiselle!'

I had only half a dozen yards to go. The office in which the boss sat was smaller than the one I had just left, but it was arranged in the same way with the same kind of counter and a window through which the branches of the lime-tree in the garden of St Mary the Virgin could be seen.

'Well,' asked Mr Meller in excellent French, 'have you a great deal of experience?'

Had they not told him about my speeds? What was I to say? A girl of seventeen does not know how to lie, nor even to gloss over her defects, so I answered, blushing:

'I have no experience at all.'

'In that case,' answered Mr Meller, who did not seem at all surprised, 'I shall dictate a letter which you can take next door and type. Then we shall see.'

Arthur was sent out to find a note-book and a pencil. My fingers had turned limp, and my hat was uncomfortably tight, but it was too late for me to take it off, and the only mirror I had noticed so far was beside the gas-ring in the big office.

The letter was an easy one, and I was able to read it back without any trouble. The fact that it dealt with a consignment of silk from Lyons had made it interesting to me. I took it to the boss, who read it carefully, and said:

'That seems very nice. I think you will do!'

My heart thumped with pleasure. What an important man he seemed. What a blessed relief to know that I would do!

'Every morning,' Mr Meller was saying, 'I dictate my letters, and then I go off to call on my customers. During that time you will type the letters and classify them. When Arthur is out, you will answer the telephone. The hours are from nine to six, with an hour off for lunch.'

'The wages?'

'Two pounds a week.'

I murmured my thanks. Two pounds were not a great deal, but mother would do wonders with them, and I now had what I wanted.

I quickly realized that Mr Meller was no ordinary man. How quick and resourceful he was! It did not take him a moment, if I was busy on other things, to whip out his typewriter, for he also had a portable Corona, and answer his correspondence in German, English, or French. I discovered that the man who had sat in a corner of the big room typing away on the morning of my arrival was a young brother to whom he generously offered the hospitality of his office.

My boss was the London agent for all the most beautiful silks in Lyons, and I was to see, unfolded before me on this long counter, under the shadow of the lime-tree of St Mary the Virgin, silks that seemed almost worthy of being incorporated into her saintly veil. I saw lamés with threads of real gold and silver that would have lent dignity to a queen driving through the historic streets of the City on her way to the Guildhall. I learned to recognize not merely the touch of certain silks but also their smell, as if they were living things, and I took pleasure in the acrid tang of gold and silver threads.

The soft colours of the *crêpes de Chine* were a delight to gaze upon. I think it was my appreciation of these tender and beautiful shades that made me feel such immense pity for the blind. Mr Meller gave me a love for materials which, far from diminishing, has grown with the years.

Arthur, between puffs at a pipe which he was continually mislaying, kept me in touch with what happened in the office, and proved himself an amusing and valuable ally. He immediately nicknamed me 'Mamzelle,' and I think that my accent amused him. He was married and occasionally talked about his child. He had a great ambition, and I have seldom seen anybody so utterly absorbed in his work. Even Mr Meller was impressed, and would sometimes allow him to go off and call on customers. His dream was to become a traveller.

Our office was closed during the lunch hour. Arthur used to lock up and slip the key in his pocket. I tried at first to squeeze into one or other of the City tea-shops for a poached egg on toast, but either because I was too young and shy, or because I was not accustomed to the habits of City workers, I never managed to get served, or if I did, it was after such heartbreak and exertion that I quickly suffered from indigestion. I decided to go without lunch. Far too many girls still try to do this. They think, as I did, that at seventeen they can do anything. What humiliated me was that I, a Parisian girl, managed so unsuccessfully amongst London girls. I thought I must be unusually stupid.

Having given up trying to crowd into tea-shops, which did not serve what was my idea of a lunch anyway, I went to sit under the friendly branches of the lime-tree in the garden of St Mary the Virgin. I loved the statue of Our Lady in her niche above the door. She had been there unchanging, ever as lovely, for nearly three hundred years, and I imagined that she would still be there in another three hundred years. I could not guess that in so short a time, whilst I was still comparatively young, with a baby of my own, her church would be reduced to ashes, and she herself would be missing from her shrine.

In spring the wallflowers and tulips smelt delicious, and young women of my own age came to sit here round the statue of Shakespeare. Avidly they read their fashion and film magazines, from time to time plunging a hand into a paper bag containing an apple and sandwiches, then munching without ceasing to read.

As they hardly ever spoke to one another, I decided that

to look grown up in the City one must cultivate a distant air, which I did, though I must have seemed ridiculous.

The grass was green and clipped; the earth the colour of soot. I learned to associate Shakespeare's England with a garden sweet with wallflowers and tulips.

Two o'clock rang out from all the towers and spires in the City, sending crowds of pigeons billowing into the sky. In an instant also, the girls in the garden, myself included, flew away. The lunch hour was over.

Our office door was unlocked, and Arthur would invariably be behind the counter, his bowler hat neatly put away on the shelf. I took my own hat off and placed it beside his.

'Had a good lunch?' he would ask while eating a sandwich.

'Yes, thank you.'

My pride would not allow me to admit that I had eaten nothing at all.

'What did you have?'

'An egg on toast,' I lied.

I would much rather have had something more substantial but this sounded plausible.

'Lucky you!' he exclaimed, with his mouth full of sandwich. 'I bring these from home to save money, and eat them in the office with a bottle of beer.'

Arthur, having finished his sandwich, covered the counter with rolls of silk, and began snipping off small squares of *crêpe de Chine* and georgette, which he doubled over and pinned lightly to a sheet of white paper. When he had made several of these, he looked up at me, and announced importantly:

'Shade cards!'

'What a pity to spoil such wonderful silk!' I objected, thinking of the many garments my mother and I could have made with these precious materials.

'This is how we carry on our business,' Arthur explained.

He was shocked at my lack of comprehension, and added:

'*Crêpe de Chine* and georgette are not known by colours but by the numbers we write against them.'

The boss seldom came back before four or five in the afternoon. It was he, Arthur confided in me, who called on the really important customers. Sometimes he had to wait quite a long time before they could see him.

He had become such a fabulous figure in my mind, that I found it difficult to picture him waiting his turn with other manufacturer's agents and travellers, to offer his materials to the buyers of wealthy firms. Was he really made to wait, as I was when I wanted anything? At seventeen one invests the boss, even though he has only two or three people working under him, with the importance of a monarch. One trembles at his approach or knocks at his door with an anxious heart. Youth is a mixture of insolence and timidity. I was often impatient and rude to my mother. I liked to pretend that I was old enough to know as much as she did. When Mr Meller called me to take dictation, I was absolutely terrified.

Fear, however, was not the only sentiment he inspired in me. I was intrigued by his lucidity, a quality I was not yet familiar with, and his commercial ability. He knew all the ways in which payments could be made, exactly how long it took for merchandise to come from various parts of Europe. This sort of thing, together with his astonishing command of languages, could not be common in so young a man.

Most of the large corporations finished work at five; many of the small firms went on till six. I learned to make up for the days when I had no lunch by having a bun at tea-time, a meal which Arthur and I observed together while waiting for Mr Meller to come back from his rounds. I was only occasionally envious of the girls who worked in banks and insurance companies. Though their offices were palatial and their hours shorter, I would console myself by saying: 'Later, perhaps, the day will come.'

After a few weeks with Mr Meller I still felt deliriously happy. The summer continued fine, and every Friday I received my pay. I now brought sandwiches from home which I ate in the garden of St Mary the Virgin. I began to love the statue of the Blessed Virgin more and more.

I felt such a tender love that I used to imagine I could take it home and have it in my bedroom. And indeed it was small enough for me to have done so.

I had not yet started to read women's magazines. *Picture Show* was the only magazine I saw at all regularly. Mother and I did not bother to buy a newspaper, either in the morning or in the evening, the little news I picked up being mostly gathered from a quick glance at the headlines of the papers which my fellow travellers read in the bus or in the tube on my way to and from work. At home our own problems seemed the only ones of any importance, and Hollywood provided us with the colour and romance we needed.

I began to set aside the second half-hour of my lunch-time in the garden for embroidery—to making napkins in broderie Anglaise or Richelieu. The craze for knitting had not yet overcome us.

Friday was not only pay day; I remember it for the fact that at lunch-time the doors under my statue of the Virgin would be open, and organ music would waft out to those of us who were lunching, reading, or sewing in the garden. These are amongst my most tender memories of the City, and they come back to me when people, as they so often do, claim that these churches and their quiet gardens no longer serve a purpose in the City of To-day. Sacred music, music by Wagner, coming out to a little group of people sitting under the boughs of a lime-tree. Is there not an old-world village atmosphere about this? Had the spirit of the garden changed so very much since Shakespeare came to sit here with his friends? Then two would strike. Like Cinderella, called away from the ball, I left my garden and my dreams and returned to the office.

To wash my hands I had to climb to the top of the building, and there I would find other young women who worked in offices under the same roof. We never spoke to one another, none of us considering it worth while to start friendships that could only with difficulty be continued between one office and another. Nevertheless, our duties were the same wherever we worked, those that were invariably the lot of junior shorthand-typists in small concerns, filing the correspondence, buying the biscuits and buns, serving tea, making ourselves housewives in embryo.

The boss's business grew in importance. One brother who was a manufacturers' agent in Paris occasionally crossed the Channel to see us. The other, the one whom I had seen the first morning with the typewriter on his knees, continued to take advantage of the big room. Now and again the father, who had set up his sons in business, called to see them. He was the patriarch who had sent them to Paris, to Lyons, to Hamburg to learn languages. All of these pronounced the word 'business' as if it were the most beautiful word in the language.

When Arthur opened one of the compartments under the long counter mice ran out, and I stood shrieking on top of my chair, but when the mice had disappeared, and Arthur pulled out the treasures he kept in these dark recesses, my curiosity would bring me off my perch.

There were boxes full of samples, cards on which were stuck bedroom slipper pom-poms, furniture braid in wonderful colours, and gold- and silver-threaded slipper satin. The first rayons filled us with surprise and fear; did they foretell the end of real silk? In Lyons and in Macclesfield, manufacturers surpassed themselves not to be out-dated, but our boss neither curtailed his orders for real silk nor underestimated the importance of the new invention. He was long sighted.

When a neighbouring office, a single room, became vacant, he immediately rented it, built a communicating door, and had the place done up as an office for himself. We looked with admiration at the thick carpet, the fine desk, the arm-chair, and the ingenious wash-basin which swung open at a touch. Mr Meller would wash his hands while Arthur stood beside him, proffering a hired towel. Then I would be called in for dictation.

His memory was too accurate for my inexperience. He noted immediately the altered word, the carefully modified sentence.

A new traveller joined us, a man of considerable experience, who wore beautiful light suits. Every morning he had a fresh flower in his buttonhole. His bowler hat took its place beside the others until he was ready to start on his daily rounds in the greatest city in the world. None of the travellers owned a car in those days. They set off toward ten and did not come back till tea-time or just afterwards. Then began for me the busiest moment of the day, for it was only then, after the travellers had brought in their orders, that Mr Meller dictated his letters to France and to Germany which I later took round to the late fee box at the General Post Office in King Edward Street.

Sometimes a Frenchman would arrive from a Lyons silk manufacturer.

Mr Meller would take him to meet his most important customers; in the evening they would have supper at the Trocadero, famed for its excellent wines, its splendid floor show, and the fact that business men were not obliged to change into a dinner jacket or tails, which were insisted on in so many other places.

Summer came to an end, and I still remained with Mr Meller. I had made up my mind to remain for at least six months in the City. I watched the glories of my garden fade into autumn browns and curled leaves. Mists, rising from the wide river, gave new beauty to the domes and towers of Wren churches; rain turned the pavements of narrow, congested streets into mirrors. Then came dense fogs which, on occasion, made even Arthur arrive late at the office.

Once, when I was alone in the big room, with all the lights on because of the fog, the door opened and a German came in. He had left his hotel very early under the impression, poor man, that people in England were at their desks as early as they were in his own country, and he was surprised to find that at eight o'clock the financial centre of the world was only half awake.

Full of energy and courage he burst in on me, his round face smiling, his podgy fingers clasping a green hat. I looked up in amused expectancy. His tie was green and so was his waistcoat. Having introduced himself, he offered me a bar of milk chocolate, and immediately started to eat one himself. Talking and eating incessantly, his gaiety was prodigious.

His bag, which, as soon as the others arrived, he opened in front of us, contained a great wonder—the very first leather skins of gold and silver, soft and infinitely beautiful, which before long would replace, for our evening dance shoes, the more delicate French lamés with their gold or silver threads which had been the fashion.

These skins filled our room with a smell of nail varnish, and it was the strangest sight to see entire kid skins laid out as at the furriers, but smooth, glittering sheets of gold or silver.

Mr Meller showed great delight in this innovation, and talked to the German traveller, who stayed several days with us, as easily and as fluently in his language as he did with the Frenchmen from Lyons in theirs. During the day he introduced him to all the most important British shoe manufacturers; in the evening they went to the Trocadero. Everything amused our Teuton, who continued throughout his visit to produce bars of milk chocolate which he offered round. This was in the early days of the German air lines, and it was arranged that the German firm which he represented would send us skins by air mail, two at a time.

We now had an office boy called Bill, brought to us one morning by his father, a workman who had stood, cap in hand, while introducing his son to us. Arthur looked important and made them sit down at a table, facing each other. Bill was shy and well brought up, with hair that stood straight up. After a few moments Mr Meller sent for them both and they were taken, by Arthur, into his new office.

'My boy is real clever,' I heard Bill's father say. 'He knows French and German and all.'

Mr Meller, well acquainted with the intricacies of these languages, listened with an indulgent smile, and immediately engaged Bill.

Bill became a charming member of our staff. We sent him to the A.B.C. to buy buns and cups of coffee, which he learned to bring up the stairs with speed and dexterity. Mr Meller also arranged with Arthur to hire a push trolley by the hour which Bill could use fetching and delivering rolls of silk and rayon, which added to the picturesqueness of the City streets.

Arthur no longer stayed in the office at lunch-time, and in his absence I was put in charge of the office key. He set off with his sample card of slipper pom-poms and furniture braid into the wilds of Hackney and Commercial Road.

Bill and I lunched on coffee and rolls and butter, and afterwards, while I embroidered, I would correct his French exercises, or we would try to learn German together in order to emulate the boss, whose fluency in that language I envied. Bill also practised typewriting while telling me stories about his school which, in spite of his pride in now working in the City, he obviously regretted leaving.

He was strong and healthy but his cheviot suit of cheap wool was creased and ill fitting, and when he came back from pushing his trolley through the driving rain, smelling of wet sheep, I used to try to warm him with a cup of very hot tea.

'My poor Bill!' I would exclaim.

'Oh yes, mamzelle,' he would answer. 'You don't know how lucky you are to be able to stay indoors.'

His dream was to sit at a desk and do office work, and very soon, finding a place where he would be able to do this, he left us.

The lime-tree in the garden of St Mary the Virgin had turned dark and grimy. All the City also was dark. Often we were obliged to put on the lights at lunch-time. Another office boy arrived with his father, who introduced us to him, and though he was thin and pale Mr Meller engaged him. I feared to think how he would fare behind the trolley, dodging the traffic in the streets, but I never learned the end of the story because my health, weakened by too many buns and strong tea, and an insufficiency of fresh air, began to worry my mother, who made me leave. The boss became increasingly important but I was not there to see his successes grow.

The next time I saw Aldermanbury Street was during the Second World War, a few months after the fire of

December 1940. The church of St Mary was now nothing but a singed skeleton. There were no longer any windows left in what had been our building but the statue of the Virgin remained glowingly white and absolutely undamaged in her niche above the shattered church door, and Shakespeare still sat in the gardens under the lime-tree. I was accompanied by my son who was then three. The streets along which I had so often run with Mr Meller's 'late fee' letters were now torn and desolate. Weeds grew on the pavements. An eerie silence reigned, and all about us was the dampness of destruction and death. The organ to which I had so often listened during the lunch hour on Fridays, while I read or embroidered in the peaceful garden, was reduced, together with everything else in the church, to pieces of charred and floating wreckage dimly seen at the bottom of a filthy pit.

Where was Bill? And his pale successor? And the man with the green hat who had come to visit us so early in the morning?

# 4

THERE was a time just after the great fire of December 1940 when all the land between St Mary-le-Bow in Cheapside and St Paul's Cathedral was wasteland. On sunny days office girls in summer frocks sat talking or reading in the long grass, which was criss-crossed by paths bearing such famous names as Old Change, Friday Street, Bread Street, and Watling Street. Traffic continued to run, of course, along Cheapside and Cannon Street, but everywhere between these two thoroughfares grew long grass and wild flowers. Occasionally one would come across a mason chipping stone as peacefully as if he were in the middle of a Yorkshire moor, and he would have made a very pretty subject for a seventeenth-century print. The only landmark to remain standing was the tower of St Augustine's, Watling Street, which nestles up against the gardens of St Paul's Churchyard. This was another church built by Wren on the site of one destroyed in the Great Fire of 1666. The Fraternity of St Austin's used to meet here in the fourteenth century when high mass was celebrated on the eve of St Austin's. Every brother contributed a penny and after mass there was feasting. Stow gives us a very picturesque description of this. Wren built a dome and small steeple above his tower, but only the tower survived the bombing. There is a curious story about a cat called Faith which is thought to have had premonition of the bombing, for it kept on bringing its baby down from a basket in the rector's rooms to a pigeon-hole filled with music three floors below. The Rev. H. Ross has described its antics and rescue in a famous booklet, and Faith and its kitten are now almost as legendary as that other City cat one associates with Dick Whittington. The other Wren church in Watling Street, St Antholin, was pulled down in 1870. The Victorians might not have been so anxious to demolish Wren City churches had they been able to foretell the future.

This large area of wasteland due south of Gresham Street and Silver Street, and the much wilder and more countrified area round Cripplegate and London Wall, were too important to be left for long as grassland. The giants of to-morrow were impatient to turn their lofty heads skywards. There was a popular feeling too that the spaces east of St Paul's should be filled as quickly as possible in a manner worthy of the cathedral which was Wren's most majestic achievement. For although far too few Londoners use it as a place of worship, it is yet a subject of pride to them, a national landmark.

The tower of the wrecked St Augustine's was left temporarily as it was. Between this extreme western end of Watling Street and Cannon Street, the Corporation of London laid out a garden. Here fountains flushed from the mouths of bronze lions and a magnificent rectangular lawn, delicately green even in the heat of summer, was banked with yellow wallflowers and white tulips in spring and lined with young trees.

This narrow strip, encompassed by Watling Street to the north, Cannon Street to the south, St Paul's to the west, and a short passage called New Change to the east, leads on to a great and beautiful new building, Gateway House, the first of the giants to go up in this vital area.

Gateway House is a foretaste of what the City of to-morrow will be like. The southern front, with a lawn facing Cannon Street, rises ninety feet above the ground. The entrance hall is on the north side, facing Watling Street. There are tall columns of gold-veined marble from the Gulf of Spezia and walls of a yet more richly coloured marble from the Apuan Alps. It would seem that Italy had again been searched for these beautiful building materials, just as nearly two thousand years earlier the Romans of Hadrian's day must have brought over treasures to beautify their homes and temples. Watling Street, the oldest street in London, and part of the old Roman military road to Dover, is indeed the most evocative of all the City's links with Italy.

A plaque in the hall is inscribed as follows:

The ceremonial opening of this building was performed on June 5, 1956, by the Rt Hon. the Lord Mayor of London, Alderman Sir Cuthbert Ackroyd Bart, . . . a benediction was afterwards given by the Dean of St Paul's, Very Rev. W. R. Matthews. The Posterne Stone set in this wall formed a part of the Ancient Gateway of the City of London known as Aldgate which adjoined the original home of Wiggins Teape.

Just above the first floor on the outside of the building are panels of Venetian glass made at Pietrasanta. The top storey has a sweep of continuous windows, the walls being faced with quartzite from a mountain south of Turin. This stone, which glistens like granite, contains many colours, and appears again as the paving stone of Friday Street, which runs through the centre of Gateway House. It is used as a right of way, a glass screen separating the public from the richly coloured entrance hall.

While 600 employees of Wiggins Teape, the paper-makers, were moving into this building, the Bank of England was putting up an even more costly one on the other side of Watling Street. This was an extension to its own famous home, so large that it would stretch all the way to Cheapside, and cover a great part of what, such a short time ago, had been grassland. Long before it was finished Watling House, separated from Gateway House by Bread Street, had gone up and became new offices for Brooke Bond, the tea merchants.

The magnificence of these buildings is the phenomenon of the age. The palaces of ancient kings, the villas of the Romans, the rich houses of the Lombards, the palaces all along the Strand, the fabulous mansion, in the reign of Charles II, of his Lord Chancellor, the Earl of Clarendon, were as nothing in comparison with such modern wonders. Ebony-coloured bricks from Leicestershire, buff-coloured bricks from Tunbridge Wells, stone from Portland, floors of Gurjun wood from Africa, lifts lined with plastic laminate, windows floodlit from inside, offices for the directors and their private secretaries of a compactness and elegance that princes did not know before, suites for employees spending a night in town, probably to catch an aeroplane to some distant corner of the globe, sound-proof telephone exchanges with a drawing-room for the girls to rest in—what fairy story gave us glimpses such as these?

This then is the City of to-morrow, the City of half a million by day, and of scarcely anybody by night.

What would it be like to live in a snug apartment at the very top of one of these monster buildings? To feel the throb of a great city all about one from nine till six, and then to be as lonely as an eagle in its eyrie on the summit of a wild sea cliff? All the bells of the City would ring out the nocturnal hours for you alone. How Lilliputian would appear the domes and spires of Wren churches as you looked down upon them. The moon would shine on the vessels anchored in the pool, and perhaps, as other monster buildings of steel and glass reared their heads into the sky, watchers perched on top of them would wave good night. Watchman to watchman, crying 'All is well!' from the roof of Gateway House, with its frieze of multi-coloured Italian quartzite, to the giddy top of Fountain House, that wonder of the modern world which, with sheet upon sheet of blinding glass, rises as with arms stretched upwards to heaven between Fenchurch Street and the scarcely less sensational new extension of Lloyds in Fenchurch Avenue.

Observe that in the replanning of the City the private apartment house has no place whatever.

'What folly even to imagine such a thing!' cry the architects. 'Nobody would be rich enough to live in it.'

So only a few couples will be allowed to live above this square mile, and to breathe in its two thousand years of history. Here, unlike in New York, the individual will be banished. He will not see the myriad lights, the gliding ships. He does not count except in the mass. Marble palace and glass cage will be for work, not recreation or repose.

Who will be the fortunate ones? The housekeepers.

Whereas in olden days housekeepers mostly lived in basements, now, in these marvellous new buildings, they will live in penthouses, the rents of which, if they had to pay them, only millionaires could afford.

'The reason,' says Mr George Hanson, who lives with his wife in a magnificent apartment at the very top of Gateway House, 'is that a man can keep a much better eye on a vast building from the top than from the bottom. The fire brigade prefers it that way.'

One Sunday night I rang his bell in Watling Street. As soon as the building is empty the telephone is switched to his apartment. He had said to me:

'Ring the bell in Watling Street, and then give me time to come down.'

These words came to me as something of a shock. I had not realized that the eagle needs a little time to come down from his eyrie.

As Mr Hanson stepped out of the lift into the reception hall, he switched on all the lights, as a householder might do when answering the front door bell on a Sunday night at his home in Richmond or in Wimbledon. Heavens, what a sight! The gold-veined Portoro marble columns, the grey-green marble walls, the tiles, the deep-red carpet by the windows, and the profusion of flowers and plants produced a fairy-like scene.

'I hope I did not keep you waiting,' said Mr Hanson.

This, at least, was a millionaire's welcome.

His voice was gentle and I found him extremely good looking, but he added quickly, as if to excuse himself:

'I lost my right eye when a V1 exploded in front of our fire-engine. It was in Eastern Avenue, Ilford. My eye just watered. I thought it was the smoke. What a silly business! To think I had gone through all the great raids on the City without a scratch. I was over in Farringdon Road on the historic 29th December 1940. A land-mine fell in Little Britain, and St Bartholomew's Hospital was ringed with a hundred fires. None of us expected to live till morning. The Salvation Army did a grand job.'

'The Salvation Army?'

'Why, yes, always being right next to us, giving us tea and buns. Not even stopping when policemen were killed in front of them. The Salvation Army did a fine job.'

'You all did, I expect. Have you always been in the fire brigade?'

'No, I was a dining-car attendant on the old Great Western Railway, mostly on the runs to Torquay and Plymouth.'

'And then?'

'I was always saying to myself, bearing in mind what I had seen in the First World War, that flame throwing would lead to something worse. I got interested in the art of putting out fires. The accident to my eye put an end to that. Well, that's enough about myself. Mrs Hanson is looking forward to knowing you.'

'Did you meet her while you were in the fire brigade?'

'I met her at Ilford just before my accident. She looked after me and we were married.'

Mrs Hanson sprang up quickly from the arm-chair in which she had been looking at television.

'Gracie Fields was just coming on.' she exclaimed. 'Please forgive me.'

This greeting made me stammer an apology. Should I disappear and let her see Gracie Fields? Would she take a dislike to me because of this? I decided this time to be thoroughly selfish and to pursue my visit. Even if I abandoned my evening on the roof of the City, promising to come back another time, there would always be something on television.

Besides, Mrs Hanson's spaniel had almost knocked me over in its delight to have a visitor, after which it jumped up on the settee, which it was obviously anxious to keep for itself. I thought it prudent not to disturb it, and so I sat in the chair opposite Mrs Hanson.

I started by expressing my admiration for this magnificent apartment decorated in delicate shades of beige and almond green, with its wide bay windows overlooking all south London as far as the Crystal Palace. I exclaimed in delight that this is the sort of view one dreams about. I imagined myself as a young wife starting in a home like this.

'No,' she said. 'I know it 's very beautiful, and a far more wonderful home than we could afford, but I am not sure that I appreciate this life so high above the streets. Besides, it is a bit far for the shopping.'

'For provisions?'

'Not so much for provisions. There is everything one needs in the way of food. I was thinking of shops, just shops. One does like to do a bit of shop-gazing, don't you think? There 's nothing like the West End or a good suburban high street for looking at the shops.'

A bell tinkled above her soft, friendly voice. Joey, the budgerigar, was showing off.

'We had a cat until a few weeks ago,' said Mrs Hanson. 'Such a nice friend for the spaniel. They got on wonderfully together, but you know what a cat is. I was always afraid for Joey. Now that the cat is not here any more I open Joey's cage so that he can fly out, but he has lost the habit of being free. He won't leave his cage.'

'Your husband tells me that he courted you at Ilford,' I interposed, changing the subject.

'That 's right. I had a greengrocer's shop. Such fun it was. One met so many people. Of course, my husband loves being here. This is a splendid job for him.'

'My wife would exchange all this,' said Mr Hanson, pointing in the direction of the Crystal Palace, 'for a bit of garden. She does hanker after a piece of garden to plant things in.'

'We can't even have a window-box,' explained Mrs Hanson, smiling. 'I don't suppose it would look right from outside.'

'And what would be the use of it?' asked Mr Hanson appeasingly. 'Nothing grows in the City.'

'Surely?'

'Not at this height. Plants seem to get burned up by the sun and the wind.'

'Come and see my kitchen.' exclaimed Mrs Hanson.

Here was every woman's dream—perfect lighting, giant refrigerator, constant hot water, and something that if I were fortunate enough to live here I would never tire of, a magnificent view across the kitchen sink of the Thames winding majestically through the City.

'Oh!' I cried. 'I do envy you.'

'The only thing is,' objected Mrs Hanson, 'that I have nowhere to hang out the wash. My balcony would be perfect, but I could not do that at the top of a building like this one, could I?'

'No,' I answered, sympathizing. 'I suppose you could not.'

I suddenly recalled a cruise I once made on a famous liner across the Caribbean Sea in tropical heat. I had struck on the happy idea of drying my bathing-dress by hanging it by the shoulder straps out of my port-hole. Every time this happened a steward would knock at my suite and say:

'Captain's compliments, madame, but please to haul in your bathing-suit.'

A rose-coloured door led to the Hansons' bedroom, a blue one to their daughter's.

'My daughter does the exact contrary to what hundreds of thousands of young women do every day,' said Mrs Hanson. 'She leaves the City every morning to work in the West End—she is very brilliant, and works at a publisher's—and comes back to the City in the evening.'

'And brings manuscripts back to this lovely room?' I queried.

'Yes,' answered her mother with justified pride.

The apartment was full of light. The paint-work was gloriously fresh, and would always be kept in this condition. Cupboards were built into the walls. I have always dreamed of built-in cupboards, not only in my bedroom, but in all the rooms of the apartment, to keep my dresses and skirts tidy. I was beginning to think that Mrs Hanson had succeeded in obtaining all my dearest wishes, when suddenly she said:

'I am up every morning at five. I take the dog down for a walk.'

'At five, Mrs Hanson?'

'Oh, I can't stay in bed in the mornings. I got used to getting up early at Ilford. My dog and I go for a stroll through the streets.'

'Along Watling Street, perhaps. How tremendously romantic.'

'I suppose so,' she answered gaily, 'and I am never tired.'

We went back into the sitting-room. The bird was playing with its toys in the pretty cage. The spaniel was given a biscuit which it guarded jealously. Before Mrs Hanson drew the curtains, I stood with her for a moment looking down into Cannon Street. The omnibuses looked tiny. One wondered what the rare passers-by were doing in the City at this time of night.

'To-morrow morning,' said Mrs Hanson, 'the pneumatic drills will start up again. Everywhere one turns buildings are going up.'

'Have you friends at the top of other great buildings?' I asked.

'Ours was the first one finished,' said Mr Hanson. 'Then came Watling House on the other side of Bread Street, our neighbour. Major Drew and his wife live on the top of that one. We exchange visits from time to time.'

'Who leaves you your morning milk?' I asked, thinking of the milkman in my district who came round in his little electric trolley every morning. But how did one persuade the milkman to deliver a pint of milk so high up in the sky?

Mr Hanson laughed.

'You are forgetting that we have a magnificent staff restaurant,' he said. 'Mr Jones, from Lemon Street, Aldgate, leaves forty gallons at seven in the morning.'

'In a churn?'

'No, in bottles. Then, at seven-thirty, the bread arrives.'

'Of course.'

'Would you like to see the restaurant?'

Imagine a great room with glass on both sides, curving to a point like the prow of a ship. At the end of this we all stood for a moment, looking at St Paul's Cathedral, gigantic, a few hundred yards straight ahead of us. We were so high up that our eyes seemed level with a point just below the dome. The cathedral was floodlit and, while the dome was bathed in a milky glow, the gold cross at the summit gleamed in the night.

'Oh!' I gasped. 'What a superb sight!'

Mr Hanson seemed to turn the matter over in his mind.

'Do you think so?' he asked. Then glancing at his wrist-watch:

'I must go downstairs and let the girls in.'

'What girls?'

'We have a staff of fourteen women who come in at 9.30 p.m. to clean the building. They go home at 6 a.m. Most of them come from quite a distance—from Deptford, for example—so if we started them at dawn they might not find the necessary transport. They work all night, get very big wages, and sometimes, but not always, I suspect, sleep during the day. Women have great resilience. I bet half of them carry on with their usual occupations as soon as they get home in the morning, breakfast for the husband and the children, and so on . . .'

'I expect they do,' I said.

Mr Hanson's fourteen girls were waiting in Watling Street for him to open the glass doors.

They trooped in, and while I was saying good-bye they sat down in the chairs round the Italian marble pillars, laughing and gossiping. Some were very young and pretty. They had string bags with them, and I supposed they had brought their breakfasts. How I would have liked to sit round the breakfast table with them at midnight.

On Saturday mornings I took to doing my marketing

in Leadenhall Street—partly, I think, because I wanted to get the feel of the City over the week-end, partly because Leadenhall Market is the nearest approach to what one is accustomed to in a French town. The ordinary London street market has nothing in common with its French equivalent, the barrow boys giving it so essentially a cockney air that even Berwick Market in Soho, which might, because of its population of Cypriots, Italians, and West Indians, radiate a foreign atmosphere, remains the very essence of cockney trading. But Leadenhall Market has a cachet; the accent is on the freshness and high quality of the food. Here are to be found the best salmon and turbot, the finest Aberdeen beef, and English home-grown vegetables. The most particular and knowledgeable French servant, buying for church dignitary or difficult housewife, would find nothing to criticize.

There has, of course, been a market here since medieval times, though not in its present form. A large building, roofed with lead, was converted into a granary in the fifteenth century, and the market people had their own church attached to it. It became successively a market for meat and fish, for raw hides, for wool, for herbs, and for cloth. One suspects that at times it did not look so very different from the market at Rouen, still so rich and picturesque, in the centre of which one may see the spot where the English burned Joan of Arc. Fish may well have been brought here from the Thames below London Bridge, as it was taken at one time to the market at Cheapside. At the time of the Restoration the Spanish ambassador, Don Pedro de Ronquillo, was telling Charles II that he firmly believed that more meat was sold here than in all the kingdom of Spain.

I like it better now than any other market in London. It is under cover and yet virtually out of doors. The fact that it links four important streets, Whittington Avenue, coming out of Leadenhall Street, with Fenchurch Street, and Gracechurch Street with Lime Street, gives it the form of a cross. Its roof and fluted columns and its colour scheme of pale yellow, crimson, and gold are beautiful

*Leadenhall Market*

and dignified. The City arms are everywhere, the scarlet cross of St George on its silver background, arms never registered but going back into the mists of time.

What poetical names one comes across! Lime Street Passage, Beehive Passage, glimpses of Asia House. The coloured tiles of the Lamb Tavern (1780) at the entrance to the grill-room and private bar depict Wren explaining his plans for the building of the Monument in 1671. In front of Hotine, the fishmonger, sleeps Victor II, the firm's famous cat, who a year ago replaced his still more celebrated predecessor, Victor I, who died at the age of nineteen. Victor II is under a canopy of plovers' eggs, not far from eight great salmon in a basket. We wake him. He is fastidious. He only likes prawns.

Here are 'budgies,' six to seven weeks old and easy to train. A few yards farther along a crowd of City men are examining the plants and gardening equipment on pavement and alley outside Henderson's—Alpine fuchsias, viola Apricot Queen, East Lothian stocks, verbena, and French marigolds; salvia Blaze of Fire, alyssum, and geraniums; chives and roses; lawn-mowers and hanging baskets; cacti plants and raspberry canes. Among the gazers are several postmen puffing contentedly at their pipes, their empty mail bags slung across their shoulders. A little boy on a tricycle, with a piece of his mother's knitting attached to the handlebars, came silently behind me several times during my walk through the market. With a sharp ring of his bell he had glided past me, amused to see the agility with which I was obliged to make way for him. At midday, when the market closed, he disappeared, doubtless into the streets and alleys in the neighbourhood of Gracechurch Street. About one o'clock I decided to sit down for a moment in the tiny rose-garden in Fen Court. Here the sun was reflected like a fiery red ball in the great expanse of glass which is Fountain House, the most spectacular of all the new buildings in the City. A few moments later back came my little tricyclist.

'Hallo!' I said.

'Hallo!' he answered, without stopping.

The garden was full of roses in their first bloom of the year, a lovely spot for a flower-hungry London woman. I like the juxtaposition of what is old and poetical with what is breath-takingly new. The main upright portion of Fountain House gave me, when I first saw it, the same feeling of excitement as Rockefeller Centre in New York when it had the dazzling whiteness of an absolutely new building.

The stone of the Rockefeller Centre shimmered in the clear air of New York. It startled everyone by the daringness of its conception, the narrowness of the blade. Fountain House is equally new and bold. The main upright is thirteen storeys of glass, and this giant finger, pointing skywards, is balanced in the most incredibly delicate way across the lower section. One wonders, as one does at Stonehenge, if giants have not been at play.

Modern achievements of this kind are things of pure beauty, and enhance what is old and lovely round them. The garden of Fen Court, is, of course, the burial ground of an old City church.

One is vexed at the number of City churches that the Church of England has allowed to be pulled down. There was one across the way in Fenchurch Street, for instance, called St Dionis Backchurch. St Dionis was the St Denis of France, and the church was given the added name of Backchurch from there having originally been a church of St Gabriel in the centre of the roadway so that St Dionis stood behind it. Mentioned as early as 1288, rebuilt in the reign of Henry VI, and again after the Great Fire—this time by Wren—it was pulled down for no very good reason in 1876.

At all events, here is the garden, and so the little boy on his tricycle and I are able to enjoy the sunshine and the scent of the roses. There is a notice which reads:

St Edmund the King
with St Nicholas Acons,
All Hallows, Lombard Street, St Benet Gracechurch,
St Leonard Eastcheap and St Dionis Backchurch.

There are two or three tombs covered with moss that bring to one's mind those sentimental poems written in a churchyard which were so popular in the early part of the nineteenth century, and indeed, if one looks carefully at the inscriptions, which have become extremely difficult to read, one sees that the people buried in these tombs died at about the time that Napoleon was marching across

Europe. Young willows hang their branches sorrowfully over them.

Back comes my little boy on the tricycle.

'Hallo!' he says, stopping beside me.

'Hallo!' I repeat. 'What is your name?'

'I am James.'

'Well, that is a good name, a good Scots name. Does your daddy live near here?'

'Of course. Daddy works the lift.'

'And mother?'

'Mother doesn't work. She looks after my baby sister. We 've also got a cat with two kittens, and they are blind.'

'They will soon open their eyes.'

My young friend rang the bell on his tricycle and answered:

'I am terribly busy. Good-bye!'

'Good-bye, James.'

Although I did not intend at first to make this part of the City at all my own, repeated visits to Leadenhall Market made me fall in love with the neighbourhood, especially at week-ends when the handful of residents came out of their houses to gossip, or to sun themselves on their doorsteps.

I was soon to discover that though some housekeepers like Mr Hanson and Mr Drew lived on the peaks of their mountains of porphyry and stone, there were others in the quieter regions behind Leadenhall Street and Cornhill who could easily have imagined themselves to be in a forgotten backwater of a sleepy cathedral town.

The loveliest and most picturesque of these retreats lies away from the traffic and the din of the road in the shadow of St Michael's, Cornhill. The tower of St Michael's so closely resembles that of Magdalen College, Oxford, on the top of which choristers sing hymns on May morning, that one instinctively looks round for a glimpse of the Cherwell with its may-trees which dip their branches of heavily scented white and pink blossom into the cool water.

There has been a church on the site of St Michael's since the reign of Edward the Confessor, and the enclosed garden with its beautiful flower-beds and lawn and softly rustling trees occupies the site of Norman and medieval cloisters. The present church was started in 1672 by Wren; the tower was not added till 1721. Stow's father and grandfather, the tallow chandler, were buried in the church on this site which was destroyed in the Great Fire of 1666. Stow himself, the sixteenth-century chronicler, who is buried across the way in the beautiful church of St Andrew Undershaft, tells a queer story of how the devil visited St Michael's belfry on a stormy night when lightning was breaking over the City. There are tales enough to make this garden a place of dreams.

The entrance is from Cheapside by a narrow lane, St Michael's Alley, famed for its vintners and coffee-houses. The garden is reached by turning to the left under the tower, through a covered passage whose ceiling is curiously vaulted. St Michael's Alley itself leads through devious other passages and courts into Lombard Street. On the left stands the Jamaica Wine House where once was London's first coffee-house. It was opened during the Commonwealth by a servant and coachman of a Turkish merchant. They were named Pasqua Rosee and Bowman, and had learned from their master to appreciate the delicious drink which the lampooners dubbed 'sooty.'

On the right, Castle Court leads with twists and turns to Simpson's Tavern in Bell Court. Straight ahead you can make your way through a covered passage called George Yard where is the entrance to the George and Vulture (Thomas's Chop House), which dates from 1600. As you emerge from the sultry history of George Yard, there is Bengal Court on your right, and the open part of George Yard in front of you. Facing you are the pillars and pink and blue hydrangeas of Barclays Bank. Mr J. Devereux, the bank's chief messenger, sits at a desk by the Lombard Street entrance, and it was he who saved St Michael's, Cornhill, when an incendiary fell on the roof during the war. To the right is the garden with a very beautiful green lawn, a young tree, and lots of red geraniums, and so to the church of St Edmund the King. Over its porch in Lombard Street is a black-and-gold clock, surmounted by a golden crown.

Looking up and down Lombard Street, the eye is caught by the many and fascinating signs that hang over the pavements—a nostalgic evocation of a more picturesque city.

Let us return to my garden of St Michael's, hidden away, as a rare jewel should be.

My favourite seat is against the wall of the Jamaica Wine House, through whose back windows I can see the Jamaica's cat asleep amongst picturesque wine bottles which I amuse myself by pretending are full of Elizabethan sack. To my left is the wall of the church with its stained-glass windows, which strike me as needing a good wash. By turning half round, and craning my neck, I can obtain from here a superb view of the tower which looks so much like the one above Magdalen Bridge at Oxford.

Thanks to Mr Devereaux, no harm came to the church during the great fire of 1940, but afterwards there was talk of pulling it down, just as All Hallows, Lombard Street, was pulled down for the usual reason, to make way for City offices. I rejoice that the hand of destruction was stayed. Thus the cat of the Jamaica Wine House and I bask in our week-end sunshine.

Facing my seat is a beautiful house of the kind one might easily see in Bruges or Delft. There are dormer windows and beautiful green sun-blinds at all the windows, and the window frames and blind casings are white. This lovely house was remodelled on an older one. Although it is called St Michael's Rectory, only one beautiful oak-panelled room, on the ground floor and near the church, is at the disposal of the rector, the Rev. Norman Motley. He is young and vigorous, a former chief chaplain of Toc H, and he uses this room as his vestry. The rest of this dream house is used by a famous firm of solicitors. Thus, as in the Middle Temple, law and church stand side by side.

There are flagstones in the garden but in the centre is a circular flower bed filled with red geraniums. A woman comes out of the rectory door, wearing a light blue hand-knitted pullover. She is Mrs Percy Counsell, the caretaker's wife, and she has a charming smile for me. She and her husband occupy the rooms behind all the dormer windows at the top of the house, and at week-ends they and the clergy of St Michael's share its picturesque quiet.

Percy Counsell was born in Bethnal Green. He can remember, as a little boy, on rainy days huddling close to the drivers of horse omnibuses, whose big oilskin capes afforded him some shelter as they drove into the City. His brother, Walter, has been clerk to the solicitors, Parker Garrett & Co., for thirty-five years, and it was he who brought Percy in as housekeeper.

On Sunday mornings the bells of St Michael's, rung by the twelve St Paul's Cathedral ringers, call the devout to prayer. There are not many of them. The church, however, is famous for its director of music, Harold Darke, who plays on the organ which Albert Schweitzer used. The Rev. Norman Motley left a big textile firm in Wood Street, where his uncle was buyer, to take holy orders, and then became curate at Christchurch, Spitalfields, before coming to St Michael's. He is not the sort of man to be satisfied with small congregations. When I told him that I had found his church closed the previous Saturday, he said:

'I am sorry. I have only been rector here since the beginning of the year. For the moment it is open every day, except Saturday at lunch time, from ten till five, and my desire is to see it open for twenty-four hours in the day.'

Mr Motley, I expect, would like to see the rectory given back to the rector, and that would appear, on the surface, a very reasonable desire, for if a man has his heart in his work, he should live beside it.

I had been sunning myself in the garden one Sunday morning after service and listening to the pigeons cooing in the tower. My husband was in the vestry talking to the rector and to Mr Charles Cook, the churchwarden. There is generally a cup of tea and a biscuit to be had there at such times, for the rector lives at Brentwood, Essex, and Mr Cook in Wimbledon Park. How hard it is indeed for a City church to keep up the illusion of being a real parish! I saw the verger in his robes, crossing the garden, with a dark brown teapot clasped in the palms of his hands. Two pigeons strutted in front of him, and the smoke from the cigarette stub between his lips left a curl of smoke in his wake. He was going to fill the teapot or perhaps to empty it, I am not sure. But the sight of this man in his robes crossing what had once been cloisters, and of the rector in his panelled ground-floor room, pacing up and down (as I could see through the windows), enthralled me. The rector's door was open, the solicitor's door was closed. As with the German figurines which tell the weather, when one comes out, the other goes in!

# 5

I HAD a sudden desire one Tuesday morning to have another look at that building in Aldermanbury Street in which I had worked as a girl and which, I supposed, was now returning to some sort of normality after the damage of the war.

In the garden of the church of St Mary the Virgin, the beautiful foliage of the spreading lime-tree was turning a deep green as Whitsun approached, but the church itself was pathetically abandoned. Nobody seemed to care for it any longer. Even the boards nailed across the porch had rotted, and through the gaping holes one could see the shocking state of the interior. I began seriously to wonder if my church was going to be rebuilt after all. Had the bishop and his friends gone to sleep? I felt impotent and aggrieved. Masonry from adjoining sites was being pushed into the garden, robbing it of its cool and leafy delight. Never had I seen a loved landmark so utterly despised and neglected.

The building where I had worked, facing the garden, had fared much better than the church. Unlike the ecclesiastical authorities, those responsible in this case had quickly restored the severe damage. I thought it looked exactly as it had done during my girlhood. When I tried to go in, however, I was stopped by a porter, asking me my business.

'Once, quite a long time ago,' I answered, 'I worked as a typist in an office on the first floor, and it would amuse me to see it again. You have a lift now. I do not remember there being a lift when I was here.'

The porter looked at me suspiciously.

'I have also been here a long time,' he said, 'and there has always been a lift.'

'Perhaps I did not notice it,' I said.

'I don't recall your face,' said the porter.

'That is possible. I was seventeen.'

This appeased him a little, and he offered to take me up in the lift, saying that when I had looked round I could come down again by the stairs.

I found the first floor looking much brighter than in my time. My old office was locked but the door was freshly painted. On the way down my high heels noisily hit the wide wooden stairs as they had done so many years before.

The porter was waiting for me at the street door.

'You have made your pilgrimage just in time,' he said. 'The building is going to be pulled down soon.'

'Oh, what a pity!' I cried.

I hated to feel that all the places where I had lived and worked as a girl were disappearing one by one. Stacey Street, our Soho home, to which I hurried back every evening from this office, was completely destroyed during the war. Not a house remains to remind me of what they looked like. Now this was to go.

'Yes,' said the porter, 'it 's a shame. These old buildings had something. One became attached to them. They intend to build one of those giants like the ones in Wood Street and Gresham Street.'

He smiled down at me. At last he was beginning to believe that I really had worked here, and he said:

'I must find out about the lift, but I have been here twenty-three years.'

I made a rapid calculation and said:

'That is why you don't remember me.'

He looked puzzled.

'Oh?'

'Yes,' I said. 'I have known the house longer than you have.'

I would have liked to have asked him about the church, but there was nothing he could tell me. I had an uncomfortable idea that the Virgin of Aldermanbury had been stolen from her niche, and I walked away feeling angry and sad.

I had for a long time been meaning to call on Carrie Miller, whose flower shop was the first in that tiny row under the famous tree, at the corner of Wood Street and Cheapside. Catching sight of the tree, as I walked along Wood Street, and hearing the bells of the City strike eleven, I decided to see if she was there.

Caroline Esther Miller—that is her full name. I had imagined all sorts of stories about her. What sort of woman kept this delightful little shop where the flowers in the window brought joy to the thousands of people passing along Cheapside?

Carrie, who was born in St Pancras, has never left London. She would like to be a little taller because she is always having to reach out for the heavy and sometimes breakable vases of sweet peas, stocks, carnations, pinks, irises, and roses that stand prettily on glass shelves in her window. The shop is so small that the window takes up nearly all the space. There is no room for a table, and even less for chairs, but that hardly matters, for neither Carrie nor her delightful friend, Winifred Pearson, ever has time to sit down.

I introduced myself and we immediately became friends. I had been so afraid she would resent my coming, but here she was already telling me about her girlhood.

'We were desperately poor at home,' she said, while busily arranging her flowers, 'and we were eight children. Alas, only two of us managed to survive. I recall dismal Sundays, when we went to visit a brother or a sister at some sanatorium, for tuberculosis was a constant shadow. So six of my brothers and sisters died, and father died too at only forty-seven, but mother, fortunately, is still alive, and my friend, Winifred, and I live with her.

'I started working at fourteen in a playing-card factory, but I had really been working and earning a little money long before that. I was scarcely ten when I used to go and scrub doorsteps and whiten them with hearthstone, but as I was even smaller than I am now, and the front steps of the houses in the squares of St Pancras were long and wide, I used to drag the scrubbing-brush and floor cloth behind me, as I ran from one end to the other, so as not to leave the mark of a join in the middle of the step. Oh! I can still see myself doing that! A grown woman had, of course, a wide enough swing of the arm to do a whole step at once, but my poor little arm hardly reached half-way. A lady came to my mother during the First World War to ask if she would let me clean the doorstep of her house on Easter Bank Holiday. The lady had a daughter of about my age and she told mother she would give me one of her daughter's dresses. I was mad with joy. There were not only the front steps to do but a staircase inside the house. I scrubbed all the morning, and I was thinking so hard about the dress the lady was going to give me that I never even noticed that some German Taubes were dropping bombs. Everybody left the house but I went on scrubbing and dreaming. What were air-raids in those days anyway? And I wanted to go to Hampstead Heath in the afternoon, and ride on the roundabouts. The lady paid me my money and gave me the dress, and I was so excited that in order not to waste a minute I slipped the new dress over my old one, and set off for Hampstead Heath, where I rode triumphantly on the roundabouts and swings.

'At the playing-card factory I earned ten shillings a week. After that there were other jobs, but at sixteen I went to work at a famous florist's in Tottenham Court Road. I knew absolutely nothing about selling flowers, of course, and it is not at all easy to handle them properly. The blooms are so delicate. The girls used to make up magnificent baskets of flowers for the musical comedy stars and for famous actresses, and the prettiest little bouquets and buttonholes as well. There was a Miss Sullivan who was an absolute artist. She taught me all I know. I thought her rather old but at sixteen one is apt to think everybody over twenty rather old. I was paid a few shillings a week, when in fact it was I who should have paid them, but they were badly in need of the money at home.

'My brothers and sisters used to work till they couldn't work any more, and then they went to the sanatorium. As for myself, I am certain that flowers, and their lovely smell, saved me from falling ill. This is an idea of my own, of course. I might, on the other hand, have been merely a healthy little girl. Why not? My mother is seventy-four. All the same, I firmly believe that I owe my life to flowers, and for that reason I love them.

'Unfortunately nobody ever gives flowers to me.'

Winifred Pearson, who was arranging a beautiful bouquet that a customer had ordered, cried out:

'Yes, it 's so strange! Some friends of Carrie's once asked me what I thought she would like for her birthday. 'Send her some flowers,' I said. 'Nothing would give her more pleasure.'

Win, as Carrie calls her friend, has worked and lived with her for fourteen years. Hampstead, where they live with Carrie's mother, is their joy. In Carrie's mind, ever since she scrubbed those front steps, and went off to Hampstead Heath in her new dress, Hampstead evokes childish dreams of coco-nut shies, roundabouts, and lovely walks across the heath. For the little girl of St Pancras, Hampstead was heaven. She determined that if ever she had enough money of her own to live anywhere, that anywhere would be Hampstead.

'And now that I do live there,' says Carrie, 'and I have a little shop of my own, I feel as if life has really given me something. I get up at five every morning, and jump into a hot bath, but I go without breakfast. I never seem to have enough time. I catch a bus to the Stoll Theatre, the bus they call the Charladies' Express.

'I am in Covent Garden by six-thirty, and I take a walk through Floral Hall. Monday is a bad day because hardly anybody in the nurseries any longer works during the week-end. I try to keep a few flowers in bud over Sunday. At Covent Garden I pay for everything in cash, and this simplifies my accounts and occasionally allows me to get a box of blooms cheaper than I would otherwise. When you make a bid, and you show the money, the dealer is only human. He has bills of his own to pay.

'Credit is a thing I took a long time to understand. When I was only sixteen, a tall, elegant, beautiful woman came into the shop in Tottenham Court Road and chose some flowers. I was doubly shy because I knew that she was the most celebrated beauty of the day. When I had wrapped up the flowers, I murmured very timidly that they were three and sixpence.

'"I have an account, my child," she said haughtily. "I never have any money on me."

'I don't think I have ever felt so small in my life.

'As we all thought in terms of flowers, Miss Sullivan had nicknamed me "Carrination." Perhaps she guessed that I would never choose another profession. Thus I went from florist to florist, to one in Bond Street, to another in Mayfair. I was sent alone one day to do the flower decorations at Buckingham Palace, and it was I who used to arrange Mrs James White's flowers in Park Lane.

'Queen Mary used to like her flowers to be of pastel shades. The last time I did anything for her was at the Goldsmiths' Hall. She was old, and they arranged a chair for her in the lift.'

'Are you superstitious about flowers? Do you think that some flowers are unlucky?'

'No, indeed, I am not. How could anybody believe that flowers are not the most precious gift that God has given us? I am never tired of them. When, at the end of a long, dark winter, spring comes at last, and I am sent a great box of tuberoses, I still feel I want to plunge my nose into the midst of these living, fragrant wonders.'

All these last things she said to me joyously holding a broom in her hand. Now she swept up some leaves, and then added:

'For twelve years I was manageress of a florist's in Old Broad Street. I had employees to sweep, to fetch, to carry, and to pack. I bought, I sold, I made the business flourish. Then the manager came back and I was expected to take my place again in the ranks. When one has climbed with difficulty to the top of the ladder, it is not easy to climb down again willingly. Perhaps I was wrong, but I resented it. So I left the job, and was fortunate enough to find this little shop under the famous tree in Wood Street. Before I came it was a toy-shop. The City is in my blood now. I would not be anywhere else in the whole world.'

By now it was eleven-thirty and the bells of St Paul's rang out. We closed the shop. This was the time, Carrie explained, when the cleaner arrived to tidy up the shop. Meanwhile she and Win and I made our way to Henekeys in Lawrence Lane for a gin and tonic and a sandwich.

As we were all three more or less of the same generation, we soon found ourselves discussing the question, were things better now than before the war?

Carrie answered in a flash:

'We worked far harder but we ate so much better—that is, when there was the money for food. Everything was of better quality.'

'What about the tuberculosis you spoke of?' I asked.

'Nothing whatever to do with food,' said Carrie. 'Either it was in your family, or it was not.'

I did not wish to contradict her. She went on:

'Young people to-day ought to be much happier than we were. Their parents make so many sacrifices for their education. If anybody had told my parents to send me to a grammar-school they would have laughed. And that was the case all along our street. How we were smacked and punished! Nobody would dare do that any longer.

'The fact is that in the old days, because there was so much misery, parents could not do otherwise but send their children out to work from the tenderest age. Nowadays the parents sacrifice themselves.

'When mother and I were having a slight argument one day, a thing that happens between mother and daughter however much they love each other, I said to her:

'"Yes, when we were all working, and bringing our money home, you did not do so badly. And as for me, from the age of ten until to-day, when I am just over fifty, I have never ceased working for you."

'It was not that I blamed her at all. I just wanted to record a fact.'

We went on to talk about gardens.

'We have a tiny garden,' said Carrie, 'and when we have not been able to sell a plant we put it in our garden. Thus, last year, I had the most wonderful hydrangeas. Even those that were sickly when we planted them have become fine plants and doubled their size.'

We were now on the way back to the shop. Bow Church, without its tower, faced the giant Sun Life building. Carrie called for the key of her shop at Wooderson's, the shirt-maker, where the cleaner always left it, and we then prepared for the lunch hour rush. On a shelf were cards which customers used when they sent flowers: 'In Sincere Friendship,' 'Love to mother and baby,' 'Congratulations!'

A girl came into the shop. She bought three carnations. The postman opened the door, and thinking that I was a saleswoman, handed me the letters. I felt quite proud. More customers arrived, and I suddenly found myself memorizing the prices of the different flowers; carnations and roses, two shillings each; mixed sweet peas, three and sixpence; stocks, five and six.

'Prices at Covent Garden start going up on Wednesdays to reach their highest at the end of the week,' Carrie explained to me. 'Housewives imagine that it is we who raise the cost, but that is not true. The profit margin remains constant as far as we are concerned. Then there is the wastage. Unfortunately we never quite sell out by evening. One does not need to be very good at arithmetic to run a flower shop.'

The hairdresser up the street wanted a beautiful bouquet which cost £1 15*s*. Carrie made it up for him. He smiled at all three of us, and hurried away, because in a few minutes he too would start the rush hour. A pretty girl came in to tell us that it was her mother's birthday. 'Are you going to lunch?' asked Carrie. The girl told her that she was. 'Very well,' said Carrie. 'Come back afterwards, and I shall have it all ready for you.' The girl went over to the shelf, and taking a plain card, wrote an affectionate message for her mother. She was left-handed and I was fascinated by the speed with which she wrote.

Nurses from St Bartholomew's Hospital, employees from the Old Bailey . . .

Carrie has a soft corner in her heart for hospital nurses, and I notice that very often she gives them more flowers than they have paid for.

'Why not?' she asked, blushing. 'When the first violets come in, I occasionally slip a bunch in with the other flowers. The girls are so happy when they discover them later.'

I admired the way Carrie and Win plunged their hands into the different vases, bringing up the flowers and allowing them to drain off before wrapping them up in paper. I would be afraid to upset the vases, balanced so precariously on the top of narrow stands.

'Oh, but it does happen!' exclaimed Carrie. 'The

worst is that when one knocks a vase over others follow like ninepins. On one terrible occasion a customer, while picking out a flower he was anxious for me to include in a bouquet I was making up for him, sent all the vases in the window crashing, and as the vases were of cut glass, and the flowers particularly expensive ones, I cried like a child.

'As so few people live in the City we sell very few plants. Our most important orders are for magnificent bouquets offered by City people to a colleague who is being promoted, or who is engaged, or who is about to retire.'

Two remarkably good-looking young men, wearing glasses, came in next. They emptied their pockets and found that they had 38*s*. between them.

'We want two pretty bouquets!' one of them said.

Carrie made up the bouquets deftly to their choice, but they were in such a hurry to take them that she exclaimed:

'Give me time to dry the stalks. You will spoil your suits!'

'Ja! Ja!' answered the two young men gaily, and a moment later they disappeared down Cheapside, each proudly holding his bouquet.

I asked Carrie if it was true that to add foliage to tall stemmed roses was apt to curtail their hours of beauty.

'Yes,' she answered, 'but it is not so much the fault of the foliage as the fact that the stems of the roses often become stifled in the minute leaves. Sometimes also the roses become hung up above the water line.'

As soon as a new customer arrived, we all stopped talking, and I watched Carrie go over to the window, select a bunch of flowers from a vase, and look deeply into the blooms, breathing their sweet smell. Was she reluctant to part with these treasures? No, but they are almost like her children, and she likes to wish them good-bye. Some people might laugh at this but I notice that women, especially, who buy flowers are very understanding, and seem to know that Carrie overflows with love for her merchandise. A woman who comes into a flower shop has quite a different expression from the one she wears in any other shop, for there are so many things in a flower that flatter her femininity—its colour, its delicate beauty, its exquisite scent.

Next came a private secretary who wanted three carnations—a red one, a white one, and a pink one—to place on her table next to her typewriter. She was the second customer to make such a choice. As soon as she had gone, Carrie began to prepare the bouquet for the pretty girl who was going to give it to her mother for her birthday. Carrie took a narrow box from a pile she had brought from Covent Garden and deftly turned it into something resembling a baby's cot. Into this she put a few gladioli, some yellow and blue irises, roses, and carnations of various colours, and finally a bunch of stocks. Her lips moved almost imperceptibly as she filled the box with this riot of colour. I thought she must be counting up the value of the separate items so that her pretty customer should have good measure. Suddenly, as a gift of her own to this unknown mother, she threw in a tiny bunch of those beautiful pinks which set one dreaming of a border in an English garden—the sort of garden we think of in hot days in a big city. A sheet of cellophane, more white paper, and the 'baby' was firmly swathed in its cot. At this moment the girl entered. I had seen her pacing up and down Cheapside several times, wondering if the flowers were ready and afraid of being late at her office.

Another girl came in to ask the price of sweet peas. Carrie and Win were busy, so I answered:

'Three and sixpence, dear.'

'Thank you,' she murmured.

We smiled at each other, and I had the same wonderful feeling of belonging here when the postman handed me the letters. What an urge there is in all of us to change our personalities from time to time.

As soon as we were alone again Carrie began to talk about flower arrangements. Her theory is that every woman knows instinctively how to make flowers look pretty. The gift is natural to her womanhood. What is essential is that she should have enough money to buy them.

'Carnations are expensive,' said Carrie, 'but the ones I buy at Covent Garden will last a whole week. The young woman who bought three for her office desk just now was right. She showed taste. My roses too are still in bud. To-day they look like the lips of sleeping babies, but to-morrow they will open out almost to the size of small tea-cups. Whenever I am asked to make up a bouquet, I try to put in as many different flowers as I can so that the girl who buys it can arrange her flowers in the way she likes them best.'

'Yes, miss?' asked Carrie suddenly.

'Miss,' who had just come through the door, had the most delightful pony tail and very high heels that tapered into a point. Her thick cardigan was beautifully hand knitted. She bought two bunches of pinks, white ones and mauve ones, and as she left she sniffed at her bunch through the white paper.

The girls are all charmingly dressed in this City of to-morrow. One is reminded of a girls' college in America—bright cotton dresses, lots of hand-knitted woollies. There are few men about in the streets.

Win, who had just sold a tropical-looking plant to a girl, said as though the plant were a baby:

'Give it enough to drink but not too much or too little, and keep it out of draughts in a nice even temperature.'

'Very well,' said the girl, clutching her treasure.

Win stooped down to pick up a leaf from the floor and brought it across to me.

'Somebody once told me,' she said, 'that if you put a leaf like this face downwards on the right soil, it would take root and grow. Wouldn't that be wonderful?'

The leaf was like velvet. I remembered a market gardener at Nice showing me a similar one which took root in this way. Win was thrilled when I told her this. She stood in front of me with the communal broom from whose sweeping the little leaf had been miraculously saved.

Carrie is on excellent terms with Mr Wooderson, who owns the shirtmaker's at the corner. Not only does her cleaner leave the key with Mr Wooderson when she has finished her work, but Mr Wooderson allows his messenger, Mr Holder, to do odd jobs for Carrie, like delivering flowers to St Bartholomew's. Mr Holder, a former policeman, smiled benevolently at us and went away with his parcels. Next a City man asked for a red carnation to put in his buttonhole, and while it is being cut he puts water into the tiny container behind his lapel. I was suddenly seventeen again, for Mr Meller, my boss, and his second traveller, both wore these clever devices, which filled me with astonishment when I was a young girl.

As soon as he had gone I told Carrie and Win.

'The custom is dying out,' said Carrie. 'The City has changed so tremendously since the war. There are so many more women than men now.'

'They make the City look brighter.'

'Yes,' she agreed, 'and women love to have flowers beside them while they work. I am sure there is not a private secretary in any of these giant buildings who would be without them. They are so pretty on her table, near the typewriter and the coloured telephones. Flowers brighten an office like sunshine. They remind her of happy week-ends.'

'What do you and Win do over the week-end?'

'Win does the washing. I often do the cooking. We garden. Our neighbours in Hampstead commission us to buy flowers at Covent Garden for them. We are quite well known there.'

'There is only one Carrie Miller,' said Win mischievously. 'A woman who saw Carrie's name on the shop from the top of a bus the other day came to us saying: "I was at school with Carrie. I knew there could be no other Carrie Miller."'

Carrie had chosen two white carnations from the window. I watched her shortening the stalks, and thrusting wire through the heart of the flowers. She then twisted the wire round the shortened stalks.

'Must you really be so cruel?' I exclaimed.

'I know what you are thinking,' said Carrie. 'I was decorating the table at the Goldsmiths' Hall the other day when the Queen was going there. She also has a horror of piercing flowers with wire. But the carnation has a heavy head on a slender body. It is an aristocrat in its way. These are for a wedding at Hampstead to-morrow, and it would be a very serious matter if they were to lose their heads at a wedding!'

# 6

IN the same part of London in which buildings like Fountain House, in Fenchurch Street, with its thirteen storeys of glass, and the smooth gigantic extension of Lloyds were springing up, I experienced on this Sunday before Whitsun the strange feeling of living for a few moments in the Middle Ages.

I had for some weeks been curious about the church of St Andrew Undershaft which stands at the corner of Leadenhall Street and St Mary Axe. Like St Bartholomew the Great, it passed unscathed through the Great Fire of 1666, and that of December 1940. There was certainly a church here in 1267, if not earlier, but because Cornhill extended eastwards as far as St Mary Axe, it was then known as St Andrew upon Cornhill, or as some chroniclers spell it, Cornhull.

Every May Day, that beautiful festival of old England, a beribboned maypole was put up in the middle of the street opposite the south door, and its shaft was even taller than the church steeple. This pretty festival of music and dancing was repeated every year till early in the reign of Henry VIII, when the wife of a local citizen was seduced by a Lombard, named Francis de Bard, who lived in nearby Lombard Street. This set up a hue and cry against all rich Lombards and other foreign money-lenders, and in April 1513 the apprentices and other young citizens began to pick quarrels with strangers in the street, and a rumour began that on May Day next the City would rise against the foreigners.

These riots were known as Evil May Day. The St Andrew Shaft, or May Pole, was taken down and for thirty two years remained beneath the eaves of a row of thatched cottages in Shaft Alley.

The present church of St Andrew was built during these years. Begun in 1520, it was finished twelve years later, and owing to the fact that the earlier edifice had for so long stood under the shaft of the maypole, it was known as St Andrew Undershaft.

I had, on my first visit, pushed open the south door very quietly at about half past eleven one Sunday morning when the service had already begun. The weather was just bright enough to be calling people to a day by the sea and, except for a small trickle of holiday traffic, Leadenhall Street was deserted.

The sound of organ music came from inside. How difficult it is to creep into a City church unnoticed once the service has started. I felt uncomfortably self-conscious as the verger in his black robes came forward from his chair under the west window to meet me.

St Andrew Undershaft is not so old as St Bartholomew the Great, that tremendously impressive choir of the old priory church which still brings back to the mind of any visitor a picture of monks at mass. In a different way, however, St Andrew's is no less a beautiful jewel.

The choir here was composed of girls and men; two young boys in cassocks and white surplices knelt at either side of the communion table. The service, I realized, was a sung eucharist in the course of which the visiting clergyman gave a short sermon, since the rector was absent. He spoke about the meaning of Rogation Sunday.

I stole into a pew at the back beside two little girls. The choir outnumbered the congregation, which gave the effect of the service being held entirely for them, but this did not detract from the feeling of warmth and happiness that immediately flowed over me. I experienced much the same peace and content as in the churches of Vienna, where one can walk right up to the altar and kneel down at any time of night or day. This church also, to my great surprise, was heated in the most delightful modern way by pipes running just above the hassocks, so warm that one could scarcely put a gloved hand on them.

The stone-work of the nave and two aisles was cleaned so that it looked like new. The sixteenth- and seventeenth-century brasses shone, the stained glass let in filtered light, and the ribbed and flattened Perpendicular roof, painted and gilt with flowers and emblazoned shields, all freshly decorated, gave one the certitude that what had been loved

*St Andrew Undershaft*

and honoured in the days of Henry VIII continued so to-day. There are still a few young people of the City who worship here as their forbears did through plague and fires along the centuries.

At the close of the service the congregation was invited to tea and biscuits in the vestry. While Mr G. Fruin, the verger, led me there, the little girls ran up into the tower to chime the sixteenth-century bells. Mr R. A. Ledgerton, the choirmaster and organist, continued to play the organ, and the visiting clergyman unrobed, picked up his attaché-case, and hurried away.

The tea, strong and excellent, was brewed by Mabel MacDonald, who has something of the charm and smile of the Queen Mother, and who exclaimed:

'I am the only parishioner!'

She and her husband, Stanley, who is a sidesman, but who was not present on this occasion, live on the top floor of the Chamber of Shipping of the United Kingdom at Bury Court. So once again we have an example of City housekeepers being almost the only parishioners.

What of the girls in the choir? What connection had these young and pretty choristers with the City? Though they were hurrying away, some to lunch, some for a day's outing at Brighton, they introduced themselves charmingly one by one.

Fourteen-year-old Susan Rimmer was born at St Bartholomew's Hospital, and her father was housekeeper at the Royal Bank of Scotland in Bishopsgate. Valerie Penfold, seventeen, was at the Central Foundation Girls' School at Spital Square, while Una Butlin, a year older, was at the Sir John Cass Foundation School in Aldgate, and, until her policeman father retired, lived in the police-station at Bishopsgate.

Edna Wood worked at a stockbroker's in Old Jewry; Norma Garnham at Dr Barnardo's Home in Stepney Causeway. Marian Panzetta, Norma's married sister, was the contralto. Sheila Christian, with the choir since it first used girls' voices, lived with her mother, a housekeeper in Great St Thomas Apostle, off Cannon Street.

The two boys I had noticed kneeling on either side of the altar were servers or acolytes. The younger, John, little Susan Rimmer's brother, started as the missal boy, carrying the prayer book between the vestry and the altar.

The elder was Ian Martin, whose father was a policeman at Bishopsgate.

A charming feature about this church was that Edward Halsey, the alto and the bell-ringer, was training little girls from the Mary Datchelor Girls' School at Camberwell to chime out the bells. These are some of the loveliest bells in England and now they may be heard high over the City streets on Sunday mornings. There is a brass to Mary Datchelor, her husband, and their three daughters on the south-west wall, diagonally opposite the memorial to the chronicler John Stow, in St Andrew Undershaft, which reads:

In the hope of a blessed resurrection, in a vault near this monument, are deposited the remains of Mathias Datchelor, merchant, of this parish, and Mary, his wife, worthy examples of piety and paternal tenderness. They left behind them three daughters, Mary, Beatrix and Sarah, ladies pious and virtuous in mind, and distinguished worth, who in life and death were not divided, who bought ye ground, and built ye vault with ye consent of vestry—A.D. 1699.

Money left by these pious ladies for charities which could no longer apply to the City in its changed mode of life was used rather less than a hundred years ago to found the Mary Datchelor Girls' School in Camberwell.

The following Sunday I again went to St Andrew Undershaft and sat behind a young man, with a little girl and her elder sister. The little girl had long blonde hair gathered together by a pink satin bow, and a flowered satin dress, with puffed sleeves, set off the milky whiteness of her delicate arms as she knelt motionless, her head bowed over the prayer book. When the man and the elder girl rose to go to communion, she remained alone, and on my return I saw for the first time the beautiful features, serious, and a little pale.

The rector, the Venerable H. J. Matthews, was taking

the service this time, and afterwards we all went, as on the previous Sunday, to have tea and biscuits in the vestry. The little girl behind whom I had sat in church was introduced to me as Philliter. With two others, Carole and Jacqueline, she was on the point of going up into the tower to chime the bells, and Edward Halsey asked me to come with them.

Mr Kenneth Lindy, the architect, says that the base of the tower is certainly Norman. I passed through the little door by the east window and began to climb the narrow spiral steps leading up into the belfry. At once I became instinctively aware of that peculiar Caen stone with which so much of my ancient farm in Normandy is built and which I have learned to know and to love as a friend. The light came fitfully through loopholes between floors so that the stairs were often in complete darkness. All the same I felt almost more at home on them than on the too polished stairs of some modern buildings, which are often treacherous and slippery. The secret is to feel one's way up with a hand against the wall. I was fortunate enough, too, in this difficult ascent to have the three spirited girls in front of me and Mr Halsey just behind.

I had not guessed that I would find myself in these medieval surroundings in the very heart of the City of to-morrow.

Our first destination was a small room of stone and ancient timbers. It smelled faintly of hay and dry wood as in the country, and against one wall was set the clavier with six horizontal wooden handles, each one of which, when brought smartly down by a touch of the hand, rings the bell with which it is connected.

Four of the six bells were made in the time of Shakespeare by the celebrated Robert Mot, founder of the Whitechapel Bell Foundry. The two others were recast slightly later. These are they:

| | | *Diameter* | *Date* |
|---|---|---|---|
| 1st bell | The treble bell, recast by Anthony Burt. | 26¼″ | 1669 |
| 2nd bell | Robert Mot. | 27¾″ | 1597 |
| 3rd bell | Robert Mot. | 30″ | 1597 |

| | | *Diameter* | *Date* |
|---|---|---|---|
| 4th bell | Robert Mot. | $33\frac{1}{2}''$ | 1600 |
| 5th bell | Made by Bryans Eldridge at Chertsey. | $37\frac{1}{4}''$ | 1650 |
| 6th bell | The great tenor bell, Robert Mot. | $41\frac{1}{4}''$ | 1597 |

The bells made by Robert Mot bore this inscription in Latin:

Robertus mot me fecit

and when little Philliter put her delicate hand on the clavier, and I heard the great bell ring above our heads, I could scarcely contain my emotion.

In medieval times bells were almost people. Each bore the name of a saint and was allocated a special job. The great tenor bell was nearly always called after the patron saint of the church to which it belonged. Thus the tenor here is called Andrew. Gabriel is the Ave or Angelus bell in honour of the Annunciation, and another is called after Guthlac, a seventh-century hermit who set off to discover the most desolate spot in Britain. A man told him of an island so dreary that nobody would live on it. He made his way by boat up the Welland to Crowland in Lincolnshire in the very heart of the fen, and managed to sustain himself there on barley bread and water for fifteen years.

Mr Halsey says that getting little girls interested in bells is an excellent way to make them church conscious, and he may be right, for when I am in Normandy we women can tell all the news of the village by listening to the bells, though we may be a mile or more away, hanging up linen in the orchard. So it must have been formerly in English villages. The passing bell or death knell was rung in so many different ways that one could almost guess who had died. The tenor bell would tell you if it was a husband or wife, the second bell announced the death of a bachelor under forty, and the treble bell had a language of its own for announcing the death of a child under ten. On Shrove Tuesday there was the pancake bell, and then of course there was the right bell to call the faithful to Morrow Mass, Lady Mass, and Jesus Mass, as well as vespers and the gay wedding! Ringing bells in changes for purely musical purposes only arrived in Jacobean times. Fabian Stedman was the father of English change ringing.

But why were the bells at St Andrew Undershaft played on a clavier instead of being rung with ropes?

'The tower would not stand the strain,' said Mr Halsey.

'What is wrong with the tower?'

'It is old and the traffic of the City swirls round it. One does not sufficiently appreciate these delicate marvels left over from medieval days.'

'Yes, but explain about the bells?'

'When a bell is swung, it exerts, quite apart from its dead weight, enormous vertical and horizontal forces. The vertical forces alone are no less than four times the weight of the bell. Imagine what that means with a tenor bell weighing thirty-four hundredweight!'

'But when the clavier is played?'

'That is quite different. In that case the clapper is merely swung against the bell, which remains stationary. Thus there is no additional force other than the dead weight.'

Philliter puts her hand on the lever and releases it quickly; Carole and Jacqueline take a little more time. What wonderful sounds! My heart beats with pleasure. Nobody says a word. Heads nod in rhythm. There is a piece of music with numbers instead of notes; it is a tune composed specially for the bells by Mr Ledgerton.

When it is all over, Mr Halsey tells me that I may ring the big tenor bell. I touch the lever, and the sound reverberates over the roofs and spires of the City.

We climb farther up the spiral stone steps, which become narrower and darker, to a chamber above, where wires run criss-cross and then up to the belfry. Now we take the steepest climb of all to the top where there is a narrow gallery from which we can look down on the bells.

On the way down, in a loophole cut in the Caen stone are three little eggs, out of which, soon, I hope, three baby pigeons will emerge and fly away!

# 7

THIS was lunch-time on Friday, the last day of May, and because of a sudden spell of hot weather about a hundred people of many different nationalities were seated on the steps of St Paul's.

From time to time motor-coaches and small wagons of German make drew up by the statue of Queen Anne, whom so many people mistake for Queen Victoria. Guides shepherded small groups of sightseers, many of them youths from Scandinavian lands, and gave them brief descriptive lectures before taking them up to the great doors.

A different crowd, infinitely larger, filled that part of St Paul's Churchyard which runs parallel to the much damaged Paternoster Row. It seemed thickest in front of the shops, both small and large, which make this thoroughfare, with the cathedral garden on the other side of it, one of the most picturesque in the City.

The interesting thing about this crowd was that it was almost entirely composed of girls and young women. The shops themselves, with a few exceptions, sold such merchandise as gay blouses, cotton frocks, tempting pastel-coloured cardigans, lingerie, the prettiest shoes, and haberdashery. Once again I had the impression of being on the campus of a women's college in America, for the crowd was such an essentially youthful one, so fresh, vital, and eager, bright as paint in pretty blouses and accordion-pleated skirts or flowered dresses.

In fact this young feminine population was utterly in tune with the sunny, luxurious offices in those giant buildings rising on every side in the City from the ashes of the old ones.

Now I also plunged into this crowd, catching the fever

of its enthusiasm, its young recklessness in spending the money of the wage packet that every young woman had earned herself and could therefore spend just as she pleased, buying the clothes that would keep her looking young and fresh.

In the sombre vestry of a medieval City church I had heard two men talking. They were men of importance and money.

'The most significant change that has come over the City since the war,' said one of them, 'is the almost complete disappearance of the office boy.'

This statement came to me as a shock. I had been aware of its truth without ever pausing to consider it. I now realized that the sight of an office boy, like the one I had known at Aldermanbury, pushing a trolley under the very nosebags of cart-horses in narrow, congested City streets, was something I should never see again. Office boys like Bill, with his cheviot suit of cheap wool, cheery companion of my tea-making days, and Arthur, so fiercely determined to be like the boss and to succeed, however much it cost him in hard work, had been replaced by those young college girls with their pretty blouses and gay skirts who could afford to buy themselves something new with every wage packet. The City was no longer a stronghold of men.

'That is true,' said the other man. 'Nearly eighty per cent of the personnel is feminine.'

'Do you realize,' asked the first, 'how many heads of corporations to-day started as office boys? Who will replace them? The young men who come to us with high degrees from the universities?'

'Girls, perhaps,' said the second, laughing. 'Who knows but we shall see a lady chairwoman of Lloyds or the Baltic?'

'Not in my lifetime, I hope,' said the first.

There are other changes in the City besides the disappearance of the office boy.

The narrow jostling thoroughfares with the butcher's and the baker's, and the little chop-house down the geranium-scented alley, will soon be as much a thing of the past as was the Tudor Street scene after the Great Fire of 1666.

Bow Lane remains, in my opinion, a pure delight. It begins with St Mary-le-Bow and ends with St Mary Aldermary, which you must on no account confuse with Aldermanbury.

This village high street in miniature with a church at each end dedicated to the Virgin Mary is just as exciting to walk along as any of the old narrow streets near Rouen Cathedral, from which ancient Norman city so many of William's nobles came.

The word Aldermary to medieval Londoners suggested that St Mary Aldermary was the 'older Marie,' and St Mary-le-Bow the newer one, though if this be really the case one wonders just how far back the older one can go.

For the moment St Mary-le-Bow, Norman crypt included, is in the hands of our friend Mr George, while St Mary Aldermary, at the bottom of the lane, is almost undamaged.

My adventures in the tower of St Andrew Undershaft led me to uncover more information about bells. Mears & Stainbank (the Whitechapel Bell Foundry), whose founder, in 1597, inscribed his name on the bells which the little girls and I had rung, had now finished a set of twelve new bells for St Mary-le-Bow, and were impatiently waiting for Mr George to build the place up again in order to hang them. As they will doubtless become very famous one day, here is something about them.

BELLS FOR ST MARY-LE-BOW.

| *The Bell* | *Her Name* | *The reason for the name being chosen* |
|---|---|---|
| Treble | Katharine | This name was asked for by Mr Albert Arthur Hughes and his two sons, William and Douglas, of the Whitechapel Bell Foundry, who made the bells. Katharine has a special blessing for bell-founders, possibly because this saint was broken on a wheel, and bells are rung on a wheel. |

| *The Bell* | *Her Name* | *The reason for the name being chosen* |
|---|---|---|
| No. 2 | Fabian | Chosen by the ringers to commemorate Fabian Stedman (1590–1630), the father of English change ringing. |
| No. 3 | Christopher | Chosen by the architect in honour of Wren. |
| No. 4 | Margaret | St Margaret Moyses, one of the former parishes, now incorporated with St Mary-le-Bow. |
| No. 5 | Mildred | St Mildred, Bread Street, destroyed in 1940. |
| No. 6 | Faith | St Faith under St Paul's, incorporated. |
| No. 7 | Augustine | St Augustine, Watling Street, destroyed in 1940. |
| No. 8 | John | St John the Evangelist, incorporated. |
| No. 9 | Timothy | All Hallows, Bread Street, where Milton was baptized. The churchwarden, Col. Stuart Maxwell Roberts, has a nine-year-old son called Timothy. |
| No. 10 | Pancras | St Pancras-le-Soper, incorporated. |
| No. 11 | Cuthbert | All Hallows, Honey Lane, destroyed 1666, incorporated. The bell to be called Cuthbert because the first appeal for St Mary-le-Bow was made by Sir Cuthbert Ackroyd, when Lord Mayor of London, who asked that the bells should be made during his year of office (1955). |
| No. 12 | Tenor Bell (42 cwt) | |

Bells, incidentally, are sold by the pound like potatoes, but they are more expensive, at least for the moment. They cost 5*s*. 4*d*. a pound.

A wonderful variety of interests crowd together in the short length of Bow Lane. I have compared it with a village high street, but in truth it is more complex, for though you will find a butcher's shop (with that nice Victorian title 'Purveyors of Meat' inscribed over the window), a haberdasher, a chemist, several legal firms,

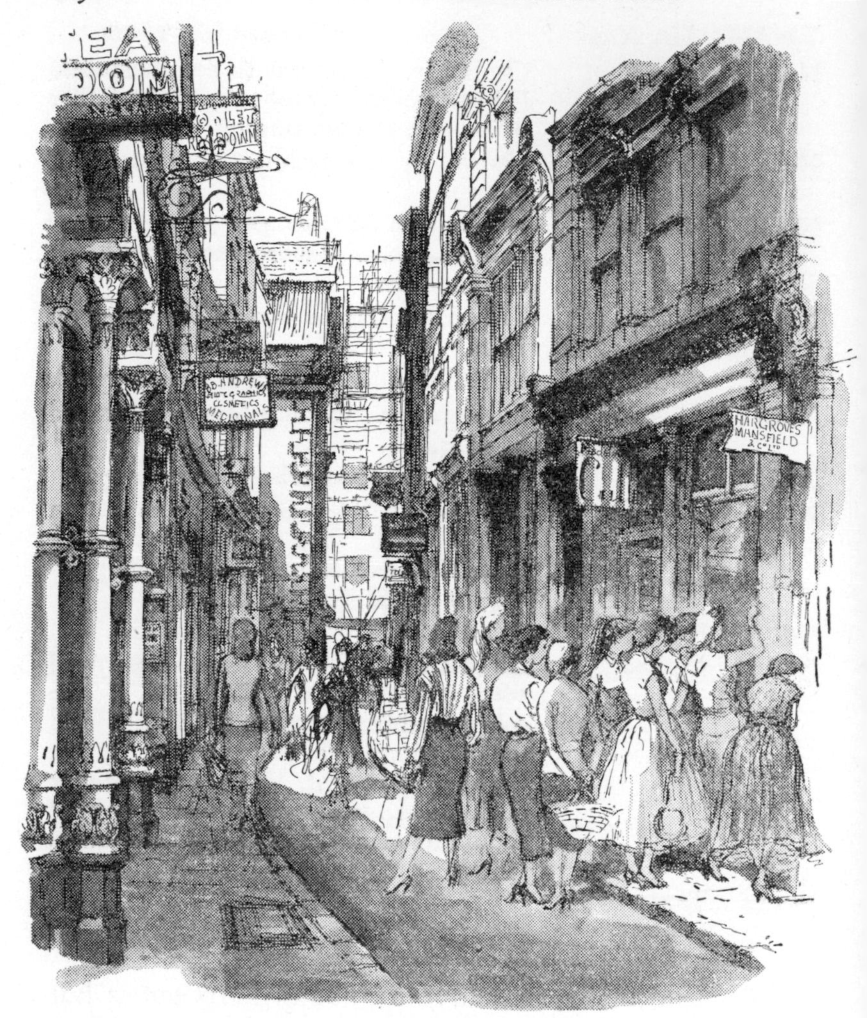


*Bow Lane*

chartered accountants, two famous old taverns, several restaurants, a barber's shop, and everything else that you would normally expect to find in an English village street, there is much else besides. There are the offices of canvas manufacturers, tie and scarf manufacturers, and engravers on steel and copper.

Cheapside, once so boisterous and bright with gilded pendant signs, has lost all its picturesqueness save for those three little shops under the tree. Not so Bow Lane, however, which still evokes the poetry of the past. Cheapside thunders with traffic and the noisy building of those giants which are soon to transform its old character, so that it will be hard to distinguish it from any similar artery in Hamburg or Philadelphia. The wind blows along it and fills your eyes and make-up with particles of brick dust. Bow Lane is delightfully narrow. From one end of it, in the reign of Henry VIII, you could have seen St Mary-le-Bow, with its medieval tower topped by four stone lanterns at the corners and a fifth held aloft in the centre by four flying buttresses, and in the distance the lovely spire of Old St Paul's. St Mary-le-Bow is just now a complete and miserable wreck. Facing it across Bow Lane is a modern tailor's shop. Further in, however, old London again makes itself felt. There is the Invicta Café, whose gargoyles were exactly opposite the temporary church built on the site of the vestry of St Mary-le-Bow, and which fascinated me when I attended service there by the monstrous shadows they made on the east window. Beyond the café is Jeanne Claey's tiny shop, whose façade, painted in light blue, frames the most enviable display of blouses and cotton dresses. Nearly always when I stop to look at them I can see at the back of the shop a good-looking woman ironing expertly on a wide board, deftly making pleats as she goes—the kind of little picture one often sees in old French towns. There are yards, courts, and passages leading out of Bow Lane. Some, like Well Court, twist and turn, affording glimpses of men being shaved and pamphlets being printed; others, like Groveland Court, are gay with daisies and geraniums banked above a red-tiled floor. A famous tavern, with the usual half timbering, faces the quiet offices of chartered accountants. Farther along in Bow Lane a shop, bearing my Christian name, sells separates and bright lingerie, another sells umbrellas, while on the other side of the street a gramophone shop, a chemist's, and an employment agency stand elbow to elbow. When heavy lorries come along Bow Lane they almost scrape the façades of the shops, and as they can only crawl along, their young, good-humoured drivers invariably keep up a diverting conversation with the passers-by.

A butcher has his establishment at the corner of Watling Street, and crossing the road from here you come upon the blackened oak beams of Ye Olde Watling Inn, which claims to have been built in the historic year of 1666, presumably after the Great Fire. Next comes a men's hairdressing establishment, overlooking the quiet precincts of St Mary Aldermanbury.

On pushing open the door of this church, in which Milton was married to his third wife two years before the Plague, I was met by a little wizened woman wearing a green cotton dress, a yachting coat of the same colour with gold buttons, and a dark brown straw cloche hat with a veil. She had brown shoes with flat heels and said, in the sweetest voice:

'I am Gertrude McVitty, the sacristan.'

I looked round, saw lighted candles, holy water, and a confessional, and exclaimed in a low voice:

'I did not know that any of the City churches had gone back to the old faith. How angry John Milton would have been!'

It had been a blind Milton who was led here with his bride in 1663. At home in Jewin Street things had been going from bad to worse under the mismanagement of his three daughters and his servant. Elizabeth Minshull was a young woman, never before married. While on a visit to London from her home in Cheshire, she had been persuaded to become the wife of a blind man of fifty-four. Milton's signature at the bottom of his declaration of intended marriage, almost illegible as it falls crookedly down the paper, is one of the most pathetic relics ever left by a man of genius.

Which day personally appeared John Milton, of ye parish of St Giles, Cripplegate, London, gentleman, aged about 50 years, and a widower, and alledged that he intendeth to marry with Elizabeth Minshull . . . aged about 25 years . . .

When this intention of marriage became known in Jewin Street, it naturally caused some consternation among the daughters. The maidservant told the second daughter, Mary, that she heard her father was to be married; to which the said Mary replied to the said maidservant that 'that was no news, to hear of his wedding, but if she could hear of his death, *that* was something.' Of Elizabeth Minshull we know little. There is a tradition that her hair was of a fair gold colour.

Gertrude McVitty looked up at me, and said quietly:

'This is not a Roman Catholic church. It is an Anglo-Catholic one.'

'Oh!' I said, waking out of my dream. 'I should have guessed. Even so Milton would not have liked it. Even Wren might have found it strange. They were so intolerant in those days about holy water, incense, and the confessional.'

'They say that just now there might be even fewer people if it were not like this.'

'I expect you are right. Do you have many people on Sundays?'

'Oh no! We are closed on Sundays. This is a guild church.'

'Of course, I simply cannot get accustomed to this modern idea of closing a church on Sundays. It sounds like the Shops Act. Are you also an Anglo-Catholic?'

Gertrude McVitty answered quietly:

'Oh, it doesn't worry me! I have seen so many changes here. When I was a girl it was very low church.'

'You have been here a long time?'

She laughed.

'I was born in Cheapside.'

'How exciting. Where?'

'In front of St Mary-le-Bow. Mother was a housekeeper above a jeweller's; father was a police officer in Cloak Lane. Mother was very low church, and when I was little we had a wonderful rector who taught us all sorts of things at Sunday-school; the church was so full on Sunday mornings that we had to put chairs here by the font. What a sight it was!'

'I suppose more people lived in the City?'

'All the girls I was at school with lived in the City. Some were daughters of housekeepers, others of policemen, others of shopkeepers who lived above their premises. We had great fun. And people enjoyed coming to church.'

'Do you still live in Cheapside.'

'No, the night St Mary-le-Bow went up in flames I had sent mother away. She was a bit nervous. I went into a shelter myself for a few minutes. When I came out there was nothing left of our building. It had fallen to the ground and was burning. We lost everything.'

'That is bad. I know what it means.'

A young man came up and beckoned to Gertrude McVitty, who stood listening to him with great attention for several minutes; he then opened a thick case, from which he brought out a duster and a tin containing some sort of liquid polish, a few drops of which he hastily poured on the floor. The next moment he was down on his knees polishing away with the duster, and almost before we knew what was happening a large circle of miraculous cleanliness appeared at our feet, so that the sacristan, whose aged features had remained motionless up till now, smiled in childish wonder. I was myself not a little impressed. The traveller, looking up at us, broke into the persuasive patter of an itinerant vendor in a French country fair. He suddenly became aware that people only a few yards away were dipping their fingers into holy water, and sprang up, thrusting his paraphernalia back into his bag, promising to come back another day.

The sacristan appeared to turn the matter over in her mind, but suddenly reverting to our earlier conversation, said abruptly:

'We all loved our Sunday-school.'

'Yes,' I agreed. 'It is fun for children.'

'Oh, but children don't go to Sunday-school any more

now!' she exclaimed. 'Most of them don't even know the Lord's Prayer, whereas we learned the collect by heart every Sunday.'

'Where do you live now?'

'In Golden Lane, at the back of St Giles, Cripplegate.'

I had promised to lunch at the George and Vulture, the early seventeenth-century tavern and chop-house in George Yard, half-way between Cornhill and Lombard street. I was pleased to find the lunch was to be at my favourite table in front of the grill where the chef, having asked one to choose from the steaks and chops laid out on a table in front of him, grills them immediately above his sizzling fire. How good it all smells! The mushrooms and tomatoes are turned over with a flick of his wrist as he manipulates his long fork. The Burgundy and claret wines attain their correct temperatures in the long cage between the crackling fire and the cash-desk, giving an air of contentment to the whole room. The knife-board seats and the narrow tables are evocative of an England which ate better than we do now. One needs to come to a place like this to realize what a pleasure good food can be. A waiter, in a scrupulously clean white coat, presents a tiny saddle of lamb to a gentleman lunching with friends, and murmurs:

'Does this meet with your approval, my lord?'

The banker from Lombard Street nods his head. He and his friends are drinking wine from Bordeaux. Voices are low, and people do not smoke while they eat. I suddenly realize that I am the only woman in the room and that men, when they are bankers from world-famous board-rooms, have advantages that women will never have. They are also, as far as food is concerned, much more civilized, and do not puff the smoke of cigarettes into the faces of their companions.

On my way home after lunch I decided to go through

St Swithin's Lane. Jutting out into the narrow street hangs the brilliantly coloured Five Arrows shield of the House of Rothschild. During the Battle of Britain my husband used to lunch here once a week with his cousin, Anthony de Rothschild, head of the London House. Hither, for instance, he made his way on foot over rubble and burning debris on the historic morning after the great fire of 30th December 1940, and that day the two of them lunched alone in a room hung with the portraits of former Rothschilds. The building was miraculously saved when flames raged all round.

Opposite the great doors which lead into these historic premises of New Court has arisen the beautifully proportioned Chetwynd House, with its four dark green lampposts, its shining white façade decorated with fuchsias, red geraniums, and tall marguerites, and its magnificent carvings of Apollo, the handsome Greek sun-god, with his lyre, and of Poseidon, with his trident, their names writ beside them in Greek letters. Here on the ground floor, and in the new muniment rooms below, N. M. Rothschild & Sons have extended their kingdom. A magnificent marble bust of the founder, placed here lately by Edmund de Rothschild, allows his illustrious forbear of Napoleonic times to survey the modern scene. Farther on, on the same side as New Court, on the way to Cannon Street, is new St Swithin's House, with its fine iron gates, its well-proportioned courtyards with a fountain in the form of a little child emptying water from her jug. In this lane also is what I think must be the smallest and most picturesque shop in the City, the prettiest shop you can imagine, with a door so narrow, and yet so elegant, that anybody can see that it was made for maidens who work in the palaces of millionaires.

Over door and window of this miniature shop, under the figure 21 in a pretty half-circle, you may read:

Ruth Rochelle

Hand-bags, gloves, hosiery
and leather goods.

The window is gay with artificial flowers, and on the door is a notice which reads: *Hand-bag and Stocking Repairs. Twenty-four-hour service.* I must come back here. I have stockings in need of mending.

Next to Ruth Rochelle hangs the sign of SANDEMAN, that sinister Spaniard with his black cloak and hat. Sandeman—Oporto, Jerez, and Lisbon, you may read on the fine brasses, and through the wrought-iron gates port casks gleam in the courtyard.

I walked slowly along Cannon Street, remembering the times I so often had to negotiate wreckage during the war, and another occasion, not so long ago, when I came here one evening to examine the temple of Mithras upon which now stands that gigantic new building, Bucklersbury House.

How much London history, in addition to the Roman temple, must have been shaken when the excavators dug down into the soil to lay the foundations of the new building. There was a strong tower of stone, called by Edward III the Cornets Tower. In the reign of Elizabeth a certain Buckle, a grocer, decided to pull it down in order to build a goodly house of wood. He so greedily laboured to pull down the tower that a piece of stone fell upon him, and we are told that his life was considerably shortened thereby, whereupon another man married his widow, finished pulling down the tower, and built the wood house himself.

I was reflecting upon the injustice of this story when

I noticed two plane-trees in lovely thick foliage, standing in front of the prettiest Adam house. A very jolly looking woman, wearing spectacles, a striped dress, and a flowered cotton apron, was sweeping the top step, and the whole picture was so unexpected, so reposeful in the busy hum of the City, that as I drew near to her I said, smiling:

'What a lovely house!'

'Yes,' she answered, 'it is.'

'Are you the housekeeper?'

'That 's right.'

'A real City-born housekeeper?'

'Well, yes and no. I was born in Shepherdess Walk, off the City Road.'

She suddenly began to sing for my benefit:

> 'Up and down the City road,
> In and out the Eagle.
> That's the way the money goes,
> Pop goes the weasel!'

Then, in order that I should not miss the point of the popular song, she explained:

'The Eagle was a beerhouse, and housewives used to pop their flat irons on a Saturday.'

I told her my name, and asked:

'What is yours?'

'Ruth Roach.'

'Do you live here with your family?'

'Yes, my husband is the commissionaire, and we have two little girls, Patricia, aged fourteen, and Ginette, aged twelve. They are upstairs now. We have a four-roomed apartment.'

She came down to the bottom of the ten wide steps to point out the beauties of the house from where I stood, adding, with a touch of pride, that as it was on the site of the church of St Thomas the Apostle, destroyed during the Great Fire of 1666, it was consecrated ground, and that the trees which so greatly added to its beauty could not be cut down. Inside the house, she said, there was a beautiful Adam fire-place and some doors on the first floor which lead nowhere. They were built against the south wall and it was her opinion that in times gone by they had been used as trap-doors for the people who lived in the house to push their enemies into the void. Under the house there were curious vaults which belonged to the church of St Thomas which must have been of great antiquity. Someone had told her that it had been at least five hundred years old when it was burned down. There was a burial ground on the other side of the street and a plaque next to the house they called the old vicarage.

I asked her where she did her shopping. She said that the City was too expensive, especially Leadenhall Market, and pointing down the road, she added:

'I cross the water and shop in Southwark.'

I now realized that we were within a hundred yards of the bridge and I was quite captivated by the idea of this woman crossing the bridge every time she wanted a packet of tea or a cauliflower. Then I made another discovery. Standing in the middle of the street I could see the façade of the Guildhall to the north and the bridge across to Southwark to the south. The effect is extremely curious. Most of us have known the excitement of walking down the street of a seaside village which seems to end up in the sea. The Thames to the Londoner is as romantic as the ocean, and here it was lapping the mud beach almost beside us while straight ahead of it in the opposite direction rose the Guildhall.

A policeman came along and turned down a street running parallel with the water.

'He is going to the station in Cloak Lane,' said Mrs Roach.

Cloak Lane. Where had I heard the name before? Why, yes, of course. That was the police-station to which the father of Gertrude McVitty, the sacristan of St Mary Aldermary, was attached.

Mrs Roach was pointing to the south wall of her lovely house.

'I would not be surprised,' she said, 'if the river in flood time did not come right up to the house two centuries ago. So if those false doors did open into the void, the enemy could have been pushed into the water.'

I looked at her in admiration, thinking that she might well have the imagination of a Dumas or a Scott. Should I advise her to write an historical romance about her house? Looking up to the flat roof, we suddenly saw two golden-haired little girls waving to us.

'Patricia! Ginette!' she called.

I waved my hand and they waved back.

'Come up a moment?' said Mrs Roach, who was still holding her broom.

Alas, people were waiting for me at home. That exquisite moment of a friendship just begun would have to be renewed another day.

# 8

THE FIRST of the new bells came to the church of St Lawrence Jewry on Whit Saturday, and by eleven in the morning the big tenor bell, weighing twenty-five hundredweight, was already hanging from a steel cable at the foot of the tower, waiting to be hoisted aloft.

How magnificent it looked! Suspended some four feet from the ground, it seemed to be pulsating with emotion. One could read the various signs and words that were engraved on it, and even, though I got into trouble for doing so, peer underneath at the fiery golden portion cut out from the metal to give the bell its tone.

Mr George, fluttering in the background, greeted me with a preoccupied look, and I guessed that it would be safer not to worry him. Important men would be arriving at any moment, and he would have to be there to answer their questions. This building had, under his direction, risen from the ashes, growing month by month more blindingly beautiful. It was now a modern masterpiece, witnessing to all that builders have not lost their art—as yet a silent achievement, but to-day to be supplied with a musical voice in which to proclaim how puny is the power of bomb and incendiary against the will of man to render honour to God's glory. What a wonderful, solemn moment!

Here, about the bell, and on either side of the powerful winch, were the craftsmen from the Whitechapel Bell Foundry:

William Theobald, aged 43, the bell-hanger, with Ernest Rowe, 35, his mate; A. Oram, 31, born at Jarrow-on-Tyne, the frame builder, with J. Paddon, 40, born at West Ham, his mate.

The four men turned the bell slightly so that I could read

what was on it. Their strong hands, stained by the plumbago which gave the great bell its dull, sombre glow, stroked its surface with affection. At the top was engraved a gridiron to recall the fact that St Lawrence was martyred on a gridiron over burning coals in the year A.D. 258 in Rome, at the time of the Emperor Valerian.

Then came the sign of the makers: a crown over a large bell, with the intitials ${}^{A}_{H}{}^{A}$ (Albert Arthur Hughes, the father) on the left of it, and ${}^{W}_{H}{}^{A}$ (William Arthur Hughes, the elder son) on the right of it. Below this, framed between two smaller bells, DH (Douglas Hughes, the younger son). And the date 1957 encircling them.

Next came this inscription:

> These bells replace the former ring of eight,
> cast 1679, 1687, and 1710, destroyed by enemy
> action, 29 December 1940.

William Theobald and Ernest Rowe, the bell-hangers, brought to their craft an understanding love, for they had both been bell-ringers and had chosen the work to which their hobby had naturally led them. Mr Theobald had been an engineer who rang bells for his amusement, chiefly at St Thomas's, the thirteenth-century church at Salisbury, and on occasion at St Paul's Cathedral and at Westminster Abbey. He it was who put back the bells at St Andrew Undershaft, which had been placed for safety during the war in Cleeve Abbey, Somerset. Ernest Rowe, born in Cheapside, and therefore a man who had a particular reason to love the bells of St Mary-le-Bow and St Lawrence Jewry, had rung those at St Ann's, Stamford Hill.

The tenor bell, still swinging gently at the end of its steel cable, was immediately under the bell-ringing chamber, the sound-deadening floor, and the bell chamber. Soon the men would bend over the winch, two others guide the rope, and very gently the bell would start its eighty-foot ascent. Then would come the anxious moment as it rose through the gaping holes above, the timber trap-doors.

Now for the first time I caught sight of the vicar, the Rev. J. F. Trimingham, doubtless in the throes of considerable emotion, for very soon the church would be his to use to the best advantage. Cecil Brown, the tall, gifted architect, was perhaps remembering the day when, so shortly after the fire, he had looked down at the pile of melted bell metal. The new St Lawrence Jewry was as much the result of his genius as the previous one had been due to Christopher Wren.

Cecil Brown started life as a chorister at St Paul's Cathedral, which shows that City choristers can on occasion, as in medieval times, rise to the point where their name will go down to posterity. He was anxious to stress that whereas the new St Lawrence Jewry was in the Wren tradition yet the interior arrangements were quite different. Like the architects of the Italian Renaissance, Michelangelo in particular, Cecil Brown is a painter as well as being an architect. His central panel of the reredos, an oil-painting on plywood, is one of the outstanding wonders of the new church. I was never tired of admiring it.

I now became aware of a small man standing all by himself in a corner. His gaze was kindly but stern.

'You must not keep the men from working,' he said quietly.

He answered most courteously, however, the questions I particularly asked. Why, for instance, was the new tenor bell smaller than the old one. Whereas this one weighed twenty-five hundredweight, the original had weighed thirty-four.

'The old peal was too large for the tower,' he answered, 'and encroached on the window space. In addition, bells tuned on modern lines are more powerful than in the days when there was no calculated harmonic tuning.'

'You have already made the bells for St Mary-le-Bow?'

'Yes, they are waiting for the church to be rebuilt.'

'At how great a distance, in your opinion, can bells like these be heard? When a person says that he was born within the sound of Bow Bells, what exactly does that mean?'

'On a quiet Saturday evening I have heard Bow Bells well up in Cornhill, and years ago, when the City was quieter, I once heard the bells of Southwark Cathedral at our foundry in Whitechapel.'

'So even in the quiet of the night it would be impossible to hear the sound of Bow Bells in the West End?'

'Yes, I think that would be impossible.'

'When bells are chimed as they are at St Andrew Undershaft, because the tower is not strong enough to stand the vibration, is the sound as effective as when bells are rung?'

'No, certainly not. The effect of chiming is feeble compared with ringing.'

Now the men turned the handles of the winch and the great tenor bell began very slowly to rise.

On the other side of tarpaulins, carpenters and polishers were working in the church where the great brass chandeliers already hung from the white-and-gold ceiling. Here I discovered Joe Thwaites, a french polisher, and his mate, polishing the pulpit and the choir stalls.

Joe Thwaites, aged forty-five, started by polishing pianos at the age of fourteen, but he says:

'Piano polishers are fewer than they were. Most modern pianos are sprayed with cellulose and burnished. That satisfies some people, but it would not take me in.'

His stained hand fondled the exquisite carving on the pulpit, and he went on:

'This pulpit was made by George Harrington of our firm (George M. Hammer & Co. of Hermitage Road, London, N.4), and I will stake my reputation that no finer piece of craftsmanship was produced in Wren's time. The wood carving was carried out by A. W. Banks, aged fifty, and a small group of craftsmen, and is certainly no less impressive than the work of the carvers employed by Grinling Gibbons, whose name we so closely associate with that of Wren.'

'How long did it take him to make?'

'About seven months. You should have seen it when it was still natural oak. To my way of thinking, they were wrong to adopt what is known as "old English colour."

I know it was like this before, but it is too black for my liking.'

'I agree. Incidentally, how do you turn natural oak into old English?'

'The natural is stained with bichromate, brushed in with white polish and chalk to bring up the grain. Then we paper it down and polish it.'

Joe Thwaites looked up at the ceiling, and the tops of the Corinthian columns, and said:

'Lovely, isn't it? They put more than one thousand books of gold-leaf into this job. It 's a treat when a man reaches my age to work on something so worth while.'

Mr Hughes had mounted the stairs leading to the organ-loft and was looking at the great tenor bell going up through the trap-door of the bell-ringing chamber. There was an anxious expression on his face, as so often happens when a man witnesses the completion of a great work.

A cold wind whistled through the boarded doors, but outside the sun was warm, and I decided to sit for half an hour in the garden of St Mary the Virgin, Aldermanbury, where I would be out of the way.

The tulips and wallflowers had been replaced by magnificent rose-trees whose deep red and yellow buds were a joy to look at. Who was the gardener of this abandoned church, and if I could discover him would he be able to tell me what had happened to the statue of the Virgin?

A girl was reading the information written at the back of Shakespeare's statue about his two friends Heminge and Condell. Heminge had lived in the parish for over forty-two years, was married here, and had fourteen children, thirteen of whom had been baptized in the church. He was buried in 1630—presumably somewhere under these rose-trees. Condell, on the other hand, who had lived in the parish thirty years, had nine children, eight of whom were baptized here. He had died three years before his friend and his wife was buried beside him. Both men were co-partners with Shakespeare in the Globe Theatre,

Southwark, and had decided after Shakespeare's death in 1616 to publish a collection of his plays.

When the rebuilding of Aldermanbury is finished we are not likely to find any small, picturesque shops as in Bow Lane to break the monotony of giant office buildings. Bookshops, for instance. How charming if one could see them clustering round the rebuilt church of St Mary the Virgin! Those first editions of Shakespeare's plays so diligently collected by Heminge and Condell were first sold in bookshops round St Paul's Churchyard. The curious shape of this has been compared with that of a bow and string—the south side being the bow, the north side the string. *The Merry Wives of Windsor* was sold at the Flower de Luce and the Crown; *The Merchant of Venice* at the Green Dragon; *Richard II* at the Fox; *King Lear* at the Red Bull. Certainly, long before there was any question of collecting his plays, Shakespeare and his companions must have frequented the booksellers of St Paul's Churchyard, and discussed what they saw there on their way to Southwark or Aldermanbury. The Great Fire of 1666 dispersed the trade, which went to Little Britain, next to my father-in-law's church, St Botolph, Aldersgate.

What is one to do with oneself in London on Whit Monday, when all the rest of the world is away in the country? My thoughts turned to the annual 'flower sermon' which for centuries past on Whit Monday has been preached at a church in Leadenhall Street just beyond St Andrew Undershaft; exactly one bus stop farther east, in fact.

This church, called St Catherine Cree, whose picturesque sun-dial is seldom noticed by busy crowds, is divided by narrow Creechurch Lane from the mighty Cunard Steamship building. With its enchanting and hardly known monastery garden, it stands in what were formerly the precincts of the priory of Holy Trinity, Aldgate. The garden, a relic of monastic days, is only twenty yards square and quite hidden from the road. Sitting here one cannot but dream of the fruit-trees, vegetables, sweet herbs, and flowers which must all have grown here when the gardens were bigger and in the care of its monks. Now, one of

*St Catherine Cree*

the tallest plane-trees in London stands guard here over ancient tombs.

Until the end of the thirteenth century people who lived in the neighbourhood were accustomed to worship at an altar in the priory church, but the prior, anxious that his monks should not continually be disturbed at mass by strangers, drew up an agreement with Richard de Gravesend, then Bishop of London, whereby St Catherine Cree was built as a parish church at the western extremity of the monastery. That was in about 1290.

The two churches, the great church of the priory and the smaller parish church, stood quietly side by side through the years. St Catherine Cree had a new steeple early in the reign of Henry VIII, but soon that monarch began to plunder and dissolve the monasteries. The priory church was pulled down. The parish church of St Catherine Cree must slowly, in Elizabethan times, have deteriorated. The body of the church was rebuilt during the reign of Charles I, but not the steeple. The steeple remains to this day as it was.

Inigo Jones, the once poor London boy (his parents lived at Smithfield) who was sent by the Earl of Pembroke to study architecture in Italy, and who acquired there a great admiration for the work of Palladio, is generally thought to have designed the body of the church. Extremely unconventional, a mixture of Gothic and Classical styles, it shows us what St Paul's Cathedral might have looked if Inigo Jones had been able to finish rebuilding it. St Paul's perished in the Great Fire of 1666; St Catherine withstood the fire and again, almost miraculously, emerged triumphant from the perils of the Second World War. Precious, therefore, should it be to Londoners. The rebuilt church was consecrated on 16th January 1630 by Archbishop Laud who stood near the communion table, and taking a written book in his hand, pronounced curses on those who should afterwards profane it. That book still exists. The church is larger than the thirteenth-century one because it takes in one of the cloisters of the monastery garden. The east window is constructed in the shape of St Catherine's wheel; the pulpit and communion table are of cedar wood, and here is the tomb of Sir Nicholas Throckmorton, after whom Throgmorton Street is called, who narrowly missed having his head cut off on Tower Hill because of his connection with Lady Jane Grey.

Every Whit Monday, from earliest times, there has been a flower service here. The congregation bring bouquets or wear flowers. How interesting, I thought, to attend such a service.

I found to my dismay that the entrance to the church was boarded up and a notice declared it to be an unsafe building. In Leadenhall Street a ladder stood against the wall on which is the curious old sun-dial. What had happened?

The Rev. S. F. Linsley told me the strange story. Previously prebendary of Lichfield Cathedral, he was licensed to St Catherine Cree, a City guild church, on 5th May 1954, but already the church was out of commission, and there was no vicarage for the vicar to go to. The authorities gave no evidence of being in any hurry to put the church in order again. Seldom had there been such a ludicrous or wretched situation.

The vicar was not willing to discuss the rights or wrongs of the case, but he explained very clearly the reasons why this church, which had functioned normally right through the Second World War and for several years afterwards, was suddenly closed to the public.

A bomb which had dropped in Leadenhall Street in 1940 blew out the fine old south windows, and did some minor damage to the parapet of the wall, but the interior was not hurt and services were quickly resumed. There was nothing to suggest that the famous church would not continue for many centuries to be a jewel in the City's crown.

But during the months that preceded the prebendary of Lichfield's arrival, while repairs were being effected to the parapet, the beams of the ornate plaster ceiling were found to be infested with death-watch beetle, and by August 1953 the City surveyor declared the church a dangerous structure into which nobody must go. The Rev. S. F. Linsley, therefore, from the time he was licensed till the time I spoke to him, had never been able to enter his church, three long years of frustration.

There were even suggestions now that, as the cost would certainly exceed £50,000, this link with thirteenth-century London would either be demolished or moved elsewhere, and that in either case the site would be sold to some commercial undertaking. What then would happen to the celebrated Bishop Laud's curse: 'We consecrate this church, and separate it unto Thee, as holy ground, not to be profaned any more to common use'?

Meanwhile the vicar was frustrated, as well he might be. With all the fervour of his young heart he prayed that his church might be saved for the City of to-morrow. He also, like all other guild church vicars, received an annual stipend of £750, and an extra £250 because he had no vicarage to live in. He had bought, in the expectation of his work, a small house just outside London.

Later in the week I went back to the tiny hand-bag and stocking shop in St Swithin's Lane which had so intrigued me over Whitsun. I expected to find a woman behind the diminutive counter; instead, I discovered a young man.

Joseph Frackowiak was born in Pomorze, which Prussia was made to give back to Poland after the First World War.

'I was born in territory which had become temporarily German,' he said, 'as I might just as easily have been born in territory which the Russians had annexed. Much of my childhood was spent in France with my parents, who live in the Pas-de-Calais, my father being a coal-miner, but I left them to do my studies in Poland.

'In 1940 I arrived in England with the remnants of the Polish army and went with them to Scotland. At the end of the war I decided to stay in London and become a British subject. I lodged for a time with friends, and it was in their house that I met a young Polish girl with whom I fell in love. She accepted me and we were married, but as she was working very hard to pass an examination, her aunt was anxious that I should do the housework and the cooking so that she could get on with her studies. I had not married her to help her pass examinations but to found a home and be the mother of our children. She failed in her examination, and soon our first son, Richard, was born, and so there was no longer any question of studies.

'As I speak three languages, English, French, and German, as well as Polish, I now work on the continental telephone exchange. Before that I had tried my hand at many things. I used to collect stockings for repair, and it was in the course of my rounds that I came to know Ruth Rochelle, a young woman whose parents, the owners of the little jeweller's shop on the other side of the lane, had taken this place for her in order to set her up in business. When she left to get married, we bought her business.

'My wife, Wanda, was learning to mend ladders in nylons. I used to see her crying with vexation at the beginning because she found it so hard to acquire the right touch; then suddenly she found it, and everything became simple.'

'One needs excellent eyesight, I suppose?'

'No, that has nothing to do with it. Wanda is short-sighted, and wears glasses.'

'So am I. Did it worry you to marry a girl with short sight?'

'I never gave it a thought. When a man falls in love, he loves everything about a girl.'

'How nice of you so say that.'

'I adore my wife. She is extraordinary. And so brave!'

He paused a moment, and then added:

'She was at Belsen, a mere girl!'

'At Belsen!'

Here, in the heart of the City rising from its ruins, the name of this German horror camp made me feel faint. The young man went on:

'Yes, for two months, until Belsen was liberated by the Americans. Wanda did not tell me for some time. That shows how brave she is. She was able to survive because she was young and strong. We have two little boys now. Did I tell you? Every winter, the children and I have colds, but Wanda never has one.'

'Does she ever dream of the past?'

'I don't think so. She forces herself to forget.'

A moment later the young man and I were laughing about something he had said. What a strange conversation! No, on the contrary, it is life itself. We all pass from tragedy to the lightest, most flippant subjects. The young man and I faced each other across the tiny counter. There was no room either to sit or to turn round.

A young woman wearing a white blouse and a black tailor-made came in for a hand-bag which she had left to be mended, and while the young man was taking it down from a shelf she emptied out the hand-bag she was carrying on the narrow counter because she wanted this one mended also. The handle was broken. So she began putting all the things that she had emptied on the counter into the mended one, exclaiming:

'I shall never get all this in!'

She knew, of course, that the seemingly impossible would happen. So, smiling at the young man, she said:

'I will come back in a week's time.'

'The bag will be ready for you,' he answered.

This shop is wonderfully situated for the convenience of girls who work in St Swithin's Lane, King William Street, and in the great banks of Lombard Street. Now that nylons are stronger and cheaper, not quite so many are brought in for mending as happened in the early days, the young man told me. But accidents happen—a stocking is laddered during the morning's work—and often in the evenings a private secretary who has been suddenly invited to a cocktail party or a dance needs to buy a new pair, perhaps of finer mesh, in a hurry.

Shelves with different coloured hand-bags cover the walls of the shop, but black bags predominate, for though, says Mr Frackowiak, he sells a few coloured bags at the beginning of the season, black ones sell all the year round.

This little shop is really no more than a porch which has been built up and given a door. It is so absurdly small that when a group of girls stop to look at a bag or a pair of gloves in the window their remarks are clearly heard inside, which is very useful to the owner of a business who wants to know what potential customers think about his merchandise.

Underneath Mr Frackowiak is a trap-door leading to a basement, and now and then he disappears down it like a jack-in-the-box. He told me that the young women who frequent his shop are so honest that he never minds leaving them alone while he does this. Are they not, for the most part, highly confidential private secretaries? They would not dream of stealing any of the alluring things that fill the shelves and decorate the window.

'When a man comes to buy a hand-bag for his wife he generally knows just what he wants; if he hesitates, and asks for advice, it is probable that he is choosing a gift for his secretary,' said Mr Frackowiak.

'Wanda looks after the shop in the morning; I relieve her after lunch. My working hours at the telephone exchange are rather complicated. Twice a week I work all night; the rest of the time from 6 p.m. till 10.30 p.m. When I am on night duty I leave the exchange, which is near St Paul's, at 8.30 a.m. and go straight home to Chiswick where we live. I generally see Wanda on the station platform waiting to come up to town. We cross like ships in the morning.

'I go to bed after breakfast, and get up at midday. We have a charming house with a lovely garden filled with flowers, near the Thames. Sunday is our nicest day: all our little family is at home, Wanda, the boys, and myself. Wanda does the washing, the sewing, the ironing. I look after the fires and do the heavy work. When my mother comes over from France to stay with us she works harder than any of us. We try to make her rest, but she is so unhappy when she is not working.

'Wanda's mother, who is a widow—her husband was taken away as a hostage by the Germans during the war, and never seen again—lives in Poland with another daughter. My mother-in-law also comes over to stay with us from time to time.

'We all speak Polish at home, even the children, but they play in English.'

A young girl came in for some nylons; my eyes rested on the names of the different kinds: Riviera . . . Mystery.

'You run a car, I suppose?'

'No, it would not be worth it, as we never travel together. We both want to work hard and put money aside. That ought to be possible with my job at the telephone exchange and Wanda and myself working at the shop.'

'I would love to see her,' I said.

'Then come to-morrow morning.'

Riviera and Mystery—Sandeman's black-cloaked, black-hatted figure, whose glass of red port, because I am so short-sighted, I always mistook in my youth for a red rose—symbol of love, the tango, and the flaming sun—romantic wrought-iron gates, with casks beyond them and those magic words on brass tablets: Lisbon, Oporto, Cadiz—the Five Arrows of the Rothschild shield overhanging the pavement outside New Court—Apollo and Poseidon carved on the façade of newly built, shining Chetwynd House—what glamour the City holds in a single narrow street!

The Percy Counsells, housekeepers of St Michael's Rectory, Cornhill, had invited me to tea in their dormer-windowed apartment on the top floor. The beautiful building has the twin doors I had seen earlier, one leading to the church vestry, the other to the offices of the solicitors who now occupy the house, which is a rectory no longer.

Having walked too quickly across from St Swithin's Lane, and finding myself a few minutes early, I sat opposite the bed of scarlet geraniums, which were so uniform in size and colour that I had the impression of looking down on a cardinal's cloak.

From time to time the door opened and a young secretary in a cotton dress came running out, her high heels tapping on the paving stones. When the last employee had gone the garden assumed its evening calm. Mr Counsell, who had spied me from within, came out to welcome me.

'I did so much gardening during the Whitsun holiday,' he said, waving a hand in the direction of the flower beds, 'that I am paying for it now with an attack of lumbago.'

The house was adorable and filled with sunshine. The polished wood of the narrow curved banisters shone, and smelt of beeswax. I was reminded of Kew Palace, the house having something of a Georgian air. The partners' rooms faced each other on the first floor. Their beautiful polished doors stood ajar, affording a glimpse of thick carpets, brocade curtains, and period furniture. Ancestral portraits and old prints decorated the walls, which were painted green.

Some time before this Mr Hanson had allowed me to peep into the room of Mr L. W. Farrow, chairman of Wiggins Teape, at Gateway House, that magnificent new giant between Cannon Street and Watling Street, and I had uttered a little cry of admiration at the magnificence of this office with its vast windows, shaped rather like the bridge of a liner, facing the full mightiness of St Paul's Cathedral. In these buildings of to-morrow the chairmen of great industrial concerns will certainly occupy fabulously expensive and lavishly decorated rooms. Here, however, in St Michael's Rectory, was something beautiful in quite a different way. These solicitors were perpetuating a link with an older aspect of the City. I told myself that Soames, Galsworthy's hero of the *Forsyte Saga*, had an office like this. These rooms had nothing princely about them; they were merely filled with the well-being of an English gentleman's home. The father's portrait looked down upon the son who was carrying on the family tradition in the comfortable unhurried atmosphere of a country house. The garden was full of flowers and birds sang in the trees. I could not tell whether these men got up early in the morning to fly to different capitals in Europe and across the Atlantic, but here were the peace and beauty of a corner of England. The only signs of life visible through the windows were the flagons and pewter at the back of the Jamaica Wine House, and the upright figure of the new rector of St Michael's thoughtfully crossing over to his church.

There was no passenger lift but a curiously archaic contraption with wires and pulleys for hauling up coal and law books, as one might have expected to see in the older buildings of the Middle Temple. When we reached the Counsells' apartment under the eaves I was charmed by the gay paper in the living-room. A budgerigar flew toward us from its perch by the window. A flutter of soft wings against my cheek, and he settled for a moment on my shoulder.

Mrs Counsell arrived from the kitchen, where she had been brewing tea, and as soon as the budgerigar saw her he left my shoulder for hers, the blue of the soft under-feathers matching exactly the blue of the cardigan she was wearing.

A radio was playing softly. A pigeon darted out of the tower of St Michael's Church to perch on the outer window-sill, whereupon the budgerigar flew over to meet it, and to engage it in a curious tapping conversation, each on its own side of the window-pane. This bird, flying about so freely in the apartment, and the comfortable old-fashioned furniture, and Mrs Counsell laying the tea, all enhanced this feeling of setting back the hands of the clock.

'Look at Peter!' she exclaimed.

'Peter is your budgerigar?' I inquired.

'Yes, but Peter is a girl. We had christened her before we discovered that. Now, how do you like your tea? No, indeed, it is no trouble at all. It is I who make tea for the partners and everybody else in the house twice a day, at ten forty-five in the morning and at three forty-five in the afternoon. No, an occasional biscuit but no cakes. I rather frown on cakes because of crumbs which are such an invitation to mice. Talking of mice, when we first came here there was a mouse here in the sitting-room, and Percy, my husband, arranged little pieces of bread and bacon smeared with poison which disappeared almost as soon as he put them down. "Oh dear," I thought. "What a lot of mice we must have!" Then one morning, when I was taking up the cushions of the arm-chair to give them a beating as one does from time to time, what should I see but all Percy's little pieces of bread and bacon carefully arranged in rows! I really do believe that mice are cleverer than we take them for. I think ours had merely hidden this poisoned food under the cushion to get rid of it.'

She laughed so gaily, and her husband, who was sitting meanwhile in the arm-chair in which the mouse had hidden the poisoned food, looked at his wife with such deep and obvious affection that my heart went out to them. I asked about the girls who worked in the house, and Mrs Counsell said that whenever there was a new one she was invariably brought up to be introduced by the other secretaries and that for a week at least everybody would discuss the colour of her eyes and of her hair and whether one could call her beautiful or not, after which, in next to no time, she would become an accepted member of the large family who worked here. When one of them had upset a cup of hot tea on another's cotton dress, the unhappy scalded one had run up to Mrs Counsell, who had quickly come to the rescue, even lending her some clothes of her own till the others were dry.

These were little events, Mrs Counsell pointed out, but they went to show how much nicer it was to work in a family business rather than in one of those rather frightening palaces of marble and glass. Her personal hobby happened to be crochet, which she worked in every sort of cotton, thick or thin, and she simply must show me some examples of her work, including a set she had just made for her dressing-table. The typists all admired her work and when one of them became engaged to be married she always asked Mrs Counsell to crochet a set.

'And I must tell you . . .' she burst out.

'Yes, do!' I answered enthusiastically, quite won over by this homely talk.

'I had begun a new design and was very absorbed in it because of the stitches I was obliged to count. There was a ring at the front door and I was away about twenty minutes. On my return my piece of work had quite disappeared. I looked all over the place for it, and where do you suppose I found it? Peter had stolen it and had tried to drop it out of the window. I suddenly noticed it hanging from the window bolt. He—I mean *she*—looked sly and very proud of herself. I had refused to kiss her when she was perched behind my ear while I was busy counting my stitches, and as soon as I had turned my back she had flown off with my crochet. Jealousy, that is what it was! Birds are just like people. The fact that they are jealous proves it. Now here, under this bowl of roses, is a piece of crochet with a stitch I have invented. Is it not pretty?'

From crochet our talk turned to food and I asked her what sort of things her husband liked.

'Percy was a cook!' she exclaimed.

'A cook!'

I am not sure why I was so surprised to hear that her husband had been a cook. In France one is always meeting men who are, or have been, chefs, but in England one is naïvely surprised to hear that a man can cook. I looked at Mr Counsell, still comfortably seated in his arm-chair, with new interest, but Mrs Counsell was momentarily telling me about her own family. Her father's name was Fred and by the time he was five years old he was already working on his grandparents' farm near Colchester and at that tender age drank half a gallon of beer a day with a chunk of home-made bread, made by his grandmother, and a lump of pork fat.

'Everything they ate in those days was made on the farm,' said Mrs Counsell. 'Food was healthier then—real bread, home-made cheese, butter, and milk from one's own cows.'

'What were his own parents doing?'

'They were working on the railway at King's Cross. My dad left his grandparents' farm at the age of twelve to work in a grocer's shop in London, first in Islington, then in Kentish Town, where he later married my mother, also the daughter of a railway man. Dad soon had a grocer's shop of his own, but when I was sixteen I went to work with my grandparents who, having retired from the railway, had a lovely old inn at Clay Hill. What a beautiful place! The country was so much prettier when I was a girl.'

'Is your mother still alive?'

'She died last year but Dad is over eighty, and still opens his grocer's shop every morning at eight-thirty and closes it at 6 p.m.'

'That seems to show that half a gallon of beer, a slice of bread, and a lump of cold pork are what children need at the age of five,' I said, laughing.

'And you see how things come in useful,' continued Mrs Counsell. 'When Percy was working as a cook at an hotel in the Isle of Wight, and I was there as a waitress in the restaurant, the management needed somebody to manage a new cocktail bar. I applied for the job and was able to make a success of it because I had worked at Grandad's lovely place at Clay Hill.'

She turned to her husband and asked:

'Isn't that right, Percy?'

'Of course,' beamed Mr Counsell.

'I had a little trouble at the beginning,' said Mrs Counsell, 'for cocktails did not exist at Grandad's place. I was obliged to improvise.'

She laughed. Her laugh was soft and captivating.

'After that,' she went on, 'Percy went as cook at the Constitutional Club. We became Londoners again.'

The evening sun filled the apartment with a soft golden glow. I was taken to visit the bedroom, the kitchen, and pretty bath-room. Peter followed us from room to room. From time to time, when the budgerigar could no longer retain its bursting affection, it hopped on Mrs Counsell's shoulder to kiss her. All this conspired to make me fall in love with St Michael's Rectory.

The next morning I went back to the shop in St Swithin's Lane.

Mrs Frackowiak, her elbows resting on the tiny counter,

was reading a book like a good little girl. I felt slightly embarrassed, but she came to my help, and said:

'My husband told me that you might be coming. I have put out a stool. Do please sit down.'

Wanda, behind her spectacles, has the prettiest eyes. She is dark but her skin is fair and her white teeth sparkle. I was a great deal shyer than I had expected to be. Wanda is pretty. At an age when other girls are debutantes, flitting from dance to dance, Wanda was at Belsen. I am always surprised to discover what an ocean separates the youth of one person from the youth of another. Mary Counsell at sixteen was working in her grandparents' inn, Wanda Frackowiak was at Belsen.

'I was born in Warsaw,' she said. 'My parents separated, and what with the war and family quarrels, I had a sad girlhood. One of my sisters was able to escape from Poland in 1939 when the Germans overran the country. Fighting went on for a long time and we kept on changing our lodgings. My father came back to us and for a while father, mother, another sister, and I were under the same roof. My sister and I enjoyed the sort of liberty that is born of disorder, when time, school, and food have all ceased to have any well-defined meaning. Then one day, when life had become quite unreal, she and I decided to go off by ourselves. One of her eyes began to swell. She suffered atrociously, and three days later was dead. I was swept up in a group of fleeing people, but after we had crossed a bridge, the Germans drew a net round us, and that was the beginning of a nightmare existence as we were sent from camp to camp. There was one camp at which prisoners were packed into boats, and rowed out into deep water. The boats were holed and the people left to drown. Corpses were strewn along the shore.

'Those of us who survived were put into cattle trucks and sent to an aeroplane factory in Hanover, but one night the sirens wailed and we were locked up in a fortress in which there were prisoners in solitary confinement. On our release the next morning we saw that both our camp and the factory had been destroyed.'

A workman wearing jeans came into the shop with a package containing a salmon-coloured hand-bag.

'Have you a pair of gloves that would match this bag?' he asked.

Wanda looked through a box of gloves and discovered a pair that both she and I, as women, thought were a good match, but the young workman, having examined them carefully, said:

'No, they will not do. She has shoes of the same colour as the bag so everything must be exactly right. I had better try one or two other places. We live in a suburb where there are not many shops but even in London it is not easy to please a lady.'

We both laughed but the customer remained thoughtful and perplexed.

'I tell you,' he repeated. 'It 's a great responsibility.'

'They gave us some dry bread and packed us all back into cattle trucks,' she went on. 'I have no idea how long the journey lasted. Time did not count. Except for our ability to talk, we had become animals. We were taken to another aeroplane factory, and there was another bombardment. On this occasion we continued our journey on foot, sleeping in the fields, eating practically nothing. Many fell by the roadside and died. We passed a men's prison camp and here something happened to me that I shall never forget. A man slipped a piece of bread into my hand.

'I continued to live because I was so young and I did not want to die. I ate everything that came my way, green apples and raw potatoes. Then they divided us into two sections. One never knew what that might lead to.

'Then we set off again. We walked so far that our feet started to bleed, and when those of us who did not collapse on the way reached our destination, we were at Belsen.

'The name of the camp meant nothing to us at that time but I remember most vividly two things, a great pile of clogs, and the fact that the prisoners looked like walking skeletons. We wore striped cotton dresses, with the addition of a sweater in winter, and we tried to stuff old newspapers under these sweaters when the cold was unbearable.'

A young woman came into the shop for a black leather purse, and she paid for it with a new ten-shilling note, of which she had quite a large number. She wasted no time in making her purchase and soon her high heels were echoing on the pavement of St Swithin's Lane.

'Really,' I exclaimed to Wanda, 'City girls are beautifully shod these days!'

'Yes, indeed!' Wanda answered. 'And so many of them are really pretty, and they do their hair so nicely.'

She paused for a moment, and went on:

'What I found most unbearable was the smell. There were smells I shall never forget. Occasionally, when rubbish is being burned, I am reminded of Belsen. There are body odours also that bring back to me the nightmare of interminable journeys in cattle trucks.

'We did nothing at Belsen. That was one of the worst features. We were made to get up at five, and we waited standing, till seven, sometimes longer, and then, after the roll call, we were given dishwater to drink. The Jewish women had their heads shaved and they remained standing for five hours or more. Sometimes also we used to see a convoy of people being taken to the gas rooms. None uttered a sound. There was nobody to come to their aid. Some of the warders were sadistically cruel; a few tried to give us a little bread. We starved, and yet I went on living, and when the Americans arrived we, who could no longer cry, found tears streaming down our cheeks. They gave us wonderful things to eat but I caught paratyphoid. We had lost the habit of good food.

'I never close a door. However cold it is here, for instance, I leave the door wide open. When I am closed in I feel as if I am being smothered. Fresh air gives me an impression of liberty.'

Another young woman came in. She wanted some gloves but could not make up her mind, and left without making a purchase.

'I am like her,' said Wanda. 'I can never make up my mind. As I am so timid I have a great deal of patience with other girls who are timid. Young English girls are tall and slim. I find them beautiful. When I first came to England from Poland I was nothing but a bag of bones. I could not stop eating. I became quite fat. Now I slim, for though my husband is always telling me that he likes plump women, he quickly lets me know when I put on weight.

'My husband did much to teach me how to be a woman. My mother-in-law used to be angry when she saw him ironing and doing such jobs but I had not had the chance to learn these things. I had to be re-educated. My joy is reading, and I never complain of the time it takes me to travel between here and Chiswick. I look at the people on the District railway, and I admire their calm, happy faces. They give me strength to enjoy life. I also obtain a great deal of satisfaction out of the women's magazines, and I notice that when they write enthusiastically about some fashion the girls in the City come to ask me for it.

'How right young women are to take seriously the unimportant things of life, a new colour, the length of a pair of gloves. That is the real joy of being free. I have learned to appreciate what is frivolous, to be thankful for all the little nothings.'

# 9

AT NO PART of the City's circumference is its frontier so geographically obvious as at its eastern extremity. Leadenhall Street, born out of Cornhill, and Fenchurch Street, born out of Lombard Street, merge like forked branches of the same tree into Aldgate; two lower lateral branches, Houndsditch and the Minories, converge a few hundred yards farther. Then comes the site of the City gate—Aldgate, and beyond what would have been the ditch the present church of St Botolph. It stands, with its pretty emerald painted door, its dark green tubs of red geraniums and two huge leafy plane-trees, between the dark, wealthy, sober City, speaking one language, and picturesque, noisy Petticoat Lane, grand and joyous sight on a Sunday morning, speaking another. Beyond this lie the mysterious plains of Whitechapel.

Between the church of St Catherine Cree, by the Cunard building in Leadenhall Street, and the City gate, Aldgate, lay the priory of Holy Trinity. It was founded in 1107, and dissolved by Henry VIII in 1531. Norman, the first prior, extended the cloisters and the gardens, caused books to be written, ordered new ornaments and precious vestments for the church. The priory began to extend its operations, like a vine putting forth its branches, sending canons to all parts—Bernard to Dunstable, other monks to Launceston in Cornwall, to Plympton in Devon, to St Frideswide in Oxford. William Tarbuit, afterwards Archbishop of Canterbury, went to the church of St Osyth in Essex. The priory is said to have been the richest conventual house in England.

Later, in 1293, the Earl of Lancaster, Edward I's brother, founded the convent of St Clare in the Minories, to receive nuns who were brought from Spain by his wife Blanche, Queen of Navarre. The City gate had marked the Roman vicinal way to the ferry at Old Ford. Much of the life of the neighbourhood clustered round it. In 1374 it was let as a residence to the poet Chaucer, and his London, the London of Edward III's reign, was a city of monasteries and beautiful gardens. When the prioress of a country nunnery came up to visit the prioress of St Clare, she would amble through the City on her mule, behind her would ride a nun and three priests and by her side would run greyhounds whom she fed.

Henry VIII in his insatiable greed was to dissolve both the magnificent priory of the Holy Trinity and the nunnery of St Clare. Stow, when he was about ten years old, used to fetch milk at a farm belonging to the nunnery. He wrote:

> Near adjoining to this abbey, called the Minories, on the south side thereof, was some time a farm belonging to the said nunnery; at the which farm myself (in my youth) have fetched many a halfpenny worth of milk, and never had less than three ale-pints for a halfpenny in the summer, nor less than one ale-quart for a halfpenny in the winter, always hot from the cow, as the same was milked and strained. One Trolop, and afterwards Goodman, were the farmers there, and had thirty or forty kine to the pail. Goodman's son being heir thereof, let out the ground, first for grazing of horses, and then for garden plots, and lived like a gentleman thereby. He lieth buried in St Botolph's church.

The priory of the Holy Trinity was the first to be dissolved. Nicholas Hancock, the prior, was made to hand it over to Henry VIII on 4th February 1531, the monks having first been assembled in the chapter house to witness a formal deed. The pretence assigned for their action was poverty. In short, they were invited to hand over their property for their own good, as the Poles and the Austrians were invited to hand over their countries to Hitler in our own day.

Henry VIII, having taken what he wanted, gave the priory to Sir Thomas Audley, afterwards Lord Chancellor, who was in royal favour because of his personal dislike for Cardinal Wolsey. Sir Thomas offered the great priory church to whomsoever would pull it down and take it away, but there was so little demand for stone, most of the houses in the City being constructed of brick and timber, that no man wanted it and he was thus compelled to carry out the work of destruction himself. The workmen with great labour threw it down stone by stone, beginning at the top. Any man could have a cart-load of the stone for sixpence, and have it brought to his own door for one penny more. Sir Thomas built a mansion on the site, and lived in it till he died in 1544. His daughter married Thomas, Duke of Norfolk, and the estate went to the duke. That is the origin of the present Duke's Place which runs into Aldgate from the north.

Meanwhile the abbey of St Clare in the Minories was surrendered by Dame Elizabeth Salvage, the last abbess, to Henry VIII in 1539. In place of this house of nuns were built 'divers fair and large storehouses for armour and habiliments of war,' and early in 1552 Edward VI gave part of it to Henry, Duke of Suffolk, father of Lady Jane Grey. There was a small parish church for inhabitants of the Close, called St Trinities, which continued to exist in various forms till it was burned down in the Second World War, when the church became attached to St Botolph, Aldgate.

Though Henry VIII plundered the monasteries, he gave no specific instructions about religious worship to the churches, but as soon as he died the Council, which acted during the minority of Edward VI, appointed a commission to pull down statues and destroy church ornaments.

The records of St Botolph, Aldgate, date back to 1547, the year of Edward VI's accession. They shed a very human light on the enforced change from the old faith to the new. William Rofford, then curate, showed a certain amount of resistance, for which he was made to depart the following Christmas. William Dabbes, a much more amenable man, was appointed in his place.

By the first set of injunctions, ministers were to preach at least one sermon every quarter against candles or tapers, relics or images, or kissing and licking the same, praying upon beads, or suchlike superstition. No lights were to be burned before any picture or image, and the clergy were to destroy all candlesticks, trindles, and rolls of wax. Mr Dabbes, entering into the spirit of the injunction, sold off all the candles to Joan Sawkins, a wax-chandler.

He then set about selling the magnificent vestments, many of which came from the dissolved priory of Holy Trinity, to a tailor called Robert Donkin, of Cornhill, and to another called Humphrey Allen, of Whitechapel. The descriptions allow one to imagine their beauty.

Three copes of red, with lions and flowers, sold for 41*s.*

A cope of blue badekyn with birds of gold, sold for 9*s.*

Two copes of purple velvet garnished with flowers of gold, sold for £4. 5*s.* 4*d.*

Two old copes of blue silk branched with birds in them, sold for 10*s.*

The church plate went the same way, the sale having been agreed upon by 'a vestry of honest men for the parish of St Botolph, without Aldgate, in the City of London, on the 18th day of October 1551, in the fifth year of the reign of our Sovereign Lord, King Edward VI.'

The sale, at which the cross of silver and gilt, weighing 61 oz, was disposed of at the rate of 5*s.* 2*d.* an ounce, was attended with considerable merrymaking, the beer and ale being charged to the vestry.

With the accession of Queen Mary in 1553 things went into reverse. 'Mary and Elizabeth,' it is recorded, 'made their public entry together into the City through Aldgate, amidst the plaudits of the people and the pealing of the church bells.' Gravel was spread before the church door. The following year new copes, new candlesticks, and new altar cloths of a very inferior quality were purchased to replace those sold too hurriedly during the previous reign. Moneys paid for missals and frankincense once more begin to figure on the church accounts.

With the accession of Elizabeth the faith changes again. The Queen presented the church with a set of silken bell ropes. The chimes of St Botolph had cheered her solitary hours when, as princess, she had been imprisoned in the Tower, and this was her charming way of rewarding them.

Though Defoe was only four during the Plague of 1665, he later wrote in his *Journal of the Plague Year* this fictionized account:

I lived without Aldgate, about midway between Aldgate Church and Whitechapel Bars, on the left hand or north side of the street; and as the distemper had not reached to that side of the city, our neighbourhood continued very easy. But at the other end of the town their consternation was very great; and the richer sort of people, especially the nobility and gentry from the west part of the city, thronged out of town with their families and servants in an unusual manner; and this was more particularly seen in Whitechapel; that is to say, the Broad Street where I lived; indeed, nothing was to be seen but waggons and carts with goods, women, servants, children, etc.; coaches filled with people of the better sort, and horsemen attending them, and all hurrying away. . . .

I went all the first part of the time freely about the streets, though not so freely as to run myself into apparent danger, except when they dug the great pit in the churchyard of our parish of Aldgate. A terrible pit it was . . . about 40 feet in length, and about 15 or 16 feet broad, and at the time I first looked at it, about 9 feet deep; but it was said they dug it near 20 feet deep afterwards in one part of it, till they could get no deeper for the water; for they had, it seems, dug several large pits before this. For though the plague was long a-coming to our parish, yet, when it did come, there was no parish in or about London where it raged with such violence as in the two parishes of Aldgate and Whitechapel.

I say they had dug several pits in another ground when the distemper began to spread in our parish, and especially when the dead-carts began to go about, which was not, in our parish, till the beginning of August. Into these pits they had put perhaps fifty or sixty bodies each; then they made larger holes, wherein they buried all that the cart brought in a week, which, by the middle to the end of August, came to from two hundred to four hundred a week; and they could not well dig them larger, because of the order of the magistrates confining them to leave no bodies within six feet of the surface; and the water coming on at about 17 or 18 feet, they could not well, I say, put more in one pit. But now, at the beginning of September, the plague raging in a dreadful manner, and the number of burials increasing to more than was ever buried in any other parish about London of no larger extent, they ordered this dreadful gulf to be dug, for such it was rather than a pit.

They had supposed this pit would have supplied them for a month, or more, when they had dug it, and some blamed the churchwardens for suffering such a frightful thing, telling them that they were making preparations to bury the whole parish, and the like; but time made it appear the churchwardens knew the condition of the parish better than they did, for the pit being finished on the 4th September, I think, they began to bury in it on the 6th, and by the 20th, which was just two weeks, they had thrown into it 1,114 bodies, when they were obliged to fill it up, the bodies being then come to lie within six feet of the surface. . . . The mark of it also was many years to be seen in the churchyard on the surface, lying in length parallel with the passage which goes by the west wall of the churchyard out of Houndsditch, and turns east again into Whitechapel, coming out near the Three Nuns Inn.

It was about the 10th September that my curiosity led, or rather drove, me to go and see this pit again, when there had been near 400 people buried in it; and I was not content to see it in the day time . . . but I resolved to go in the night and see some of them thrown in. . . .

I got admittance into the churchyard by being acquainted with the sexton who attended, who, though he did not refuse me at all, yet earnestly persuaded me not to go, telling me very seriously, for he was a good, religious, and sensible man, that it was indeed their business and duty to venture, and to run all hazards, and that in it they might hope to be preserved; but that I had no apparent call to it, but my own curiosity, which, he said, he believed I would not pretend was sufficient to justify my running that hazard. I told him I had been pressed in my mind to go, and that it might be an instructive sight, that might not be without its uses. 'Nay,' says the good man, 'if you will venture upon that score, name of God go in; for depend upon it, 'twill be a sermon to you, it may be, the best that ever you heard in your life. 'Tis a speaking sight,' says he, 'and has a voice with it, and a loud one, to call us all to repentance;' and with that he opened the door, and said, 'Go if you will.'

His discourse had shocked my resolution a little, and I stood wavering for a good while, but just at that interval I saw two links come over from the end of the Minories, and heard the bellman, and then appeared a dead-cart, as they called it, coming over the streets; so I could no longer resist my desire of seeing it, and went in. . . .

. . . The cart had in it 16 or 17 bodies; some were wrapt up in linen sheets, some in rags, some little other than naked, or so loose that what covering they had fell from them in the shooting out of the cart, and they fell quite naked among the rest. . . .

Let us pass over the centuries and visit this same church, or to be more exact, its successor, on Holy Trinity Sunday 1957.

The morning was magnificently hot, and leaving the bus where the Cunard Steamship Building dwarfs the ancient church of St Catherine Cree, I walked to the end of Leadenhall Street, past the pump at its junction with Fenchurch Street, into that short piece of Aldgate which leads to the church of St Botolph without the City Wall.

This stretch of Aldgate, scarcely two hundred yards in length, had taken on quite a new appearance since the completion four months earlier of the gay new building of the British India Steam Navigation Company, which has thus been able to move out of the overcrowded P. & O. offices in Leadenhall Street. Here, at Number One Aldgate, as the building is called, is the pleasantest example of the City of to-morrow. Taking up a great part of the south side of the street, it is a cool symphony of light green spandrels, of marble and bronze; the entrance doors are of armoured plate glass, with red and green handles, signifying port and starboard. Above the doors are four formal compass points carrying the flag masts, and in the teak-lined entrance hall are a superb marquetry mural map and illuminated coloured pictures of ships belonging to the famous company.

The loveliest feature of this airy building is the recurrent sea motif. Glass panels are patterned with illuminated sea birds and glass screens are decorated with sand-blasted pictures of British India ships from the days of the Indian mutiny, ships like the 500-ton *Cape of Good Hope*, the first one of all, a brig-rigged screw steamer which sailed and steamed round the Cape to start the Calcutta–Burma mail service.

Robert Mackenzie and William Mackinnon went out to India in the early days to seek adventure and trade. It was their enthusiasm and courage, and that of others like them, that led directly to the building of this wonderful place of marble and sea birds. Too late for them to see it, it is yet the reward of their daring, and to appreciate the immense achievements of such men is to love the City with a new love, a love that carries us on from the days of the founding of London's priories and nunneries, the poems of Chaucer, and the bravery of those who conquered plague and fire.

Robert Mackenzie was drowned when the ship in which he was returning to India from Australia foundered in 1853. His partner William Mackinnon continued the venture and won the mail contracts between Calcutta and Rangoon, and Bombay and Karachi. His ships cruised close inshore so that a merchant with his goods could stand on a clear piece of beach and hoist his umbrella to attract the captains' notice. Later they put up flagstaffs for the same purpose. At Dubai, on the Persian Gulf, a small Arab boy was posted on a tall date palm to signal the approach of a British India ship.

What other romantic stories go to the making of this Aldgate building which in the short space of eighteen months rose from nothing to its finished perfection?

The *Cashmere*, of 1,080 tons, was taken and looted by pirates near the mouth of the Shat-el-Arab in the 1860's. The pirates came aboard as passengers, knowing that the vessel was carrying gold, and at a prearranged signal they overcame the crew. The Sheik of Muhommerah, within whose territory was Abadan, modern oil town, hunted the pirates. Much gold was recovered and several pirates were hanged. British India ships that passed that way in later years fired a salute to the sheik.

Where Aldgate emerges from the City, before continuing

arrow-like to Whitechapel, stands St Botolph, well back from the street, which seems as though it drew a breath of sweet air from the church garden's lilies of the valley and fig-trees. Here too Aldgate is traversed by Houndsditch and the Minories, which, the one curving back to the north-west, the other to the south, in the direction of the Tower of London, follow the line of the old City wall.

The church, with its emerald painted doors, gave me a sudden, absurd feeling that I was in some quiet little town in Maine; it had the peculiar air of wide American hospitality. I did not intend at first to go in; I was wearing a cotton frock and was not feeling dressed for church, but the geraniums in their dark green tubs, the wide-open green doors beckoned me in. I went up the path, and saw a notice which read:

> The Lord Bishop of London signifies that he proposes to collate the Rev. George Appleton, clerk, M.A. to the benefice of St Botolph, Aldgate, and Holy Trinity Minories.

So there was to be a new rector. Perhaps he was already inducted. Who could he be?

The Bishop of London had thoughtfully set out the rector's previous preferments, amongst which I read that he had been a curate in Stepney, examining chaplain to the Bishop of Rangoon, principal of the Divinity School there, and finally Archdeacon of Rangoon.

I had been vaguely surprised to find the church open, for it was only a quarter past ten, and on my way in the bus I had noticed that neither St Michael, Cornhill, nor St Andrew Undershaft appeared to be open yet. Their services did not start till eleven.

There was a sort of vestibule before one entered the church proper, with a screen surmounted by the royal coat of arms, and on this screen were the words: All Seats Free. Books provided.

Beyond the screen were doors with glass panes through which I could see that an early communion service had just begun. I fell in love with the church at first sight. I loved the deep blue glass of the altar window which—and this is unusual—faces north. I loved the ochre walls and fluted pillars, the reredos with a biblical painting, the galleries on the east, west, and south sides, the last of which contains the organ. A sidesman, noticing me behind the door, rose quickly and straightway conducted me to a pew, but not before I had paused an instant to read these words written in a very large letters on the floor under the gallery:

MAY
10th–11th
1941

I said to myself: 'That was nearly the end of the first period of intensive bombing. I must remember to ask the sidesman about it on my way out.' After this I gave myself up entirely to the beautiful English of the communion service. Long ago, in the reign of Edward VI, these words had angered those who preferred the Latin that was used in the old faith. Now, for many, the words are a heritage more priceless than Shakespeare.

The clergyman came to the door to shake hands with us and I told him how moved I had been by the thought that the service I had just attended was being held only a few yards away from the great pits into which the bodies of Londoners had been thrown at the rate of a thousand a week when the plague was raging. I felt like saying with the sexton of Defoe: '''Tis a speaking sight, and has a voice with it!'

'I feel the same way about it,' said the clergyman, 'but it is not so much a question of being near the pit as standing right over it. The church was rebuilt in 1744.'

I said I supposed he was the new rector and had come from Rangoon.

'Good gracious, no,' he answered. 'I am too old for that. I am merely filling in the interval.'

He added that he was the Rev. P. D. Ellis, and that he was a Welshman.

'I am a Welshman also,' put in the sidesman. 'Dyfrig Lewis is my name, a porter at the London Hospital.'

'I have been wondering about the date written into the floor on which we are standing,' I said. 'Were you here when the church was bombed, Mr Lewis?'

'I was immediately underneath with six other fire-watchers in a very small crypt or cellar, which the then rector had arranged for us,' he answered. 'A land-mine crashed through the roof and embedded itself into the floor here without exploding. The machinery for exploding it had been injured when it grazed the organ on its way down. So the thing could not go off. The organ, therefore, was the cause of a miraculous escape, for without its help we and the entire church would have been blown into eternity. I find it a sobering fact to reflect that such a miracle should have taken place on the exact spot of the great plague pit, for we in the cellar were standing inside what was then the pit.'

'Yes, indeed,' I answered, 'another Defoe will have to describe the moments of terror through which you and your companions lived. Were you very frightened?'

'We felt the bump!' smiled Mr Lewis.

'I imagine you did.'

I then turned to the Rev. P. D. Ellis.

'I take it that you were not here in those days? Were you also a freelance during the war?'

'No,' he answered, a trifle sadly. 'I had a church of my own, a City church, one of the loveliest, until it was destroyed.'

'Really?' I asked. 'Which one?'

'St Mary the Virgin, Aldermanbury,' he said.

'You are a sort of missing link if you will pardon the expression,' I said, smiling. 'I have been searching for you without quite knowing where to look, and now here you are, and it is for me the happiest of accidents that we have met.'

'If you had not come here this morning,' said Mr Ellis,

'we might indeed never have met because the new rector will soon be taking over and, as I say, I am a freelance for the Bishop of London.'

'Do you live in the City?'

'Not now. I live at Woodcote Road, Wanstead, but early in the war while I was rector of St Mary, Aldermanbury, I lived at 5 Amen Court, which I rented from the organist of St Paul's Cathedral.'

'So you were in the City on the night of 30th December 1940. Did you see your church catch fire?'

'No, my wife and I were trapped in Amen Court. There were flames everywhere. We could not get out, not till the morning. When we reached Aldermanbury Street the church was a smoking ruin.'

'What did you do? Did you cry?'

'No, but I may have wanted to. I am not sure what I did. The whole district was in ruins. The church itself smouldered for three days and three nights.'

'Do you remember the small statue of the Virgin in her niche above the church door?'

'Of course I remember her.'

'Quite lately it has disappeared.'

'I do not often go back to Aldermanbury. I did not know it had gone. Would it be a good thing to ask somebody at the London Diocesan Fund? The trouble is that they can't make up their minds what to do with the church. Perhaps they took down the statue of the Virgin to put it in a safer place.'

'Let me take you into the garden,' suggested Mr Dyfrig Lewis.

'That would be a good idea,' said Mr Ellis, 'but you ought to come into the vestry first, and I will unlock the black deed box in which they keep the head of Henry Grey, Duke of Suffolk, father of Lady Jane Grey, who was beheaded on Tower Hill in 1554.'

'How horrible!' I exclaimed.

'Horrible, perhaps, but interesting. There is also a portrait of the duke which you can compare with the head. The effect is most strange.'

We went into the vestry, where Mr Ellis unlocked a japanned box and brought out the head, which he held in the hollow of his hands. I stepped back involuntarily. The effect was indeed strange. The features, even the expression, a slight wisp of hair, the protruding teeth, everything was extremely vivid and distinct.

'Anybody who knew him,' I murmured, 'would certainly have no difficulty in recognizing him.'

I suddenly recalled what Mr George had said about being able to see clearly the features of people buried several centuries earlier, but those he spoke of had been preserved in lead coffins. The duke's head had doubtless been thrown by the executioner into a pile of sawdust. That may have been the reason for this extraordinary preservation.

'Where does it come from?' I asked.

'Workmen found it more than a hundred years ago in the vaults of Holy Trinity, Minories, an unpretentious little church that stood to the left just across Aldgate High Street here, hard against what was once the nunnery of St Clare.'

The nunnery of St Clare, you will remember, was dissolved by Henry VIII in 1539. After that several officers of the Tower resided there, but five years after the young King Edward VI came to the throne, when the monarch was fifteen years old, he gave it to the newly created Duke of Suffolk. The fact that the duke's head was discovered in the vaults of Holy Trinity, Minories, confirms its authenticity. When the little church was destroyed by a bomb during the Second World War, traces of a window belonging to the chapel of the nunnery were found in the ruins of the bombed church.

To what extent had Edward VI encouraged the project to set aside his sisters, Mary and Elizabeth, in favour of Suffolk's daughter, Lady Jane Grey? Suffolk had taken a prominent part in the government during Edward's minority, and actively championed the cause of the Reformation. On 9th July 1553, three days after Edward's death, Suffolk, Northumberland, and others went to Sion House to hail Jane as Queen.

Lady Jane and her husband, Lord Guildford Dudley, fourth son of Northumberland, were both beheaded on Tower Hill on 12th February 1554. The young woman, so beautiful and learned, who had read Plato's *Phaedo* at the age of thirteen, and at fifteen added Hebrew to her studies, which already included Greek, Latin, Italian, and French, gazed upon the bleeding body of her husband as she herself went to the scaffold.

Suffolk and his younger brother, John, had hidden in a gamekeeper's cottage on the duke's estate in Warwickshire but the keeper betrayed them, and Suffolk, who was very ill, was discovered in a hollow tree. He was executed on Tower Hill on Friday, 23rd February 1554, meeting death with the same dignity and courage as his daughter and son-in-law had done.

The British India building in Aldgate had set me thinking about the men who had sent those first little steamships across the globe to trade from port to port. Words which I read in St Botolph as I followed Mr Dyfrig Lewis into the garden shed light on another aspect of the story:

To the memory of
William Symington
born October 1763
He constructed the Charlotte Dundas,
the first steam boat fitted for practical use.
Dying in want, he was buried in the
adjacent churchyard, March 22
1831

How pretty the wild fig-trees looked, the juice smelling so strongly in the hot sun, and the many coloured irises in this garden where tombstones lay half hidden under the dark leaves of the lilies of the valley. At the back of the church two or three people were quietly reading under the spreading branches of the old trees.

But what a bustle in Aldgate High Street! Barrows

were piled high with ripe strawberries. All the shops were open, even the restaurants and milk bars, and from Middlesex Street, which is the modern name for Petticoat Lane, came the sound of a brass band that made me hurry toward the noisy fun. Is there anything in all London more riotously gay than Petticoat Lane on a bright Sunday morning?

What is strange is that, however much London changes, scenes like this have gone on for more than a century. Even the inns keep their original names, like the Three Nuns next to Aldgate underground station. Originally the Three Nuns is thought to have been upon a messuage given to the abbey of St Clare; it was a well-known coaching and carriers' inn. One supposes that, except for the difference which fashion makes in clothes, Petticoat Lane, and the streets and alleys adjacent to it, much blasted and bombed though they are now, looked the same on Sunday mornings in Dickens's time. There would doubtless have been a much greater variety in male as well as female attire, including articles such as dress coats, frock coats, livery and gamekeepers' coats, paletots, tunics, linen and satin waistcoats, capes, and knee-breeches. Some of the narrow streets now had men's suits and raincoats hanging from all the lower windows. A new feature was the enormous number of coloured people freshly arrived in London from the West Indies who were apparently outfitting themselves completely; otherwise the great crowds that thronged the streets were probably more prosperous and better dressed than at any time in history. Business was so good that one was no longer importuned by over-eager traders, as one used to be at Seven Dials, for instance, when that market, so similar to this one, still existed on a Sunday morning.

That people have more money to spend was evidenced everywhere also by the youthful gaiety, the ready smiles, the politeness. I threaded my way as far as Houndsditch, where there is a store as large as any in the West End. Here I went to buy what I needed to make some curtains. What a fine sight this immense store was with its mountain of knitting wool, its cotton dresses, scarves, and blouses, and all the thousand and one other things.

At the corner of Duke Place and Creechurch Place was the burned-out shell of the Great Synagogue; in front of the gate was a poster bearing these words from Isaiah:

> The grass withereth, the flower fadeth,
> but the word of our God shall stand
> for ever. Isaiah XL. 8.

Turning the corner into Creechurch Place, however, I saw a number of young people going into the office for marriage authorization. Out of curiosity, I followed them. Instead of going upstairs as they did, I peeped into the board-room, on the walls of which hung portraits of former wardens, amongst whom was Solomon Hirschel, Chief Rabbi in 1802, with the inscription in Hebrew and English underneath: 'Although elected in preference to other candidates because of his English birth, Solomon Hirschel had left London at the age of four, to return here thirty-seven years later, and he never succeeded in learning English.'

Five generations of those Rothschilds of New Court whose red shield hangs outside the entrance to the bank over St Swithin's Lane have held the office of warden. Yes, no fewer than five generations of this family which since Napoleonic times has never ceased to occupy such an honoured and vital role in the City of London. Gazing down upon me from the wall are the gentle, kindly eyes of Mr Lionel de Rothschild, whose son, Edmund, now a partner in the bank, has been warden since 1942.

# 10

MANY PEOPLE think of the City in terms of the Stock Exchange. Throgmorton Street is the narrow, congested nerve which actuates the City broker. By a miracle neither the great fire in the night of 30th December 1940 which swept across Cripplegate and London Wall like a malicious, bloody flame, nor that intermittent onslaught of high explosives which destroyed so many medieval splendours, did more than singe this street of resonant telephones and shouted prices. Picturesque alleys, avenues, and courts remain virtually unchanged. For a few more years, therefore, one can expect this piece of the old City to remain within the new one. Throgmorton Street will not, like Wall Street, be a canyon of towering stone, and our children will possibly attach to it some of the historic glamour which they will be unable to find in that area of gigantic new buildings that stretches from Cannon Street to Cheapside.

The good fortune of Throgmorton Street is only part of a wider phenomenon. The terrors of war, as far as the City is concerned, by a frightening coincidence fell at their cruellest on religious and historical treasures. No major financial building suffered the agony that overcame nineteen churches, three medieval, sixteen by Wren, and thirty-one precious halls of ancient City companies. The Bank of England, the Stock Exchange, the Royal Exchange, Lombard Street with its banks, Cornhill with its insurance companies, Leadenhall Street with its world-wide shipping interests were safely guarded by an angel that appeared to prefer the temples of money to those of God. That in these circumstances anybody should consider, even for an instant, the willing sacrifice of such jewels as St Mary Aldermanbury or St Catherine Cree is utterly bewildering.

Some people like Throgmorton Street when, because the stock market is boiling over, the narrow thoroughfare has an excited air about it; some find it more picturesque during the lunch hour; others prefer to descend upon it in the quiet of a Sunday morning when, as once happened when I was there, the only living thing in sight was a black cat walking toward me down the centre of Lothbury, the church of St Margaret Lothbury on its left, the garage of the Bank of England on its right. It walked slowly but deliberately towards me, its tail held high, expectancy written all over its person.

On week-days traffic flies past here. A Bank of England porter, in the traditional uniform of pink tailcoat with silver buttons, scarlet waistcoat, black trousers, and tall silk hat, stands in front of the garage entrance. There is one I know with upturned moustaches which give him a fierce expression. Opposite the porter, between Founders Court and the church, is a branch of the Royal Bank of Canada with its painted crest and Spanish-looking windows with wrought-iron bars through which marguerites, geraniums, and forget-me-nots peep prettily. This summer the church wall was being cleaned by the usual system of spraying it for hours with cold water. The effect was miraculous. Soot and filth disappeared; the white stone gleamed. This church, like a mother bird, has collected under its wing the parishes of six other churches. Two of these, St Martin Pomary and St Mary Colechurch, were not rebuilt after the Great Fire of 1666; four were thoughtlessly pulled down to make way for other things—St Christopher le Stocks in 1781 to enlarge the Bank of England, St Bartholomew by the Exchange in 1841 to make way for the Sun Fire Office; St Mildred in the Poultry was pulled down in 1872 and St Olave Jewry in 1888.

Employees of the Bank of England and one or two City brokers with an ear for music steal in here for a few moments during lunch-time to listen to William Tubbs playing Bach on the organ built in 1801. The Rev. A. John Drewitt is the rector.

To the east of the church is a narrow passage, St Margaret's Close, which, skirting the high east wall in which there is no window, will lead you to the peaceful vestry garden with its tall plane-tree and wrought-iron gates; fig-trees nestle up against the side of that same Royal Bank of Canada whose pretty façade is in Lothbury. Stone steps come to a sudden halt on the edge of a bomb crater.

Token House Yard is the next turning beyond the church in Lothbury. Here is the Bank of England Club, whose milk churns and empty lemonade bottles overflow into the side of the bombed site behind the church. At lunch-time the smell of cooking comes from the kitchens, into which you can peep through low windows at pavement level.

I like to enter Throgmorton Street from Lothbury; with Bartholomew Lane on the right, flanked on one side by the Bank of England, and on the other by the Alliance Assurance; and on the left the magnificent Westminster Bank building with its great lantern swinging in the entrance, and high above it the swooping, gleaming white cornice banked with massed geraniums of the same colour as the pink coats of the Bank of England porters. A plaque at the entrance reads:

1836–1936
This stone was placed here
to commemorate the centenary
of Westminster Bank.

The Capel Court entrance into the Stock Exchange is off Bartholomew Lane; the Shorter's Court entrance is off Throgmorton Street; with the cable and wireless office at the corner from which messages fly to every corner of the world. Eight pints of milk stand in a row outside the cable office. Has the milkman just left them there, or are the employees too busy to take them in? A line of men, youths, and commissionaires file under the archway and walk hurriedly across the courtyard, where they disappear through a door. Other men, some carrying slips of paper, walk with the same preoccupied air but in the opposite direction, and when these reach Throgmorton Street they scatter to various brokerage houses. Similarly you may sometimes see two lines of ants keeping up a ceaseless trek along a garden path.

Throgmorton Street, though open to one way traffic west to east, remains reasonably free of cars, but there is a barrow of strawberries of a very superior kind, in expensive punnets, which tempt prosperous-looking jobbers and brokers who are doubtless anxious to bring something home to their wives in the country. On our left is Angel Court, picturesque and mysterious, with a man in a smart black suit and an Alexandra rose in the lapel of his jacket seated in the tiniest theatre ticket office imaginable. Spot-lighted by the brilliant light of his shop against a background of theatre posters, he looks as if he himself were on a stage. A few yards farther along is a barber's shop visible through long basement windows. Men are having their hair trimmed or are being shaved, rapidly for fear that Shell Transport or Hudson Bay should get out of hand during their short absence. Hair cut 1*s.* 6*d.*—says the notice above them. Now here is Birch's Restaurant (established 1690), with its creaking signs over the pavement of the court. Jobbers and brokers, some bare-headed, others wearing bowler hats, one or two wearing tall silk hats, may be seen in the picturesque room into which you can peep through old-fashioned windows. A few are seated at little tables with a glass of sherry and a piece of cheddar; many stand by the window talking shop.

Out in Throgmorton Street again I come across a nun threading her way through the crowd of men. She has an open book in her hand, not a devotional book but a large copy book in which are typewritten the names and addresses of firms who are in the habit of giving something to the poor.

On the right are the steps leading to the Stock Exchange visitors' gallery. Here is one of the marvels of the City of to-day, a realization on the part of the Stock Exchange Committee that this temple is no secret place but an institution to be proud of, a national asset to be visited and

*The Stock Exchange : entrance to the visitors' gallery*

admired by all who pass by. What a great change has come over the City man!

You would not imagine, if it were not for the notice, that this would be the way up to the visitors' gallery; you would more easily think that this led to some small office—a broker's office or perhaps the office of the City editor of a newspaper. One might have a similar surprise when entering some rather humble dependence built against a castle. One would climb to the first floor where, through an opening in the wall, one would look down at knights gathered in the castle's banqueting hall.

In this case, you find yourself in a suite of reception rooms done up in African mahogany with concealed lighting. Is this the entrance to a rich corporation, some very modern bank? No, this is the tastefully designed lounge which has been arranged to put you in the right mood to proceed further. There are arm-chairs, pretty tables, and a map of the world on glass with lines radiating from London to the capitals of the various lands which, like ourselves, are financially minded. 'The Stock Exchanges of the world are all linked with London,' it says. And again: 'The Stock Exchange provides the public with a market in which twenty-five thousand million pounds' worth of securities can be exchanged from hand to hand.'

Until September 1954 the London Stock Exchange could only be seen when it was closed on Saturdays. Conducted tours were organized. To-day you may look down upon it through glass from a long and commodious gallery at any time it is open.

The gallery is just dark enough to allow all the light to be concentrated on the floor of the exchange, which at first sight gives the impression of a huge circular stage broken up by veined marble pillars with passages or alleys between them in which men sit or stand.

There is a ledge against which to lean and space for one's hand-bag and gloves. Every few yards there is a map with a key to explain what all these men are doing, where exactly they job in brewery shares, oil shares, South African mines, Canadians, Americans, and so on. On the extreme right there is the Capel Court entrance (leading into Bartholomew Lane), and in another corner the Shorter's Court door through which had passed, and now continues to pass, that endless stream of men. I have a growing impression of looking down on a surge of black. Men's dark suits are extraordinarily sombre when seen unrelieved by colour. In front of me, if my eyesight were good enough, I might be able to read on a board against a pillar the Sterling Exchange against New York and Montreal. The picture is fascinating, crowded, but not animated. Some men are yawning. They are probably hungry, for it is lunch-time. I decided to go back to Throgmorton Street. As I passed through the lobby, I found workmen building a tiny, beautifully upholstered cinema, and I read:

> The Stock Market is a market for everybody. It is two to one that you are an investor either DIRECTLY, if you own stocks and shares yourself, as a private investor, or INDIRECTLY, if you have money in, or pay into, any of the following: Bank, Savings Bank, Building Society, Co-operative Society, Insurance Company, Pension Fund, Trade Union.

On the other side of Throgmorton Street is Copthall Court, with ever turning swing doors leading into the Stock Exchange Restaurant.

I entered and suddenly had the strange feeling of stepping into one of those long bars that one sees in American cowboy films. The room is very long, low-ceilinged, deliciously old-fashioned, lit by hanging lamps, and, apart from the barmaids behind the various bars, I noticed with a thrill of pleasure that I was the only woman.

There is a great round clock over the swing doors, for time is important to the City broker; to my right are a number of telephones into which men are shouting. The noise in the room is terrific. Two barmaids serve behind the first of the long bars, the one to the left, where beer on draught has linen covers over the barrels, and where there are bottles in a tub of ice on the counter. The walls are marble and there is a life-size picture let into the wall of the Stock Exchange in the days when all the men had whiskers and beards and top hats. Three barmaids are behind a longer bar on the right, against a background of mirrors, toby jugs, and cut flowers in vases. Beyond that again is a snack bar with two young white-coated, white-hatted chefs or carvers—and everywhere men, men, men!

Back in Throgmorton Street a man brushed past me carrying a guitar over his shoulder; he was walking briskly in the direction of Old Broad Street. There were no cars in sight, and for the moment, with this crowd of City men hurrying to and from their offices, the nun with her book open in front of her, the musician with his guitar over his shoulder, there was a faint echo of medievalism in this narrow street, which at the same time throbs with modern life, and from which each pulsation of the Stock Exchange is flashed all over the globe.

Here on my left is Throgmorton Avenue and the Drapers' Hall with its two great carved figures on either side of the Throgmorton Street entrance; its motto is most appropriate in this centre of money:

Unto God only be honour and glory.

How calm and beautiful is Throgmorton Avenue. The red brick of the 1898 wing of the Drapers' Hall has been rubbed new and now glows with colourful warmth; the stone beyond is being washed down by hoses to make it gleam like the south wall of St Margaret, Lothbury. A moment later I came upon the magnificent gardens of this ancient City company. Tall plane-trees cast their cool shade over the avenue. There are mulberry-trees, fig-trees, and deep-red geraniums. Birds chirruped and a gardener was watering young rose bushes. The air seemed sweet and pure; here was the City at its loveliest.

I turned into Austin Friars. In the days of Henry III a certain Humphrey de Bohun, Earl of Hereford and Essex, who a few years earlier had held the future Edward I as a baby at the font, came back to England from a crusade. On this spot he founded a monastery for Friar Hermits of the order of St Augustine of Hippo. A century later a descendant who bore the same name rebuilt the church in the magnificent style of a cathedral.

The glory of the monastery lasted rather less than two hundred years. In 1538, just seven years after forcing

Nicholas Hancock to hand over the priory of the Holy Trinity, Aldgate, and a year before the dissolution of the convent of St Clare in the Minories, Henry VIII dissolved this Augustinian monastery. All over England monastic life was being suppressed.

Edward VI was to find an unexpected use for the Augustinian monastery. Archbishop Cranmer, in his anxiety to promote the Reformation, had brought over a number of Protestant divines from the Continent, amongst them Johannes à Lasco and Johannes Utenhove, who took under their wing the Protestant fugitives from the Low Countries. Edward VI not only granted them the right of free worship, but in 1550 presented them with the choir and aisles of the Augustine friars' church, repaired at the expense of the Crown.

With the accession of Queen Mary, Johannes à Lasco, Johannes Utenhove, Dr Micron, the first minister, and about 175 persons set sail from Gravesend in two Danish vessels, one of which reached Elsinore after being a month at sea, the other not arriving till it had experienced many adventures along the Norwegian coast. They were finally reunited at Emden. Queen Elizabeth I gave them back their property, and from thenceforth until the Second World War Dutch Protestant ministers preached their sermons in the beautiful fourteenth-century nave built by a de Bohun for his friars.

On the night of 15th–16th October 1940 the church was completely destroyed by a land mine dropped by a German bomber.

The foundation stone of the new church was laid by Princess Irene of the Netherlands on 23rd July 1950, the date of the four-hundredth anniversary of the charter signed by Edward VI. The church was ready for use by 1954.

The destruction of one of the last remaining links with monastic life in the City—happily we still have the church of St Bartholomew the Great—seems unnecessarily cruel. One feels that the City was being made to pay for its mistakes and lack of understanding in the past.

Austin Friars, with its gleaming new Dutch church, the clear air of this enchanting corner, the boughs of the trees rustling in the sunshine, the blue sky reflected in the smooth surface of such colourful new buildings as Augustine House, whose solid glass doors, marble facing, and flower boxes breathe the future; these things make up, to some extent, for the choir and aisles of a fourteenth-century monastery. This is a younger London, a London in which a rising generation is more at ease.

I became extraordinarily aware of this one Sunday morning late in June when, though not speaking a word of the language, I attended morning service at the Dutch church. Would it be a service virtually without a congregation as it had been at St Andrew Undershaft?

I was fortunate with the weather this June. Day after day the sun shone and it was a pleasure to walk, dressed in a light summer frock, through the City streets. There were occasions when I felt like a woman on holiday; the air is so sweet in the City at week-ends that I cannot imagine why people trouble to go out into the country.

The Dutch church seeks no inspiration from the past; wisely enough, the architect has kept the lines simple and clean, the whole feeling in tune with the period in which it was built. Beyond it, but almost at right angles, stands the newly finished Augustine House, on a wall of which, rather high up, is a life-size statue of St Augustine of Hippo which, on this particular Sunday, because it was not yet unveiled, was covered with a great linen sheet that fluttered so curiously in the breeze that one had the impression of seeing a ghost.

The doors of the church were open: I passed under the carved cipher of Edward VI. The service had begun and the church was crowded. As I looked quickly round I had, an immediate impression of something I had not seen for a long time—a very young crowd. The women were simply but extremely well dressed in gay clothes with hats of vivid, amusing colours. The men were largely of college age, and there was a sprinkling of extremely well-behaved children. I was so surprised to come across this atmosphere of youthful vitality in what, after all, was a City church, that I walked almost gaily to the back row, where I found a place behind three young Javanese girls. They were dark and unusually beautiful and wore cotton prints with Athenian rather than oriental designs—figures of Hermes and Apollo.

A very young minister in a black gown and white bands was preaching from a tall, narrow-backed pulpit placed where the altar would be in Anglican or Catholic churches, but known in the Netherlands as the Liturgical Centre.

One of the characteristics of a Presbyterian church is that so much emphasis is laid on the spoken word; for this reason the Dutch place the pulpit in this central position. There is no altar. The whole congregation sits round a table when they partake of the Lord's Supper.

The young minister talked for a very long time, and now and again I would understand a word because of its similarity with the German, but on the whole I day-dreamed, and what came most easily to me was the thought that I was no longer in the City but in Holland.

There was no collection at the end of the service; by the entrance door was a great chest, probably Elizabethan, into which one dropped a coin. The pastor, Dr R. H. Van Apeldoorn, extremely distinguished and good looking, was here, in an ordinary lounge suit; it was not he but an assistant who had taken the service. 'Where does the congregation come from?' he echoed, in answer to my query. 'There are, of course, employees of various great firms like Shell, Unilever, K.L.M.; men also who own their own businesses; students; members of the embassy and consulate; Dutch people on holiday; quite a lot of Dutch-speaking South Africans who like to meet compatriots and people from Holland after the service in the hall downstairs. Come down and have a coffee.'

'Do any of your congregation live in the City?'

'Only Al Van Duin, the verger. He has a very lovely apartment above the church.'

Al Van Duin was not at all my idea of the City verger. Of an ancient Netherlands family, he was attached to the Royal Air Force as liaison officer during the war, and is married to an English girl, a Wren, who on this particular Sunday morning was preparing coffee in a spotless kitchen for the many young people who had forgathered after the service. Some thirty young South Africans were united round a table in the middle of the room; a coach load of Dutchmen were on the point of leaving for Aylesbury. The Van Duins were anxious that I should come and see their apartment though warning me that, like the approach to the terrace at Windsor Castle, there were one hundred and twenty steps. But when one has climbed them what a magnificent residence! Al Van Duin collects paintings of the Dutch and English schools; Persian carpets lie in profusion along the corridors and in the rooms. In the dining-room stands a magnificent cabinet made of oak taken from the foundations of an ancient church in Hull. Blue Delft china bowls and early Dutch snuff-boxes decorate its shelves. 'From church to church,' says Van Duin with dry humour.

The window-sills are tiled, Dutch fashion, though the architect was English. One particularly amusing room has a painting of the cliffs of Dover entirely covering one wall.

Far above us at the summit of the delicate steeple is the weather-vane in the form of a cockerel which turns proudly with every breath of wind. Already, like the tower of St Andrew Undershaft and the grasshopper of the Royal Exchange, it is a famous City landmark.

# II

I HAD NO particular motive in mind when I walked down Ironmonger Lane that morning. It was the last Saturday in June and the hottest day, so the papers said, for twenty years.

If ever the Romans saw Londinium under such a scorching sun they must have longed for the shade of the Appian Way. Passing down Watling Street I had stopped to admire the immense activity all about the new Bank of England extension, which people were already saying would cost several million pounds before it was finished, an even greater undertaking than Bucklersbury House in Walbrook which, they said, it would dwarf, though this might be something of an exaggeration. Certainly this gigantic building, stretching from Watling Street to Cheapside, would be almost a city in itself. With its sculptures and courtyard, and the governor's roof garden, there was no fear that finance would not have a temple sufficiently big and shining to hold its own against grimy St Paul's.

I had reached the south entrance, exactly opposite Gateway House in the lounge of which on that Sunday evening two months earlier I had seen all those charwomen waiting for Mr Hanson. I suddenly noticed, rather high up against the façade of the new Bank building, a remarkable sculpture showing the coins of five reigns from Queen Victoria to Queen Elizabeth II. Close by stood a small man with a broad smile and a scarred nose. His shirt and trousers were covered with fine, white dust and his chest and arms were burned a deep red by the heat of the summer. 'Shall I get the money down for you? Nice to have in your purse!' he exclaimed, laughing.

'Whose work is it?'

'Mr David Evans, the sculptor. You might find him over by New Change.'

Should I go back and look for him? These coins were really very effective, and my informant added that one of them, the representation of a gold coin, I think, bore the date of Mr Evans's birth. Many other magnificent pieces of sculpture were to be seen at various points, not the work of one man only, but of several, all celebrated sculptors, amongst them Sir Charles Wheeler, Mr Esmond Burton, and Mr Donald Gilbert, a descendant of Sir Alfred Gilbert who sculptured our beloved Eros in Piccadilly Circus. Donald Gilbert's father, Walter, designed and made the great gates round Buckingham Palace, and on certain of them you can see his name.

I walked back a little way, as far as the corner of Watling Street and New Change, and then, overcome by the exertion, sat down on a piece of stone, my feet resting on a wooden plank. Labourers passed with wheelbarrows. The sun seemed to burn through my dress. A young man looked at me and said:

'You seem to like the sun?'

I had folded a handkerchief in four and placed it on my head, and I wondered if he took me for a tourist or a labourer's wife waiting for the midday whistle. With his white shirt, open at the neck, short sleeves which showed young sunburned arms, blue eyes under dark lashes, he was extremely good looking, but what surprised and charmed me most was the whiteness of his teeth. There is nothing so rare in a man as white teeth.

'Have you been working here long?' I asked.

'From the beginning, several years ago.'

'Married?'

'Yes, with two little children.'

'With weather like this, you will be able to take them down to the sea.'

'They are there now,' he answered, 'but as they are coming back to-morrow night I shall not go down this week-end. They have had wonderful weather all the time. I only hope I shall have it as fine for my holidays.'

'You are not a Londoner?'

'No, I come from Belfast but we live at Swiss Cottage.

The air is better and the journey doesn't worry me. Besides, when this job is finished, in a couple of years' time, I shall be sent somewhere else. I may find myself in Piccadilly Circus. Who knows?'

'What do you do?'

'I am in the engineering section, and I love my job because I am always in the open air. I don't know what it is to be ill or to catch a cold. The open air is what brings lots of young fellows into the building trades. Besides, the pay is good, which means that my wife can afford to stay at home and look after the children. When I go home she is always there. That makes me feel good; gives me a gay feeling when I am at work.'

'How much do you earn?'

'About fifteen pounds a week.'

'Do you hand your pay packet over to your wife?'

He smiled.

'No, she doesn't know what I earn. I give her eight pounds, and help out with the rent, the holidays, and so on. I like to have enough over to give her a little present from time to time.'

'What do you do for a meal at midday?'

'Normally she makes me sandwiches, and I buy a glass of beer.'

A labourer, wearing a dark shirt, looked at me as he passed, tripped over a plank, and landed at my feet.

'Well,' I said, 'at least you must admit you fell for me!'

He laughed, and now the man with the damaged nose arrived to see if I had discovered the sculptor. His expression was once again radiant. The nose had been injured in an accident on a former job. He was caught by the chain of a crane. We went off in search of the sculptor but neither he nor his pointer was there. I found myself examining some of the work of Esmond Burton, a celebrated architectural sculptor, who amused himself when a boy at Marlborough by designing furniture in the carpenters' shop; on leaving school he was apprenticed to a master stone and wood carver.

The work he has done for this building is exceptionally

fine and reveals the skill of a master who has worked in this medium for fifty-five years. He had only a few weeks earlier received international acclaim for his sculptures at the newly opened Bank of London and South America building in Queen Victoria Street. At that time it was the City's most lavishly designed bank since the war. Mr Victor Heal was the architect, as he also was for the Bank of England extension. The two men who have worked together on these two mighty projects thus march hand in hand to fame; their names will stand high in the City of to-morrow, and not only metaphorically. Esmond Burton's head of an Aztec god, representing Mexico, looms on the top of the Bank of London and South America building. Other examples of his work are a condor from the Andes, an anaconda from the tropical forests, a bull's head from the pampas, and a ram's head representing the southern plains of the Argentine.

Esmond Burton makes his models in clay, inventing them as he goes along, not incorporating the features of living models but drawing upon his imagination as a novelist does. He then casts his models and sends them to the building, stating the amount of Portland stone he requires. For each panel at the Bank of England extension something like three-quarters of a ton may have been required. The models might be as large as seven feet by five feet. The panel of the fountain of golden water above the Bread Street entrance on the east front stands about twenty-five feet from the ground. Though Esmond Burton is constantly on the spot, standing with his skilled carver on the platform built for this purpose against the façade, the carver does most of the work. Amongst his indoor work you will find a Bacchus and a satyr over the door leading to the restaurant ('I represent Bacchus as a young man. He was not a drunken old man. I like to think of him as a youth with a wreath of vine leaves'); and over the door leading to the branch bank a seated figure of Midas leaning on a burst bag of gold, and holding a cornucopia from which coins fall in cascade. At one end of the roof garden is the governor's flat; at the other a cultural hall above the entrance to which Esmond Burton has done a fine frieze with two classical figures, one with masks representing comedy and tragedy, the other poetry.

Esmond Burton thinks that young men are too apt to seek their training at art schools. They want to be sculptors immediately, and when they cannot make a living they give it up, whereas if they went about it the hard way, being apprenticed for five years, doing the humdrum work, they would always have a profitable trade to fall back on.

Just as Esmond Burton on leaving Marlborough became apprenticed to a stone cutter, so there is a foreman on this gigantic job whose story is a fairy-tale. When he was a boy of eight or nine he loved to see houses being built. His father was an army officer and they were well off, but, to his parents' consternation, he apprenticed himself at the age of fourteen to a bricklayer, working from six in the morning till six at night, and then hurrying off at half past seven to evening classes. These he attended till he was well over thirty, continuing meanwhile his meteoric rise through the many branches of the building trade.

Can the university graduate ever catch up with the practical experience of a man like this? One constantly hears this question discussed. If you ask the practical man on a gigantic job like this one whether he could personally set his hand to the many different occupations of the five hundred men under him, he is likely to answer: 'The first thing to remember is that modern technique is constantly changing. When methods are improving overnight, you have to be on the alert all the time.'

I thought I would look in at St Lawrence Jewry, but as the midday siren at the Bank of England had already gone, I hardly expected to find anybody there. The magnificent plane-trees in the church passage cast pools of shade across the white stone of the newly built church with its two natural oak doors, one leading into the vestry, the other into the vicar's quiet and beautiful flat. Here, at least, a Church of England clergyman was living in some of the dignity one associates with a past age. The water from the copper fountain overlooking the courtyard of the Guildhall splashed merrily on the two drinking cups. One might have been in a cathedral close. The only sound was the winging of birds from green bough to green bough.

The vestry door was open. The hall on the left where the craftsmen used to lunch at trestle tables was freshly painted and bright as a new pin. Mr George's office was locked. Most of his work was finished; the church was to be officially opened in three weeks' time. I suddenly realized that I would be almost sorry when this masterpiece was handed over to the ecclesiastical authorities. During all this summer I had watched it emerge from the nakedness of its four walls to a thing of increasing beauty, but most of all I had marvelled at the pride and interest of the workmen. During its re-creation it was a living thing. Men moved purposefully about every corner of it, wood-carvers, stone-masons, carpenters, bell-makers, forming together a symbol of practical faith, energetic and youthful, whereas, when it was finished, would those Sunday morning services become, as in so many City churches, stricken, like the branch of a diseased tree, with blight? Only one man was left inside the church, a master joiner. He was passing a hand lovingly over a piece of oak.

'English, and the best,' he said softly.

'Are you a country man?'

'A Londoner but of country stock. However, I know about oak.'

'Is there still plenty of oak in England?'

'They had to look round a bit to find four trees tall enough for the main timbers at the base of the tower. Each is no less than thirty-four feet long.'

Anxious to show me how they were placed, he took a piece of paper and drew a diagram.

'Thirty-four feet long,' he repeated, 'and nine inches by nine thick. The trees themselves could not have been less than fifty feet tall. They were discovered between Swaffham and Watton in Norfolk, about a hundred miles from London.'

'The church is nearly finished?'

'They still have the tenor bell to hang. If you look up into the ringing chamber you can see her.'

'Why "her"?'

'Bells are feminine. A ringer refers to his bell as "she."'

'From Norman times?'

'Perhaps.'

He went to fetch his bicycle, and a few moments later we were under the trees in the church passage.

'Well,' he said. 'I'll be going.'

'A happy week-end.'

An empty milk bottle stood by the church door. I filled it with cool water from the fountain and put it back. A minute later a sparrow, who had watched this operation from a low bough, flew down to drink thirstily from the mouth of the bottle.

A boy, seated by the window in the rector's flat, was reading a book. The calm of the week-end had begun.

I had then walked as far as Short's, the wine house, at the corner of Gresham Street and Old Jewry, and was vaguely surprised to find it still open. I thought I would go back by way of Old Jewry, which has become quite dazzling with new buildings, when I suddenly changed my mind and, retracing my steps, turned into Ironmonger Lane, which runs parallel with it but offers more shade, and is altogether a narrower and prettier street.

The Jews of London, many of whom came over with William the Conqueror from Normandy, lived in this corner of the City from the time of the Conquest till 1290. Toward the end of this period, for instance, Master Moses, an illustrious member of the community, and his wealthy son, Hagin, owned property with gardens and orchards extending from Ironmonger Lane to Old Jewry, then known as Colechurch Street. But there was hardly a generation when Jews were not fined or massacred. King John imprisoned, blinded, and tortured those who could not pay his levies. Henry III seized a third part of their furniture and turned their new synagogue in Colechurch Street into a church. Hagin, whose life was continually in danger, fled to Normandy during the London massacre of 1264, then returned to Ironmonger Lane, where he spent the rest of his life in and out of prison. Ten years later, in 1290, Edward I, the king who as a baby was held at the font by Humphrey de Bohun, finally expelled all the Jews from England. Their property was seized by the Crown. On their readmission to England three and a half centuries later they selected Jewry Street, Aldgate, for their habitation, and their former neighbourhood was then termed Old Jewry.

Half-way down Ironmonger Lane, on my left, I came across the delicate wrought-iron gates leading into the shady garden at the end of which stand the tower and porch of St Olave, Jewry. 'How strange,' I said to myself. 'I thought this church was pulled down in 1888!' I therefore passed through the garden and entered the porch like a person discovering something in a dream.

Having entered what was once the church, I found myself in a freshly painted corridor with very pretty office rooms on either side, and a wide staircase leading up to a first floor. These offices, the doors of which were open, seemed quite deserted. Having peeped into one room after another, feeling increasingly certain there must be somebody in the building, I climbed up to the first floor where more rooms were arranged in the form of a cross, two in the spacious church tower, level with the tall window immediately above the porch, two others in what would have been the body of the church. In the one on my right a man was writing at a desk.

'Are we in a church or an office?' I asked.

He looked startled.

'This is the new annexe of a firm of chartered accountants of Ironmonger Lane,' he said. 'We were getting a little crowded over there. Was this a church? It never struck me. We have not been here long.'

'You have a nice view over the churchyard. Can I have a look at the rooms in the tower?'

'Why, yes. Delighted. I will come with you. I am the only person in to-day.'

We were level with the lower branches of the plane-trees, and sunshine streamed through the enormous windows.

'Your firm has done the place up beautifully, and you must have very efficient secretaries. This one has put a notice on her filing cabinet asking people who borrow documents to put them back carefully. Is there another floor above this one?'

'Yes, but that has nothing to do with us. The Rev. John Drewett, rector of St Margaret Lothbury, has an apartment up there.'

'How does one reach it?'

'By a side entrance in the garden immediately below the window where I was sitting.'

A notice at the rectory entrance said: 'Ring the bell, advance into the outer hall, and talk into the speaking tube.'

I rang the bell but, instead of struggling with the speaking-tube, which alarmed me, I pushed open a door leading to a narrow staircase of painted oak. Almost immediately I heard descending steps.

A tall, slim, distinguished-looking man, wearing a bright tie, beautifully pressed light-coloured trousers, and a well-cut jacket, looked at me and said:

'My daughter has gone shopping in Regent Street. The sales are on and she wanted some cushion-cover material.'

'Oh, I see.'

'My son-in-law has taken the boy on the river. It 's such a lovely day.'

'Of course. I am so very sorry to have troubled you. I was intrigued by this rectory in an old church tower.'

'My name is Walter Harding. The rector is my son-in-law. They have only been living here a year. The place has been done up specially for them. You should have seen it before that. Heaven knows how many bedrooms. Nobody could have kept it up. I came to stay with my daughter and son-in-law when my wife died. Do come up if it amuses you. I shall be happy to show you round. I am afraid it is quite a climb. Do you mind?'

'Not at all. If Mrs Drewett has been successful at the sales perhaps we shall meet after all.'

So I followed Mr Harding up the beautiful new staircase.

I had not expected anything so youthful or full of colour as this delightful apartment built at the top of a commercialized church tower. A magnificent circular hall, lit by a wide glass skylight above a mauve staircase leading to the airy bedrooms and the rector's carpenter's shop, had rooms of different bright colours all round, a kitchen of royal blue, a primrose dining-room, a drawing-room with chintz curtains and easy chairs. Here were the cushions which Mr Harding had brought from his home in the country and for which Mrs Drewett had gone to buy gay material at the sales. There was a playroom for their little boy Paul, I could see his trains on the floor, and Mrs Drewett's sewing-machine in a corner. In the rector's study were three huge windows with red sills and a green carpet over a red, black, and green linoleum. The doors were red, and so was a wide table under the semicircular tower window. On this table there was set out a wonderful collection of animals and toys from all over the world. Most of them had been given to the rector when he was secretary of the Church Missionary Society. There were Scandinavian coloured wooden horses, a little train of camels from Egypt, a bust of Nefertiti, and the lion and unicorn which once decorated the Lord Mayor's pew at some no longer existing City church and which Mr Drewett had found in a cupboard at St Margaret Lothbury. The whole of one wall was covered with books, and every available space was taken up with some charming print, picture, model, or calendar.

The hall itself was so spacious and comfortable that it could count as a room on its own. A round gilt mirror hung on one wall and an icon on another, which the rector had brought back from Russia when he had gone there two years earlier.

Right at the top of the tower was the weather-vane in the form of a sailing-ship. It came from the church of St Mildred in the Poultry which was, sadly enough, pulled down in 1872. The reason for the ship is that corn used to come up the river from Thanet.

The next day I attended Sunday service at St Margaret Lothbury, after which I apologized to the rector and Mrs Drewett for having called without warning at their home the previous morning. They most graciously showed me the beauties of their church, including the reredos in the Lady Chapel from St Olave Jewry into which is fixed a tablet bearing the Hebrew word YAHWEH. Was this a relic from the synagogue in Colechurch Street, possibly from the one Henry III seized and turned into a church? St Mary Colechurch, for instance, was not rebuilt after the Great Fire of 1666 and Wren may well have incorporated this Hebrew tablet into the reredos of St Olave Jewry. The bottom half of the screen dividing the Lady Chapel from the nave was the communion rail of St Olave Jewry brought here when that church was pulled down.

The choir at the service we had just attended was composed of five women and one man. The congregation, including the rector's wife and ourselves, had numbered half a dozen. But one must remember that the church was closed from 1940 until 1952, and it is something of a miracle that those in authority have not sold the site for a quarter of a million pounds. That is the danger that overhangs these City churches. They stand on ground worth millions. Henry VIII knew something about that. I told the rector how pretty his tower and south wall looked since they had been cleaned.

'A present from the Bank of England,' he said.

'So now there is only the east wall left to be cleaned?'

The rector was not certain about the east wall. The east wall does not face the Bank of England, so perhaps the Bank of England thinks that what is out of sight is out of mind.

# 12

WHILE GIGANTIC new buildings were going up all over the City, Throgmorton Street was vibrating to the news of vast 'take-over' offers for famous businesses and departmental stores. Though such juggling of monetary power ended of necessity on the floor of the Stock Exchange, preliminary discussions took place in the quiet of private houses.

One beautiful evening during the week that followed my visit to St Margaret Lothbury I dined at a house in Hampstead. Our host had built up one of the most successful departmental stores in the country. Under the leafy trees in the garden, the men guests, who were well-known financiers, affectionately chided him for not having let them into the secret which, only a few hours earlier, had taken the financial world by surprise.

These superb houses with their pretty lawns and lofty trees are the natural successors of those which, had a magician allowed us to peep at the London of the thirteenth century, we should have found in Ironmonger Lane. Rich merchants and bankers no longer enjoy wine and cakes at midnight under the apple-trees of St Martin Pomary, but those were exactly the delights we were offered under the trees, with the coloured lamps amongst the foliage, in the Hampstead home of this wealthy City merchant.

The making of money, when discussed by men of this calibre, makes fascinating after-dinner conversation, and one is tempted to believe that the Victorian custom of banishing the women before handing round the port did much to retard our mental evolution. As in the time of the Lombards, however, many City merchants of to-day are of foreign origin; at this particular dinner, amongst six men and six women, three were born in Russia, one in Poland, two in Hungary, and one in Armenia. Yet the men were City men, known internationally for what they had done in this country.

I imagine, judging by myself, that most women dream from time to time of making money as a change from our universal desire to spend it. Before leaving my flat in Piccadilly that evening I had picked up two letters which I read on the way. The first was from a man of eighty-three who lives at Arrow Lake, British Columbia, where he had been reading *The Little Madeleine*. He said:

> After leaving school, I went on to a lawyer's office in Leadenhall Street in the City. Unfortunately I had lost my father when I was only ten. One day I was sent to a very old firm of solicitors near the Bank of England, a dusty, nasty, dingy place which it would have taken a Dickens to describe. A long desk ran the length of one wall in front of which, perched on high stools, were three elderly clerks, busy writing, heads bent down. They were all dressed alike in long-tailed office coats, black and shabby, and they looked as if they had been on these same stools for decades. I thought of them as three black crows. 'If I stay in this place,' I said to myself, 'I shall suffer a similar fate!' So in 1891 I scraped up a little money and bought an ocean ticket for Canada. In those days it cost hardly anything to cross the Atlantic. I made my way to the West and because I had no trade I had to do labouring work to live. I rambled round a lot, have been from coast to coast and then settled down on a prairie farm. In 1911 I sold out, took my wife and boy to England for a holiday and came back in 1912, and headed for British Columbia where I have been since. This is a lovely spot, mountains, trees, and water. I never get tired of looking at it. I lost my wife two years ago, a few days before we were to celebrate our fiftieth wedding anniversary. I am still lonely, lonely for her but it is all in the hands of God. Now I am in my eighty-third year waiting for the last move. May God bless you,
>
> O. J. ASPINALL.

This letter from a reader entirely unknown to me cast a curious beam of light on the City, on the way it looked to a boy working in Leadenhall Street at the end of the last century. With the Stock Exchange now so excited about investing money in Canada, the second part of the letter seemed terribly modern.

The second letter had a more personal interest for me because in some curious way it seemed to reflect what I was unable to put into words just now about the attitude of so many of our sex to money. The writer is a young New York girl, a very sweet friend:

> I have got a job which I started Monday two weeks ago and I love it. I have a two years' contract at twenty-five thousand a year and I felt very rich and smug about it until yesterday. Do you remember my telling you about a young man I used to go out with? Well, he wasn't quite good enough for me—ha ha—so yesterday he married Ann—one of the richest girls in the world, also pretty. She already has 20 million dollars. What a place they live on or at. Like Buckingham Palace only with a lot more ground around it. Well, of course, I 'm filthy jealous of the girl, and I don't know whether it 's her money or her husband I envy her most for.

And as for me, I don't know what or whom I envy most —men who create magnificent departmental stores, their wives who can just go straight in and have everything they want put down on a charge account, the money of financiers who buy up departmental stores from City merchants, houses in Hampstead with lawns as big as Central Park, or the twenty-five thousand dollars a year (as near as I can make it, £9,000 a year) which my girl friend is earning at the present time in New York City! Should I mention that she adds:

'Now look, now that I am with a job and in clover, what do you want me to send you in nylon? Would you like a blouse, or a dress, or something?'

Heavens, I would like the whole of Fifth Avenue! But mostly, though I love her, I am desperately jealous of this girl who, so young, can make herself the equivalent of nearly £9,000 a year!

I now feel almost certain that the Virgin of Aldermanbury has been stolen, and I am furious about it. On making tentative inquiries at the London Diocesan headquarters in Bedford Square, I was referred to the architect of St Mary Aldermanbury, who, having consulted his own records and talked to the contractor, gave it as his painful conclusion that the Virgin might well have been stolen by hooligans.

I also learned that the corrugated iron roof which had been erected some years earlier in an effort to preserve what little remained of the interior of the church had in turn proved dangerous. As a result of this, the corrugated iron had been taken away, leaving the ruins once again at the mercy of the elements.

Aesthetically, of course, the ruins are far prettier without the iron roof. I am even beginning to think that they are the best-looking ruins in the City. Pigeons fly out from the crenellated tower, which was scorched by the intensity of the fire. They play hide and seek in and out of the delicate stone lacework which runs along the top of the walls or perch on the top of the stone pine-cones which are presumably symbols of evergreen faith. The trees in the garden were at their shadiest and most lovely, keeping Shakespeare very cool looking! A charming and unexpected sight was a deep-red rose peeping over the top of the box hedge. No novelist could imagine a more pitiful plea for a touch of the country in this sea of cement.

Meanwhile the miracle of St Lawrence Jewry was within a few days of completion, and supposing that the tenor bell must by now be in place, and the church all ready for the dedication, I went there almost with a sense of nostalgia.

I had no sooner entered through the west door than I caught sight of Mr George accompanied by a little dark-haired boy with the prettiest brown eyes you can imagine.

'Yours?' I queried.

Mr George beamed assent.

His youngest son turned those quick, brown, intelligent eyes inquiringly upon me.

'How old are you?' I asked.

'Five.'

'Your name?'

'Donald.'

'Like the duck,' I began, but at this moment the entire church reverberated to the celestial sound of one of the new bells. The child's eyes were alight with pleasure.

'Donald,' I cried. 'Take me up into the tower!'

'Very well,' his father agreed. 'You can both go. I'll come up in a moment.'

The steps and walls of the narrow spiral staircase were gloriously, evenly white, for the stone was everywhere repaired or refaced. Within a moment, however, since no one had put on the light, we were moving in complete darkness and Donald, of course, was so far outrunning me that I could hear his little steps growing fainter in what seemed the impenetrable heights above. Light from the open door of the ringing chamber soon restored my courage, but there was nobody there and heavy weights hung from what ringers call the 'sallies' or thickened part of the ropes. So up again I climbed past the 'deadening chamber' or clock room (the mechanism of the great four-sided clock is stored in the sound-deadening chamber), with its pretty ogival door of stained wood, and up past all this to the bell chamber where Mr Theobald, the bell-hanger, and his mate, were standing on a beam, doing something to No. 3 bell, while Donald peered at them through the open door.

'Well,' said Mr Theobald, greeting me. 'Here they all are, and don't they look lovely?'

They did indeed look lovely but curiously frightening, each bell with her tall wheel round which is threaded the ringing rope; her 'stay,' the upright piece of wood attached to the headstock; and her 'slider,' the loose bar below. How heavy and powerful they seemed; I became uncountably terrified of being caught in between them and being pummelled and beaten to death before being flung down below. The four huge windows of the belfry, where I expected to see wood or slate louvres, like fixed Venetian blinds, were boarded up, beneath the clock faces, with oak planks.

'Why are the windows boarded up?' I asked Mr Theobald.

'To drive the sound upwards into the spire,' said he.

'Now that commercial buildings are as tall as church belfries, the sound of these magnificent bells, were it to escape horizontally, would deafen people working on the corresponding floors of new City offices, so by boarding up the windows of the belfry the sound will rise and travel over the tops of buildings and thus will be heard at a far greater distance.'

The bells are grouped together in a cast-iron frame on a steel base and the wheels of the various bells vary from about three and a half feet to eight feet in diameter. Notice that long experience has taught the bell-maker how the wood from different trees can best be blended together.

'For instance,' says Mr Theobald, 'the "soling," the channel for the rope round the rim of the wheel, is made of ash because ash is the most easily bent. The wood is steamed and a perfect circle made from one piece. The spokes are made of oak. Oak gives them strength. The "shroud," or rim, that keeps the rope from running off is made of elm, a good, light, hard wood. The "stay" that prevents the bell from making more than a complete revolution is also made of ash, because though it must be both light and strong, it must yet be breakable. Oak would be too strong.'

'The stay, in other words, is a safety device in case an inexperienced ringer pulls too hard on the rope? Is that right?' I queried.

'Yes, that is more or less right,' said Mr Theobald. 'If a ringer pulls too hard on the rope, and the bell is overturned, after the "stay" breaks, unless he quickly lets go of the rope, he will go right up in the air.'

'What do you call "right up in the air"?'

'On a small bell he might go up ten feet; on the tenor, anything from fifteen to twenty feet.'

'But surely that is very dangerous. Might he not smash his head against the ceiling?'

'He certainly might.'

'Does it ever happen?'

'Yes, I remember it happening some years ago at St Paul's Cathedral. A man was caught up by the tenor bell;

luckily he let go at about fifteen feet or he would have dashed his brains out. As it was, he broke both ankles in his fall.'

Donald had disappeared up more dark steps.

'Wait here,' I cried to Mr Theobald. 'I had better go after him.'

Then, as an afterthought:

'By the way, Mr Theobald, what is above us?'

Mr Theobald looked up thoughtfully.

'To the top of the spire, there might be anything from forty to fifty feet.'

I ran up after Donald but I had not got far before his father, who had arrived to look for him, called out his name, and down he sped, slipping past me like a lizard. I peeped through one of the slits in the stone at the City sky-line. Surrounded by buildings like the Bank of England extension, Gateway House, and Bucklersbury House, one loses even in a church tower the illusion of height.

Standing beside the bells had given me my only moment of fear so far. I was to have another when Mr Theobald, anxious to show me what a bell looked like when it was being rung, ran down to the ringing-chamber to pull the rope of No. 3. His assistant, who had remained with me, cried:

'Take care. The noise is deafening.'

I covered my ears and waited in trepidation. This was not to be like the chiming at St Andrew Undershaft where, because of the weakness of the tower, all that happens is that the clapper is made to strike the bell. This was the real thing, a ringer swinging on the rope below. I experienced again that feeling of impotence in front of these mighty bells, a fear of being deafened and crushed.

The bell swung almost imperceptibly. Mr Theobald was unfastening the weight. Now it swung a little higher each time, and soon the first silvery tone boomed out, followed by another and another till the mouth of the bell faced upwards, and the bell remained thus in suspense, so that looking into it one could see the scratched part, red like a copper saucepan, where it had been tuned. The modern method of tuning is this. A shaving is planed off the interior by the aid of steam power to flatten the note. As the seventeenth-century poet, known to posterity only by his initials, F. D., sang:

> Could I mould and file and tune my Lines as well
> As thou canst mould and file and tune thy Bell.

I was wearing some little black shoes with spike heels made for me by a Greek shoemaker in the Rue François Premier in Paris, and I had taken them off while running up and down the stone stairs of the tower. I sat down in the Lady Chapel to put them on again and then went into the church, where a pile of new hassocks in royal blue had just been delivered. They were stacked in a corner waiting to be put out for the opening ceremony, and as Mr George and Donald had gone on to St Mary-le-Bow, where I had promised to look them up later, I slipped into a pew and, kneeling down on a copy of a newspaper which a workman had left there, I made my first prayer in this church which I had learned to love. When finally I lifted up my eyes, it was to see my name saint, Mary Magdalene, with blue eyes and honey-coloured tresses, the sun shining behind them, looking down upon me from the stained-glass window in Gresham street. The parish church of St Mary Magdalene in Milk Street was not rebuilt after 1666.

Two or three young craftsmen were at work in the single aisle overlooking the Guildhall which is separated from the main part of the church by Corinthian columns. Now it was midday and time for them to go home. One of them, who had parked a very old motor-cycle against a pew, said good-bye to his companions and wheeled it out through the nave and the vestibule, and hence into the brilliant sunshine. This is what I loved best about this church in the making, the human sidelights, the woman who had brought in her dog, the craftsman who after his morning's work wheeled out his motor-cycle, the little boy of five careering up the steps of the tower, the fact that it was always open. I wondered if the rector would keep his church open for as many hours of the day when the men who had made it moved elsewhere.

On my way to catch a bus in Cheapside I went over as I had promised to St Mary-le-Bow. A small yellow house has been built on stilts above the entrance to the yard; this is Mr George's office. As I looked up at this edifice I saw Mr George wiping his hands on a brightly coloured towel. I waved to him, and a moment later Donald appeared with hands also freshly washed which he in turn proceeded to dry on his father's towel. Then, one after the other, they climbed down the steep ladder leading to the street, where a tall, good-looking young man was waiting for them.

'My son Leslie,' said Mr George with pride. 'He has just come over from Token House Yard—a commercial building—where he is in charge under me.'

I looked at the youthful features of the boy who was already following in the footsteps of the father. Big brother and small brother held hands and led the way down Cheapside in the direction of St Paul's Churchyard. I felt as if I were looking at the closing scene of some magnificent film in which there is all the promise of the years to come. These were the men of the City of to-morrow. How lovely to see two brothers walking hand in hand toward their destiny!

'What will you be doing this week-end?' I asked their father.

'Accounts till about seven to-night,' he answered, tapping a bulky package under his arm. 'Then to-morrow, if the weather keeps as hot, maybe we will all take a pleasure-steamer at Charing Cross pier, and go down to the sea.'

We parted at the bus stop, and as the great building yards emptied into Cheapside, along which London's traffic has flowed since medieval, nay, Roman times, I watched them merge into the crowd.

# 13

IN MEDIEVAL TIMES the fen or moor field stretching beyond the City walls all the way from Cripplegate to Bishopsgate in the direction of Islington and Finsbury was damp waste land over which, when it was frozen in winter, the London apprentices used to skate. The postern, called Moorgate, was not built until the reign of Henry V. Thomas Falconer, then mayor, had caused the wall of the City to be broken at this point for the convenience of citizens wishing to walk on causeways toward Islington and Hoxton.

Henry VIII, at about the time of his dissolution of the monasteries, drained most of the land; James I laid it out in pleasant walks, but it was not until after the Great Fire of 1666 that Londoners, fleeing from their devastated homes, started first to pitch tents, then to build there.

In Georgian times, and indeed until early in the reign of Queen Victoria, Finsbury was the fashionable medical quarter, and the many doctors and surgeons who had houses in Finsbury Square, Finsbury Pavement, Finsbury Place, Finsbury Circus, Broad Street, and St Helen's Place made much larger earnings out of prosperous City families than the West End faculty made out of the court and aristocracy. The last great physician to practise in the City was Henry Jeaffreson, senior physican of St Bartholomew's, who lived in Finsbury Square, where he is reported to have made a vast income. When wealthy City families migrated to the west, eminent doctors soon followed them, not always from choice but because City rents were already becoming prohibitive.

Moorgate leads through Finsbury Pavement and Finsbury Square to the City Road, which, by twisting sharply to the left, will eventually take you by way of Moorfields Eye Hospital to the Angel, Islington.

When, during the building of St Lawrence Jewry and

St Mary-le-Bow, I followed Mr George from crypt to nave and nave to tower, and we came across the remains of Londoners who had lived in the City four centuries ago, I used to speculate on how the women dealt with the ailments that affected themselves and their children. Because I stood about too much, I was later obliged to go to the Orthopaedic Hospital in Great Portland Street, and, though that is not in the City, I felt during those visits that I was still learning something about the character of the people of Bread Street, of Cheapside, and of Aldersgate who had lived in the days of Milton and earlier.

The office was clean and bright. A number of young women were typing or telephoning with the busy activity that one associates with such scenes in a film. One of these young women, having read the doctor's letter I handed her, waved me to a bench where half a dozen other women were waiting.

One by one our names were called, and we were directed into a waiting-room the walls of which represented the seasons. I thus found myself examining the panel devoted to winter where swift huntsmen and hounds made an unfortunate contrast with the women about me, some of whom had crutches, others varying kinds of orthopaedic appliances.

The woman next to me confided:

'I feel rather ashamed to be taking up a famous doctor's time, but perhaps you don't know what it is to have your feet hurting, however carefully you buy your shoes. Yes, of course there are far more terrifying ailments, and many people would have no pity on me for complaining about something so trivial, but all the same, when one works in an office where all the girls seem to have the most perfect feet, it is most demoralizing not to be the same as they are.'

'Oh! but I quite understand!' I said emphatically.

I, who spend my life envying the good points in other women, fully realized the joy of having the small, well-shaped foot that is shod so prettily in a little shoe. She went on:

P

'If I were to start again, it is in a hospital that I would like to work. See how pretty and gay the girls are in the office here. Their white overalls are both useful and feminine.'

There was an air of assurance in my companion's voice. She had reached that delightful moment in life when, though still young, she obviously knew exactly what she wanted. During the war she had been a blood donor.

'I was very nervous the first time they called me,' she said, 'but terribly interested. Everything interests me. I am as curious as a cat. No new experience is a waste of time. After every gift of our blood we were given a cup of tea with as much sugar as we liked. That was exquisite.'

We were now called into a room marked WOMEN, where most of my companions started to remove their stockings, for they appeared to be suffering chiefly from ailments connected with their feet and knees. One woman informed us that her knee 'sang,' and she invited us to examine this vocal joint which, because we were curious, we all lost no time in doing, but we were soon obliged to confess how ignorant we were in anatomy. The woman of the singing knee was in no way put out by this, but started to unwind a long bandage. Meanwhile we resigned ourselves to another long wait, stockingless legs very pale and white, almost indecently so.

The doctors worked in a room connected on the one side with ours, on the other with that in which the men got ready for the consultation. Young nurses called one of us every time there was a vacant place in front of the surgeon or one of his assistants. Most of those who were here for the first time were sent, after this examination, to other departments for blood tests and X-rays.

In possession of a paper on which the doctor's instructions were marked, we now joined a new group in which there were both men and women; the men wearing hospital dressing-gowns that enhanced the dreariness of socks so uninspiring that if by any chance we had come here with our hearts full of romantic thoughts they might well have suffered a rebuff.

The X-rays were now taken in full daylight; welcome

contrast with the frightening seances in the dark of earlier days. Here again a young woman in a white overall was in charge, and above the machine she, or somebody else, had perched a minute teddy-bear.

For the blood test there came yet another young woman who did her work most carefully and gently. Though I was eager not to miss any detail of this operation, I found myself a little sick at the sight of this drawing away of a minute portion of my life stream. A moment later the young woman, as in an American film, was already deep in its analysis, in front of a machine.

'Please go back and wait till you are called,' she said.

My companions were already there; all of them had been X-rayed, but I was the only one to have been given a blood test. A woman I had not noticed before was explaining that she had spent most of her life looking after an arthritic mother who had just died.

'Poor thing,' she said, 'it 's a pity!'

We nodded sympathy, and agreed that arthritis was indeed a cruel ailment that sapped a person's energy.

'Yes,' she said, 'it does, and more 's the pity, for next Wednesday Mum would have been ninety-three!'

This confession aroused smiles, but she went on:

'I was lost without the poor dear, so I thought it might be time to look after myself. I am not arthritic, mind, they say it skips a generation, but I have my bunions. So that is why I am here.'

A nurse emerged from the doctor's room with a list in her hand and started to call out a short list of names. Our features immediately took on a tense expression, as if we were afraid to miss something or not to understand. We had reverted to the mentality of schoolgirls.

'I have butterflies inside me,' whispered the woman beside me.

This nervousness was delicious, but it is sad to reflect how fearful is the human race, how little sure of itself. The daughter of the arthritic mother, hearing her name called out, jumped up and went off to show her bunions to the doctor.

The woman who had told me earlier that a hospital was, in her opinion, an excellent place for a girl to work in, described her own office, a very large one, in Holborn. She said it was moderately gay but impersonal.

'There are too many of us,' she said. 'When I began there some years ago we worked longer hours but we had the impression of being more important, and I think our advice was occasionally sought. All that is finished. There are advantages, of course. We have no responsibility. Nobody would dream of blaming us for a mistake. Nobody blames anybody for anything, but on the other hand when one is never consulted one ends by feeling a little hurt. Eventually we cease to care; then work becomes monotonous. That is why I was telling you just now that if I had my time over again I would work in a place like this. Women who work in a hospital can never be quite impersonal. See how tenderly that nurse over there is helping that old man along! You may say it is just part of her job. I know, but it is the little extra kindness she shows him that makes the difference.

'I also lived with my mother. I have a pretty suburban house, and it was lovely when I came home on winter evenings to see lights in the windows, and to know that she was waiting for me; and in the morning before I left for work I used to go round the little garden and see what she had done in it the previous day. Even in the coldest weather she found something to do in the garden. We used to spend week-ends planting things, or making alterations. She was terribly plucky and never ill; the day she went to bed it was to die.

'Now when I come home at night there are no lights in the windows, but I have a budgerigar; so you see that I am not quite alone.'

The daughter of the arthritic mother emerged from her consultation; her expression was of bitter disappointment. The surgeon had refused to operate on her bunions. She would be given corrective appliances to wear. On bidding us good-bye she looked for a moment as if she were going to cry.

By the time it was my turn to see the doctor he already had in his possession the reports on the blood test, which were normal, and the X-ray photographs, which he invited me to look at against a lighted frame.

'A slight maladjustment of the spine,' he explained. 'You were born with it but unless we do something immediately the pain may increase. I will prescribe you a course of sun-ray therapy. You will be notified as soon as there is a vacancy.'

This then was one more example of the admirable effects of the health scheme in the large London teaching hospitals. I had been aware of this maladjustment since the beginning of the war when I was wheeling my baby through the burning, stricken streets of the West End, and I now felt glad that the doctor had not prescribed for me, as he had for so many other women, corrective appliances.

I had, during the battle of London, quite accidentally hit on my own way of arresting this incipient trouble. This is how it happened. After one particularly devastating night raid, the lovely little haberdasher's shop owned by Gladys Shearn in Shepherd Market was wrecked by blast. She sold me at a generous discount some pretty knitting-wool that had been drowned in water from the firemen's hoses and at the same time an old-fashioned boned corset designed to give the wearer a twenty-inch waist.

This corset proved a miracle against backache when I did the housework and had to carry the baby. Without knowing it, I had simply had recourse to what a doctor would have called a corrective device. Gladys Shearn, going through her bombed shop, discovered a drawer full of these treasures, each decorated with tiny bows of blue ribbon. After I had taken my choice she sold the rest at ten shillings each to the 'girls' in the market.

The men who came there in search of amorous adventure were delighted, it appears, to find these ladies wearing such strange evocations of the past, which, encircling their waists with the steel grip of an Austrian waltzer, gave them unsuspected charm.

Great changes, I may add, have come over the nocturnal

aspect of Shepherd Market and Curzon Street since then. To the French 'girls' and English 'girls' must now be added the coloured 'girls' from the West Indies.

'What will you?' said one of the French 'girls,' winking at me. 'Men are so adventurous!'

A card from the hospital informed me that I would have treatment twice a week in the afternoons. I arrived on the first day rather before time. A young woman seated at a small table looked up from her files. The course, she said, would last two months, at the end of which time the surgeon would see me again. I must make the appointment now.

Having done this, and still finding myself a little early for treatment, I sat on a bench under a clock. A Chinaman arrived, and bowed to the secretary behind her table, then to me. Dressed in black, with a black trilby in his hand, he tendered his appointment card with an engaging smile that showed gold teeth.

'You have made a mistake,' said the secretary firmly but with great kindness. 'See! The card says Thursday, and to-day is Wednesday. What a pity that you have come on the wrong day!'

'For to-morrow?' said the Chinaman. 'I regret. I must have misread. I come back to-morrow.'

He continued to smile, thanked the secretary, bowed to me, and, replacing the card in his wallet, disappeared.

The next moment I was called, and passing into the room marked WOMEN, I found several patients undressing for their treatment. Seeing I was new, they told me to do the same. The treatment was carried out in the next room.

A nurse arrived, and having made certain that I had no metal on me, she unfolded a deck-chair, put some cushions on it, and told me to make myself comfortable. She then gave me a woollen blanket.

In a cubicle, a woman who had just finished her treatment was dressing.

'Is this your first time?' she asked. 'You will find it wonderful, but take care. Don't go to sleep under the sun-bath. You might burn.'

The nurse, on her return, gave me a similar warning, and I confess that it was with fear rather than with abandon that I sought relaxation under the health-giving rays.

The woman in the cubicle was bandaging her knee.

'Arthritis,' she explained. 'I have had it for seventeen years.'

Her fingers were spindly. I recognized the symptoms as those of my mother. The woman's gestures were slow, and when she walked she limped. Another woman had her feet in an enamel tub, her soles resting on metal arches which rose and fell rhythmically like the advertisements in orthopaedic shoe shops where a skeleton foot goes up and down on a steel platform. When she emerged from this, she was given a stool on which to do exercises.

Yet another woman lay face downward on a high bed, one of her legs being drawn up and down by means of a rope and a pulley; she resembled a doll in the ballet of the *Boutique fantasque*.

A curtain divided us from the men, one of whom was apparently being massaged; we found ourselves listening to snatches of his conversation.

'Nothing ever goes right with me,' we heard him say. 'I am so accustomed to things going wrong that I have given up hoping for anything good—unhappily married, no money, ill health!'

He gave a hollow laugh.

Does it happen that misfortune settles on a person like some evil bird, darkening all the years of his life? I felt sorry for this man whose voice I had just heard but whose features I might never see. Those who get little out of life should always be pitied; the odds against them are probably too heavy from the start. It is as easy for a man with good health to succeed as for a girl who is born vivacious and pretty. The fortunate ones should not take too much credit to themselves.

A little girl whose frail legs were encased in heavy

contraptions of leather and steel was doing her best to play; how unfair that this calamity should fall on a girl child who should be running after a ball as lightly as a butterfly.

'It is only in a hospital,' said my friend of the budgerigar, 'that one starts to reflect on one's own good health. The people you meet there are invariably worse off than yourself.'

That is true, but as soon as one goes out into the street again one envies the others—those who are younger, prettier, richer, better dressed.

A slim, good-looking woman I had not seen before, arrived, wished us good afternoon, and taking her place on a high bed which the nurse arranged specially for her, folded her arms and basked in the rays, appearing to go to sleep.

We finished our treatment at about the same time, and as we were dressing she began to tell me about herself.

'There is quite a sizable piece of my spine missing,' she explained. 'A bomb at the beginning of the war. My house had a direct hit. I knew nothing about it myself, of course. They told me it was a miracle that I lived.'

'Have you any children?' I asked.

'No,' she answered. 'Have you?'

I told her I had a son; she asked me in rather a curious way if he was in good health, and then she said:

'I had a daughter, but the last time I saw her she was four.'

'You mean that you lost her?'

'She was in the house with me when the bomb dropped. I was not told for months, for years. They did not think I would live. I was not conscious of anything or anybody. I did not really know I was alive. She would be twenty-one this month.'

'How terrible!'

'That is war!' she said.

Twice a week I came to this little room whose glass roof trapped the rays of the sun on hot afternoons. The nurses would occasionally leave us to look after patients in the so-called 'gymnasium,' and then we would all start to chatter like schoolgirls when the mistress has left the room.

Our 'head girl' on these occasions was the woman whom I had noticed on the first day peering down into the enamel tub in which the soles of her feet were being made to move up and down on metal disks. Her admirably styled coiffure drew my attention.

One of us asked her if she had a long way to come.

'Oh no,' she answered. 'I live in Bloomsbury, where my business is to find lodgings for students at London University. What exciting jobs there are these days! This one is immensely interesting. Young people of every country and race pass through my office, and if I were to go for a trip round the world I would be fairly certain of finding people in every part of it whom I had known in Bloomsbury.

'I have learned to recognize the different types of coloured races, mostly, I think, because I am so tremendously keen to understand them. We are still very short of accommodation. They are happier with us. We know their problems. They represent, of course, a great many different social levels but they all strive toward the same ideal of more knowledge.

'You would certainly not see any antagonism between races when the students are together. They are all bound together by the eagerness of youth. Even young Americans forget any prejudices they may still feel when at home against Negroes.

'An amusing situation does sometimes arise, however. A cockney charwoman, whose English was extremely concise and picturesque, was remarking the other day, while cleaning one of the student's rooms, on what she considered to be the "backwardness of them blacks." A young student from East Africa, the person against whom these remarks were principally directed, happened to be within earshot. Afterwards, he said to me in great high spirits:

'"I would have liked to have seen the expressions on the

faces of my parents if they had heard the remarks of my charwoman, for my father was an exhibitioner at Cambridge, and is now a magistrate; my mother was a scholar at Somerville."

'Certainly the mere fact of living amongst these vital people from all over the world keeps me feeling very young. No two of them seem alike; some are meticulous about their belongings; others are appallingly untidy. Their spare-time occupations fascinate me. There are those who compose music and play various instruments; others who are mad about jazz. There are painters and sculptors. Their different ways of looking at life continually provide me with new ideas. When a Negro paints a London street scene, for instance, his appreciation is quite different from our own. Buildings I pass every day, when painted by a Japanese artist, take on quite a new aspect. Even his sky and clouds are amusingly un-English. I love this seeing familiar things through different eyes. I get much the same fun out of it as in seeing a Greek or Italian film.'

As soon as our nurse came back into the room the conversation turned on violets. We were on the eve of mothers' day, and for the generation represented by the younger nurses this occasion was of considerable significance.

'The first time I sent a bunch of violets to mother she was so touched that she kept it,' said our nurse, 'and every time I go home she brings it out of a drawer to show me.'

Another nurse who had joined us said:

'I shall also send flowers to mother: everybody else does it. Does your son send you flowers on mothers' day, Mrs Henrey?'

'No,' I answered, 'and judging by what you all say, daughters appear to be more tender than sons.'

'Oh yes,' cried our nurse with conviction, 'especially after they have left home. We seem to appreciate our mothers even more when we are financially independent. They, of course, cease to treat us like children and it is lovely for us who, after all, are still a little afraid of them, to be consulted by our mothers.'

The second nurse said almost shyly:

'I sometimes rather miss not being scolded by mine!'

The woman lying on the high bed in a sort of tunnel of light, who had been so terribly injured when the bomb fell on her house, turned her head toward us and resting it, like a little girl, on a folded arm, began to talk.

'We would know very little about our fellow creatures if we did not frequent hospitals,' she said. 'I who have been frequenting them, alas, for seventeen years am no longer surprised by anything, and yet I am never tired of hearing people talk about themselves. There is always something a little different. I am sure that even two peas would not look the same under a microscope.'

'That is why we take so many X-ray pictures,' said our nurse. 'We are suspicious of anything which, at first sight, looks just like something we have seen before. One wonders how doctors were able to diagnose at all in the old days.'

I felt a great affection for the woman on the high bed and I asked her about her husband.

'He works in a bank,' she said, 'and is the best husband any woman could wish for. It was I,' she added laughing, 'who was wounded in the war; he was in the Eighth Army in Africa and came out of the fighting without a scar. We were separated for four years, and my letters to him were as censored as his were to me. We were kept in complete ignorance about each other, and it was only when he was on his way back to England that he learned that his little daughter was dead, his house demolished, and that the wife who was waiting for him was only a poor shadow of the young woman he had married.

'There are things one cannot write to a soldier on active service. My husband's morale might have suffered, just as mine would have done had I been told that something had happened to him. Thus our two lives were wrenched apart and I was left to cry my eyes out all alone for the daughter we had lost. In this state of dejection I was moved from one hospital to another, trying to be brave when succeeding surgeons decided on new operations.

'But at last my husband came back, and life flowed once again in the joy of companionship. He is a darling husband. Just think. I am not supposed to lift even the lightest weight, and if on occasion I do rather more than I should it is merely that I must use to the full what remains of my life.

'We might, of course, have another child, but for a mother not to be able to lift up her new-born in her arms, or out of its cot; not to be able to bathe it, or dress it, or rock it gently to sleep when it cries, what sort of a mother would that be? So you see that our life is different from what we had hoped it would be at the beginning, but we love each other, and our greatest happiness is to take walks together through the streets of the City.'

A patient I had not seen before was wheeled into the room. She was still relatively young and both her legs were encased in plaster of Paris so that she looked like a mummy in the British Museum, and we were so moved by the poignancy of her condition that conversation suddenly stopped.

Continual pain had robbed her face of expression, and she was not even able to respond to our smiles of sympathy and welcome. Terror overcame her as she tried to help herself out of her invalid chair to the crutches waiting for her, and in spite of the incredible gentleness and skill of the nurse this operation took an unconscionable time. Out of the immense sympathy in our hearts we watched with dreadful attention this tremendous misfortune.

An elderly woman in a corner of the room said suddenly:

'Oh, nurse, if only you knew how hard it is to lift this foot!'

Her words fell curiously on the silence which had fallen over us. At least she could move her foot, though with difficulty; the newcomer, behind features marked by pain, had resigned herself to worse.

'Don't be afraid. I am here!'

The young nurse's voice was vibrant with compassion;

no wonder that to-morrow, when she took that bunch of violets home, her mother would no longer think her daughter a child.

Grey skies greeted me as I left the hospital. Quite a number of people were waiting for a bus, which suggested that one was due at any moment.

A woman and a young man were in the front of the queue. She wore spectacles and was uninspiringly dressed, a plastic hood of dull colour over her mousy hair. He, tall, slim, extremely elegant, carried a walking-stick.

The first drops of rain began to fall, and as I watched this couple I saw the young man's long, well-shaped fingers run round his companion's coat collar to satisfy himself that she was adequately protected against the rain. She appeared pleased by this concern for her welfare, and gave a happy laugh. They talked incessently and gaily; his voice had in it all the melody of youth.

He wore an officer's beret, and when he turned I saw, to my consternation, that in the place of his eyes there were two scarlet holes from which tears seemed to drop.

My heart thumped with terror. I had never before found myself face to face with a blind man who had only just become blind.

When our bus arrived the woman helped the young man into it, but as she did so she called out good afternoon to a man carrying a white stick who was getting off. Before the bus moved, I looked back at him, and saw him move with assurance across the pavement. He must have been accustomed to his long night.

The woman and the young man were seated immediately opposite me; from time to time he would lift a hand to wipe a drop of moisture from the socket of an eye. His shirt collar was impeccably white, as indeed was his shirt. His neck was long and boyish, and I marvelled how affecting can be the youthful appearance of a young male, the skin so clear and smooth, so superbly free of the artifices we employ to attract the attention of the opposite sex.

He paid the fare, plunging a hand awkwardly into a pocket under his raincoat, like a man groping his way through unfamiliar labyrinths, but all the time he laughed and occasionally turned to face his companion's eyes as if, by some secret sympathy, he could read from them.

Had this young man, about whom I knew nothing, gone off with other young men one fine day—every day is a fine day for those who have their sight—to some distant war where others fell but he was saved, only to be plunged into eternal night? I kept on thinking of his mother, who must have cooed over him when he was a baby, proudly watched him growing tall and strong and tried not to cry when he left her. Was it like this that they had given him back to her? Could this happen to my son?

The woman kept on talking and laughing, and her vitality was so unusual that I began to suspect that it was not entirely spontaneous. As her companion was denied the sight of the myriad things about us which we enjoy silently, the traffic, the shop windows, the expressions of the people seated next to us in the bus, or those hurrying along pavements, costers selling fruit from barrows, a pretty hat, posters on walls—because he no longer had any of these, his companion was doing her best to replace them with a rippling, colourful torrent of words. From time to time, perhaps in gratitude, he would stretch out a hand and lightly touch hers with the endearing gesture of a blind kitten.

How I longed to know how this tragedy had happened, and my heart kept oscillating between pity for the young man and bitterness against those things that might have brought about his affliction. Had there not been only the previous winter that senseless tragedy in Egypt?

The woman and the young man had reached their destination, and as they rose—the man so tall that he bumped his head against the top of the bus—the conductor, gentle and solicitous, was beside him, guiding him safely out of the bus and on to the pavement of the London street.

Then, as our bus went forward again, there came into my mind the slowly remembered lines of Milton, the boy from Bread Street, the blind, disillusioned poet who on summer evenings sat in the little garden of his house in Jewin Street:

But, chief of all,
O loss of sight, of thee I most complain.
Blind among enemies! O worse than chains,
Dungeon, or beggary, or decrepit age!
Light, the prime work of God, to me is extinct,
And all her various objects of delight
Annulled, which might in part my grief have eased.
Inferior to the vilest now become
Of man or worm, the vilest here excel me;
They creep, yet see; I, dark in light, exposed
To daily fraud, contempt, abuse, and wrong,
Within doors or without, still as a fool
In power of others, never in my own,—
Scarce half I seem to live, dead more than half.
O dark, dark, dark, amid the blaze of noon,
Irrecoverably dark, total eclipse
Without all hope of day!
O first-created beam, and thou great Word,
'Let there be light, and light was over all,'
Why am I thus bereaved thy prime decree?
The sun to me is dark
And silent as the Moon
When she deserts the night,
Hid in her vacant interlunar cave.
Since light so necessary is to life,
And almost life itself, if it be true
That life is in the soul,
She all in every part, why was the sight
To such a tender ball as the eye confined,
So obvious and so easy to be quenched,
And not, as feeling, through all parts diffused,
That she might look at will through every pore?

# 14

THE APPEARANCE of the City was changing so fast that when I was obliged to go away, even for a short time, I felt on my return almost aggrieved to find everything looking so different.

My overhanging gardens were disappearing. Where a fortnight ago I had fondly gathered roses and lavender, I now found big cranes installed. They were clumsy, with elongated necks like prehistoric monsters. Railway lines for one-wheel trucks ran through verbena bushes and across flourishing rockeries where ivy and vine had covered picturesque eighteenth-century tombstones. I hated to think that the lilies of the valley and the marigolds which had given me such joy during this glorious summer would not come back to welcome me another year. I was too much a woman not to regret the tranquillity and the flowers, the casual meeting with other women who liked to knit and to sew in the open air. The City of to-morrow seemed to be rising up so swiftly that I was afraid. I had hoped to keep pace with it. I was impressed and I thought it increasingly beautiful, but I was overpowered.

The towers and spires of City churches, landmarks for centuries, were beginning to look insignificant. Only St Paul's was big enough to hold its own. One supposes that medieval Londoners looked with awe at the stone steeple of St Mary-le-Bow with its five lanterns glazed and having lights within them to guide travellers on the road by night. The immensely tall maypole of Cornhill vied with the tower of the church of St Andrew. Skyscrapers now looked down upon the churches. I even found myself wondering if they were really such masterpieces as I had believed. I was beginning to lack faith. I fought against this feeling, however, with all my strength.

The churches were not the only buildings to suffer from

the mighty newcomers. Indeed, one newcomer itself, one of the prettiest of all the buildings to go up, the beautiful new Saddlers' Hall in Gutter Lane, was being so tightly hemmed in that one could no longer obtain a distant view of it. I had loved, only six months earlier, to gaze at it from across the bracken which divided it from Wood Street; it glowed like a castle in a fairy-tale. I even forgave it for hiding the spire of St Vedast, Foster Lane. Now, though it would not be officially opened till Christmas, it was already so small by comparison with some of its neighbours that I was as sorry for it as I had been previously for St Vedast.

However, in all things I was fickle.

There were glimpses of the City of to-morrow that captivated me. I felt about this dazzling whiteness as I so often feel about some violent change in Paris fashions. At first sight, though I am immensely intrigued, I am slightly suspicious. My eye is not yet accustomed to what has been purposely made so different. After a short time, however, I find myself so enamoured of the new style that I want to throw out or alter everything in my wardrobe. I cut up dresses, alter the hems of skirts.

The different aspect of the City of to-morrow took hold of me in the same insidious way.

Thus I fell desperately in love with Walbrook.

Walbrook is that very short street which runs from the Mansion House to Cannon Street station. With the exception of the Mansion House and the historic church of St Stephen, Walbrook, the street looks just about as new as a freshly minted penny. Nothing in the whole world could look newer. Even the eighteenth-century Mansion House gleams with its magnificently cleaned Portland stone against which lovely flowers in window-boxes splash vivid colours, and as for the church of St Stephen, a Wren masterpiece, that also has a new look.

Here, of course, was the heart of Roman Londinium.

The Walbrook was, until the middle of the thirteenth

century, an open stream whose exact course has only recently been recharted. Until 1952 people were content to say that it followed very roughly the present street. Stow, who was merely writing from popular belief, described it as a fair brook of sweet water which came from out the north fields, through the wall and midst of the City, into the Thames. The course thereof, he adds, was from the said wall to St Margaret's Church in Lothbury; 'from thence under St Mildred's church and through Bucklersbury, by the great house built of stone and timber, called the Old Barge because barges out of the river of the Thames were rowed so far into the brook on the backside of the houses in Walbrook Street.'

In Roman times the area was evidently very wet, with thickets of birch and alder, whose pollen is abundant in the recently disturbed peat.

The temple of Mithras, whose discovery proved one of the wonders of deep post-war excavations, stood on the west bank, along which much later, in Saxon times, was to be built the first church of St Stephen, Walbrook, which had a belfry. A certain William de Clarke, while pigeon nesting, fell from one of its beams and was killed, a story which reminds me of the pigeon's nest with the eggs in it, which I discovered half-way up the Norman tower of St Andrew Undershaft the day I went up there with the little girls to chime the bells.

On the east bank, during the reign of Edward I, a fish and meat market was set up where previously a pair of stocks had stood. By this time the once sweet water no longer ran so clear. On Friday, the feast of St Margaret, in the nineteenth year of the reign of Edward I (A.D. 1291) an inquisition was made as to who is or are bound by rights to repair the bridge of Walebrok near Brokerelesbere. Eventually it was covered over and built upon.

The second church of St Stephen's was built in 1439 on the east side of the arched-over stream, and soon the market, which was called the Stocks Market, began to specialize in flowers and herbs. In the reign of Henry VIII there were rows of trees, very pleasant to the inhabitants, on the east side of the market; to the north were twenty-two covered fruit stalls; at the south-west corner were butchers' stalls, while all the rest of the space was taken up by gardeners who sold fruit, roots, herbs, and flowers. The stock, that gloriously scented flower which always reminds me of an English garden, owes its name to the fact that it was first sold in this market.

Bucklersbury, which nowadays is cut in half by Queen Victoria Street, joins Walbrook where the market used to stand. In the days of Elizabeth I, Bucklersbury was a street of chemists, druggists, and apothecaries. Shakespeare mentions Bucklersbury in *The Merry Wives of Windsor*; and Ben Jonson in *Westward Ho!*

'Go into Bucklersbury, and fetch me two ounces of preserved melons.'

When St Stephen's was destroyed in the Great Fire of 1666, Wren, who had been living in Walbrook, was asked to design a new church and he decided to experiment with the kind of dome which he was later to use in St Paul's Cathedral. This was the period when the architect, grievously overworked, frequently found himself the recipient of gifts and invitations to dinner from wardens whose churches had been burned to the ground and who were all clamouring for his services.

Wren started on St Stephen, Walbrook, in 1672, but within a year the churchwardens, in order to hasten on the work, were loading Wren with gifts. They also held a dinner in his honour, but though he was even then engaged on rebuilding St Michael, Cornhill, the churchwardens of St Stephen had no cause for alarm. Wren was building them one of his finest churches. There is an oft-repeated story of how Wren's critics were convinced that the slender columns would not support the dome, and that they all assembled outside the church on the day the scaffolding was taken down, in the hope of seeing it collapse. When later, they went in search of him to exclaim in admiration, they found him kneeling in prayer.

The Stocks Market was still in existence, and it is recorded that the smell of rotting vegetables was so strong that when the north door was left open during divine service the worshippers were overcome by the stench. The door was bricked up but its outline can still be seen in St Stephen's Row.

Bucklersbury, meanwhile, had become a street where elegant women went to buy tea, fans, and Indian goods. They also, on occasion, took advantage of these expeditions to meet their lovers. The poet Prior sang:

> The first of all the town was told,
> Where newest Indian things were sold;
> So in a morning, without boddice,
> Slipt sometimes out to Mrs Thody's,
> To cheapen tea, or buy a skreen;
> What else could so much virtue mean?

After this, in 1739, came the building of the Mansion House, on the site of the Stocks Market.

The great nocturnal raids of the Second World War ringed this area with flames. The house of Rothschild in St Swithin's Lane was miraculously saved but the adjoining hall of the Salters' Company which stood between St Swithin's Lane and Walbrook was destroyed. A friend of mine watched the church of St Swithin, London Stone, go up in flames. He saw the lead-covered spire, which was topped by a ball and vane, take on the appearance of a red-hot poker, then slowly dissolve. To the west of Walbrook the destruction was immense.

Archaeologists quickly realized that there might never again be such an opportunity for excavating the heart of Londinium and tracing the bed of the Walbrook stream.

The first ruins to be cleared were those of the Salters' Hall. The belief was still held that the stream had been navigable as far as the Bank of England; some even claimed that along the stream stood the quays where merchandise was landed from Gaul, Spain, Italy and the Near East. However, in the course of the excavations for the great new building which, with its forecourt, was to stretch all the way from St Swithin's Lane to Walbrook Street, no trace of the stream was found. Many Roman remains were discovered in the peat laid down by the flood water, mostly pieces of bronze and fragments of pottery. A Roman woman's brooch was in the same perfect condition as when she mislaid it 1800 years ago. An almost perfect Roman sandal came to light, the loop and the sole of the shoe cut from a single piece of leather, and the heel added separately. A thong was threaded through the loop in much the same way as men lace their shoes to-day.

Not until archaeologists were able to investigate the other side of Walbrook Street did things really start to happen.

Here was to arise the mighty Bucklersbury House, the very spirit of the City of to-morrow. On what sacred ground does it stand, for here, conjured up from beneath tons and tons of earth, appeared the now famous temple of Mithras!

The Walbrook stream, in its original Roman form, was also traced; it flowed along the centre of a hollow stretching from Sise Lane to Walbrook Street; it was rather shallow, the width of the channel probably between twelve and fourteen feet, a fact which seems to cast a good deal of doubt about the story of the barges. At all events, here it was, this legendary Walbrook, rediscovered in 1952, slightly to the west of the line along which it was generally supposed to have run. Now buried again some thirty-two feet below the streets along which we walk.

The Mansion House is very pretty, and I love the book which a former Lady Mayoress wrote about life within its walls, but I regret that there is no longer a market here with—as in the days of Henry VIII—a row of leafy trees, fruit stalls, and a picturesque corner where country women sell vegetables and herbs. Some future Lady Mayoress should call for more places where the girls who work in the City can amuse themselves during the lunch hour. If the

City is to become increasingly an area into which thousands of young, extremely intelligent girls flock every morning, with that magic hour for lunch during which they can shop and dream, choose their clothes, and buy the good food they will require to take home in the evening, then the City must also cater for their needs and be gay.

I met the partner of a very old City firm who told me that he had come to the City as an office boy in 1906, and what fun he had! In those days, he said, Walbrook was full of the most amusing shops—tailors and second-hand booksellers, splendid restaurants, an old-fashioned dairy, stamp shops which so delight the hearts of little boys, and I know not what else. Undoubtedly when men considered the City their personal stronghold they took good care to provide it with colour and amusement.

Walbrook to-day has a different beauty. On the east side are the Mansion House, aflame with flowers, the superbly cleaned church of St Stephen, Walbrook, which is an architectural gem. Indeed, if it were in Florence or Rome, you would fly off to see it on the advice of the guide-book!

The lovely new office block, St Swithin's House, whose forecourt faces St Swithin's Lane, now entirely covers the space formerly occupied by the Salters' Hall. Just before you reach Cannon Street stand the Banks of America and Nova Scotia with their brilliantly coloured hanging signs. The first sign shows a sailing-ship; the second includes a fish, a ship, a deer, and a unicorn. I like these evocative links with what is still, by comparison with this history-steeped ground on which I am standing, a relatively new world. I picture the blouses and shoes I would like to buy in Fifth Avenue. I feel the salt tang which blows against my make-up and entangles my hair as the liner steams into Halifax.

The church of St Swithin will apparently soon be pulled down, for the Church of England is said to be eager for the money which a valuable City site can yield. They say they can make better use of this money in newly developed areas farther afield, but they are wrong not to guard more jealously every single link with the past, and one is appalled by the thought that men in authority can consider, even for a moment, the disappearance of such jewels as St Swithin's, London Stone, St Catherine Cree, and St Mary, Aldermanbury.

I walk into the Bank of America with the assured air of a woman who might own an account in dollars. The Stars and Stripes, flying side by side with the Union Jack, give me a curious thrill. The bunting is so crisp that it looks newly washed and ironed. A poster extols the qualities of this flourishing bank. One sees a little man with a comical American hat watering an immense sunflower, and above this picture are the words: 'Still growing to serve you better.'

On the west side of Walbrook rises the gigantic Bucklersbury House, marvel of the City of to-morrow. Its foundations dig deep into the precious earth which nurtured the men and women who made this island's greatness. Here was Londinium. Here ran the sweet bubbling waters of the Walbrook. Here was the temple of Mithras. Here women who knew the same hopes and fears, dreams and disappointments as I do, bore children and kept house for their men.

When will Bucklersbury House cease growing? Is some little man standing above it with a comical hat and a watering can? Do I resent the intrusion of modern immensity on this spot hallowed by history? On the contrary, I rejoice to think of the new and wonderful opportunities that will be available within its shining walls to girls and young women—opportunities to earn more while working in beautiful surroundings. Indeed, the higher wages they will be able to command will be only a beginning. Soon the day must come when, in addition to her bright new typewriter and posy of flowers, a young woman will earn no less than a young man.

Against the roadway is a builders' shed. A man was bending over a column of figures. When he had finished totting it up, I asked him to tell me which was the highest—Bucklersbury House or the spire of St Stephen,

Walbrook. He looked at me in surprise, emerged from his little house, peered into the London sky, and answered slowly:

'Come to think of it, lady, I don't for the life of me know. From down here, they seem about the same.'

Organ music came from the church, and I climbed up the steps.

On the night of 10th May 1941 incendiary bombs set fire to the dome, which collapsed. The Lord Mayor's private secretary saw the flames from the Mansion House and summoned the firemen, who saved the building. St Stephen was the first City church to be restored. Gilbert Meaden, the architect, was asked to make it exactly as it was before, and though he did not live to see the work finished, his plans were minutely carried out.

So now this church, which Canova said he wanted to see once again before he died, is as beautiful as ever, but except for a clergyman who was obviously sightseeing the church was empty, and I hurried out into the garden, from which I could see, through the branches of the acacia-trees, people working in the house of Rothschild.

This garden is kept up by the joint interest of three renowned City firms—a distinguished firm of accountants, a famous brokers, and the house of Rothschild. What a lovely place in which to read or sew amongst the rose-trees and the blue and yellow irises! Here, under the branches of the trees, one may find peace.

At the back of the Mansion House is George Street, one of the oldest and narrowest streets in the City. In medieval days it was called Berebyndereslane which, in modern English, would be Bearbinder Lane.

Just beyond the lovely corner house, which is occupied by a brokerage firm, is an eighteenth-century house which still retains those picturesque window reflectors, so typical of the City in Victorian days.

The occupants of this magnificent house represent all that is most upright in the traditions of our land. Their desire to remain modestly anonymous behind their early Georgian façade is almost disconcerting, but though the panelled walls have something Dickensian about them, the prettiest young woman may be seen sitting at the reception desk at the foot of the oak stairs.

Narrow George Street and St Swithin's Lane all had the most picturesque old-fashioned shops until the Second World War. In this they resembled Walbrook. In George Street early this century there was a grocer's shop with such low steps at its entrance that it was easy, so people say, for a man to bump his head on the beams. In St Swithin's Lane, facing George Street, where there is now the London Assurance, stood the famous Bay Tree Inn where many a City man drank more than he could stand. City men nowadays have become much more sober. I wonder, does this make them better husbands?

Mrs Counsell, whom I met hurrying along with a loaded shopping-basket, told me that her husband was helping at the church because the verger was away on holiday, and as she was at this moment going back to her flat at the top of St Michael's Rectory, Cornhill, I decided to accompany her, at least as far as the church.

Mr Motley's vigorous tactics were already showing results. His lunch hour services were gaining adherents. The vigorous lithe gestures with which he accompanied his words as he addressed his congregation from the altar rail were very effective. There was something of the actor in him which gave picturesqueness to his voice.

Mr Counsell had arranged a posy of flowers on the stained-oak table in front of the font by the entrance door. Almost exactly overhead hung the flag of the Royal Fusiliers, City of London Regiment, with words embroidered upon it which I can never read without tears welling up in my eyes—Mons, the Marne, Arras.

A book lay open on the table beside the posy of flowers, with this invitation by the rector:

> If you have some deep concern, or if you are praying earnestly for someone, would you let us share in your prayers. If so, will you place the name of that person, or other details, in the Intercession Book.
> Bless You.

I confess that I became immediately inquisitive, for I thought it possible that from the pages of this book I might discover the real heart of the City.

I was not disappointed, for in clipped sentences these poignant cries went up from unknown people. The first wrote:

'Intercede for my fiancé to restore the sight of one eye in an operation.'

The second:

'For Paul, living alone in Australia, that God may grant him peace of mind, and that he may be reunited one day with his mother and sisters. He has known many trials through no fault of his own.'

The third:

'For myself who earnestly desire renewed faith.'

Having taken leave of Mrs Counsell on the threshold of her home, I decided to call on Mr George in his 'house on stilts' at St Mary-le-Bow, so I retraced my steps as far as the Mansion House, turning for a moment into that part of Bucklersbury which is to the north of Queen Victoria Street.

In place of the elegant women of Prior's day who bought tea and fans, and sometimes made assignments here to meet their lovers, this portion of Bucklersbury attracts, if one can judge by the lunch hour crowds, an almost entirely male following. The Green Man, a famous City inn, which forms the promontory between Bucklersbury and Pancras Lane, and Bodega, in Bucklersbury itself, are packed with men milling round with glasses in one hand and sandwiches in the other. It gives a woman the same awkward feeling of intrusion as in some of the bars near the Stock Exchange. Even the shops on the east side of the street, or at least some of them, tend to give me the impression that this is a man's street. Men come to buy their shoes here, for instance, and to stare at cameras. I realized how dangerous it is to make statements about the City becoming mainly a place for girls. Though the trend must be that way, numerically, the important posts will always be held by men. There are curious sharply defined areas which seem to be given over to the needs of one sex or the other. Here was this short street full of men. Then there is the north side of St Paul's Churchyard where the lingerie and the blouse shops are to be found—an entirely feminine quarter where I feel as much at home as here I count myself a stranger.

If one turns into Pancras Lane, skirting the Green Man, one comes upon an empty ill-tended garden with a plane-tree growing in the middle of it, and a plaque stating that this is the site of the church of St Benet Sherehog destroyed in the Great Fire of 1666. I would like to cultivate the ground myself and fill it with bulbs that would bloom in the spring, in memory of Ann Ferrar. Before the church was destroyed, here lay buried the girl wife of Nicholas Ferrar, merchant adventurer of Elizabethan times. He was a friend of Drake, Hawkins, and Raleigh, and frequently had an interest in their ventures. Stow has immortalized the lines carved on Ann's tomb:

Here was a bud,
  Beginning for her May;
Before her flower,
  Death took her hence away.
But for what cause?
  That friends might joy the more;
Where there hope is,
  She flourishes now before.
She is not lost,
  But in those joyes remaine,
Where friends may see,
  And joy in her againe.

A few days earlier someone had told me:

'I tried to buy that piece of land to put a building up on it, but the ownership is complicated.'

One day, somebody will build on it, I suppose, and when that happens, I hope they will call it Ann House!

Mr George's tiny house, built on stilts high above the roar and bustle of Cheapside, reminds me of the homes of the ancient Britons. The Gauls also, if my girlhood history books were accurate, built entire villages like this in the swamps where Paris now stands. The house is painted yellow and there is a balcony from which Mr George can watch the ebb and flow along Cheapside.

'It 's better than the front at Brighton!' he exclaimed.

Access to Mr George's house is by a very tall ladder lashed at the top with ropes, and that, if one has a tight skirt and spike heels, is an even more perilous adventure than climbing up the corkscrew tower of St Andrew Undershaft with only the light of a medieval slit window to guide you.

'How are you getting along, Mr George?'

'Well, we are getting along all right.'

The house—though we should not really call it that; it is merely a general foreman's office—is built on a platform of planks. Alongside the house on the left I noticed an iron Victorian wash-stand, with basin above and soap poised on a dish underneath. There was a towel on the rail and a bottle of milk against the wall. Inside the house, pinned above a drawing table, were notes from Dove Brothers and cartoons from the *Carpenter and Builder*. Together we examined these, and though Mr George must have seen them a hundred times, he laughed with me because the jokes were all to do with his trade; two workmen, for instance, peering down at a motor-car which had fallen into the bottom of a deep pit. One man says to the other: 'Say nothing. Fill it in quickly!'

My instinct tells me that this is going to be the biggest job in Mr George's life. The people who tread the pavements of Cheapside cannot guess the complexities of rebuilding something which in its multitudinous forms dates from Saxon, perhaps from Roman times. This will be several times more difficult than the miracle of St Lawrence Jewry.

'Have you been to see it?' asks Mr George.

'St Lawrence Jewry? Yes, it is a jewel. I can hardly believe it. When I need reassurance of England's present-day greatness, I shall go into the church you have just built. There I will say a prayer of thanks.'

Yes, indeed all that is loveliest in our land is contained within those once charred stone walls—the grass-green altar embroideries, the magnificent silver candlesticks, two on the communion table, two larger ones on the marble floor, the superb carvings, the painting on the reredos, the magnificent columns with the gold leaf that blinds the eye, the angel trumpeting the words:

> O, all ye works of the Lord, praise ye the Lord!

the superb detail of the tower chapel; the happy blend of an Elizabethan chest and a lovely modern radiator, and under the bell tower the little oak chair that looks as if it were waiting for the little brown bear!

'Yes,' said Mr George, 'it is all lovely.'

'I hope they use it,' I said. 'I hope they all realize what it has meant. I am told there are no services on Sunday.'

'It is their right,' said Mr George. 'But any rate it is open every week-day.'

'And here?' I repeated. 'How are you getting along here?'

'This will be my only job now, my very biggest job.'

He opened a wide shallow drawer from which he took out an architect's plan. What he wanted me to know were the difficulties involved in sinking deep piles, on which the church will eventually rest, into the depths of the Norman crypt. The point of his pencil danced over the architect's plan, and though I tried to follow what he was saying, I understood but little. What gigantic tasks men undertake!

'Would you like to come and see?' asked Mr George.

The church, which I had last seen as a shell, was being given a temporary roof. There were rows of planks supported by tubular steel scaffolding which made the interior very dark. We went down into the crypt where arches of Caen stone gleamed in the half light, but when one touched them the stone came off like damp face-powder. Before the piles were driven into the foundations, Roman, Saxon, and Norman brick and stone would be numbered, removed, and then faithfully set up again. I felt like a little girl in a fairy-story listening to absurd tasks being imposed. What adventurous idealists are men that they must so often seek to accomplish the almost impossible!

We came upon two heavy safes much damaged by fire and water, one of which was locked.

'What do you think is inside, Mr George?'

'I wonder. I have the key somewhere. I could try to open it.'

'Do you think there is hidden treasure? Perhaps it has not been opened for centuries?'

'How romantic you are! You may be right. Still, it depends what you mean by "treasure."'

'What did you find in the other safe?'

'You would be surprised. Did you know that in the old days water was carried in leather buckets?'

'Yes, I think I did. I seem to remember seeing them in pictures of early fire brigades.'

Mr George opened the safe and started pulling out leather buckets. I thought them slender and beautiful. Some appeared to be in excellent condition; others might have been gnawed by rats. Mr George smiled.

'Just what the ladies wear as hand-bags!' he said.

'Yes,' I agreed. 'Some women. I once chaperoned a little girl from Paris——'

This would hardly interest Mr George, so I broke off and said:

'Do you find it damp down here? I am shivering, and there is something eerie about all these things that come to us so directly from the past. These buckets, for instance? How old do you suppose they are? A hundred . . . two hundred years old?'

'More than that, I fancy,' said Mr George. 'I shall have to do something about them when we start working down here. By the way, I wonder who turned on the lights? Let us turn them off and see if anybody shouts!'

A lunch-time service was being held in the temporary chapel that Mr George had put up not far from his house on stilts. I first became aware of it by noticing how many people turned off from Cheapside, pushed open the little gate, and then proceeded to walk up the garden path past the geranium tubs.

'You should look in,' said Mr George. 'The girls decorated the place themselves.'

The room was crowded, the roof was pink and white, and pretty curtains nestled against the windows. Here was the feminine hand. A clergyman was telling his congregation, mostly typists and secretaries, about the minister of a church in Edinburgh who, besides being noted for his sermons, wrote books, all of which did not prevent this busy Scot from feeding the sparrows that flew into his study through the open windows. The minister died, and asked St Peter to let him into heaven, but Peter said that he had never heard of him.

'Nonsense!' said the minister, 'I am very well known in Edinburgh.'

'Possibly, but Edinburgh is a large city.'

'My books are read as far away as London.'

'I would not be surprised, but London is a large city also.'

'Then can't I come in?'

'I am afraid not,' said Peter.

The unfortunate minister was walking sadly away, when a sparrow flew down and perched on his shoulder.

'You wouldn't be that Scottish gentleman who used to feed the sparrows in his study every day?' Peter called out. 'Come back quickly. The master of the sparrows wants to see you!'

During all the time I had explored the City I only found one person who had known my father-in-law.

B. A. G. Norman was the owner of auction and sale rooms in Little Britain, that curiously shaped street which leads from St Botolph, Aldersgate, to St Bartholomew's Hospital. In this street, three hundred years ago when it was crowded with second-hand booksellers, the Earl of Dorset was hunting for books to his taste. He picked up *Paradise Lost* and, dipping into it, was much surprised by the passages he read. The bookseller begged him to speak in its favour if he liked it because the volumes of this poem lay on his hands as waste paper. My Lord took it home, read it, and sent it to Dryden, who in a short time returned it, saying: 'This man cuts us all out, and the ancients too.'

The firm of Norman & Son goes back to the days when men lived with their families over their places of business. John Norman, the founder, had been apprenticed in 1811 first to a tea dealer and grocer, then to a lorimer, a maker of bits and bridles. By 1819 he had opened up a business in Goswell Street, after which by various stages he became cabinet maker, upholsterer, autioneer, house agent, and appraiser.

Benjamin Gordon, the present head of the firm, the founder's grandson, sits in a basement office adjoining his auction rooms. The windows open out on to a bombed site overgrown with strongly growing ferns. The furniture in his office is sparse, but opposite his massive desk stands a heavy mahogany bookcase made by his great-grandfather during his cabinet-making days, probably in Cloak Lane.

This man of seventy-two is witty and vigorous. Amongst his many other activities he is a governor of St Bartholomew's Hospital. He wears narrow, gold-rimmed spectacles, a moustache, and a stout signet ring on the little finger of his right hand which he turns round and round thoughtfully as he puffs at a narrow dark pipe.

His son, Edward, who occupies the adjoining office, keeps running in and out, and it is delightful to see the close, good-humoured understanding between father and son.

They are both intrigued by my interest in Selby Henrey, remembered perfectly by Benjamin Gordon, whose father was in those days a churchwarden. This office is now held by Edward, the cloak of the father and grandfather having descended upon the son, for the auction rooms and the church face each other across the narrow street and are bound closely together by long years of intimacy.

Edward arrived with an unframed canvas of his great-grandfather which he rescued from the attic. The portrait has gone almost black as if it has been smoked like a kipper or an Auvergne sausage, but by peering closely at it one can fairly easily discern noble but determined features, bright eyes, and a prominent nose. Edward, excusing himself, says:

'I think it was better before mother tried to clean it with Sunlight soap!'

This is the sort of family business that I dreamed of finding in the City, for within its framework could be found all that is most romantic, vital, and picturesque.

This part of Little Britain is enchanting, for the boughs of the plane-trees reach out from the garden of St Botolph's, and overhang the narrow street, giving it the appearance of a country lane. Clusters of fig-trees push their milky leaves through the iron railings. A cat with three kittens purrs with contentment on the top of a compost heap.

I decided to peep into the church where my father-in-law so often preached, and there I found a Negro fast asleep in a pew, doubtless dreaming of sugarcanes and pineapples. I like this church enormously, and I enjoy gazing at the stained-glass windows as much as a child would. They are like the pages of a picture book, depicting scenes from the New Testament.

The Rev. S. F. Linsley, rector of St Catherine Cree, who, because it was declared a dangerous structure, was never able to hold a service in his church, has just been appointed rector here, which by many is taken to imply that St Catherine Cree is to be pulled down and the site sold for a fabulous sum, as will be doubtless the fate of St Mary, Aldermanbury—perhaps I shall never again see its beautiful little statue of the Blessed Virgin which I loved so much.

I must make do with St Botolph, Aldersgate. At least there will be a link. Victor Cray, the verger, came in, treading very softly so as not to wake the sleeping Negro, and I ask him for news about the lunch-hour services which are held here every Thursday.

'About twenty people come along,' he says. 'That makes fourteen more than we got on Sundays when the rector used to hold a morning service.'

'So you close your church on Sunday now? That explains why I could not get in on Easter morning!'

'Yes,' he answered apologetically. 'On Sunday the congregation was composed of myself, my wife, three of our grandchildren, two of whom sang in the choir, a lady from Harrow, and another from Plumstead.'

'I suppose you live near here?'

'No, we live by the Angel in Islington. This Christmas, my wife and I hope to celebrate our golden wedding.'

'Have you been verger for long?'

'Since 1929.'

'What made you come here?'

'I was out of work. I wanted a job.'

Benjamin Gordon Norman was holding an auction, and I looked forward to seeing him on the rostrum. I therefore crossed the road again, and went down into the basement.

The room was low, divided up by pillars, and densely crowded with men. Cigarette smoke at first impeded my vision. Everybody seemed to be talking at the same time, and yet above all this din rose the clear, youthful voicc of the seventy-two-year-old auctioneer.

'How much for the full-size ladies' models?'

By edging forward I became aware that between these gesticulating men stood plaster figures of naked young women whose protruding busts seemed stretched toward them. Male hands passed expertly over the plaster to see if it was intact.

'Now,' said the auctioneer. 'How much will you pay for them? There are three in this lot?'

These men in their dark suits were pressed closely up against these nude, flesh-coloured figures which were dotted all about the room. It was a strange sight to come upon in the street where the Earl of Dorset discovered *Paradise Lost*.

I tried to tell myself that these were merely showroom fittings but I found them much more disconcerting than the Chamber of Horrors. Ranged on glass-topped show-cases were busts of girls with blood-red lips and youthful breasts. Had I seen them wearing brassières in the window of a haberdasher's shop I would not have looked twice, but here I was ashamed for them because they were naked.

There were naked children too in pathetically innocent postures, and a little girl of six or seven who, though nude, still clung to the azure blue shoes they must have forgotten to take off her when she left the shop to be sold. Five female heads with no hair stood grouped together, evocative of the horrible vengeance inflicted on a number of unfortunate young women in France after the last war. A feminine figure has her lot number stuck against her navel. An attendant is carrying high above his head a couple of woman's legs.

'How much for two dozen busts?' asks Benjamin Norman.

There is a sudden silence.

'Ten shillings?'

The sun is still warm in Little Britain and the smell of fig leaves scents the air. The brightly painted sign of the White Horse Inn creaks fitfully. Two men are loading women's fur coats into a van twenty yards away from the house which, rather more than two hundred years ago, was the scene of Charles Wesley's evangelical conversion.

Three nurses from St Bartholomew's Hospital, who are housed at the bottom of the street, come tripping along, and give me broad smiles as they pass.